The Congregation as Hermeneutic of the Gospel

American Society of Missiology Monograph Series

Chair of Series Editorial Committee, James R. Krabill

The ASM Monograph Series provides a forum for publishing quality dissertations and studies in the field of missiology. Collaborating with Pickwick Publications—a division of Wipf and Stock Publishers of Eugene, Oregon—the American Society of Missiology selects high quality dissertations and other monographic studies that offer research materials in mission studies for scholars, mission and church leaders, and the academic community at large. The ASM seeks scholarly work for publication in the series that throws light on issues confronting Christian world mission in its cultural, social, historical, biblical, and theological dimensions.

Missiology is an academic field that brings together scholars whose professional training ranges from doctoral-level preparation in areas such as Scripture, history and sociology of religions, anthropology, theology, international relations, interreligious interchange, mission history, inculturation, and church law. The American Society of Missiology, which sponsors this series, is an ecumenical body drawing members from Independent and Ecumenical Protestant, Catholic, Orthodox, and other traditions. Members of the ASM are united by their commitment to reflect on and do scholarly work relating to both mission history and the present-day mission of the church. The ASM Monograph Series aims to publish works of exceptional merit on specialized topics, with particular attention given to work by younger scholars, the dissemination and publication of which is difficult under the economic pressures of standard publishing models.

Persons seeking information about the ASM or the guidelines for having their dissertations considered for publication in the ASM Monograph Series should consult the Society's website—www.asmweb.org.

Members of the ASM Monograph Committee who approved this book are:

Susan Maros, Affiliate Assistant Professor of Christian Leadership
Fuller Theological Seminary

Sue Russell, Professor of Mission and Contextual Studies
Asbury Theological Seminary

RECENTLY PUBLISHED IN THE ASM MONOGRAPH SERIES

George Shakwelele, *Explaining the Practice of Elevating an Ancestor for Veneration*

Peter T. Lee, *Hybridizing Mission: Intercultural Social Dynamics among Christian Workers on Multicultural Teams in North Africa*

The Congregation as Hermeneutic of the Gospel

Investigating Lesslie Newbigin's Answer to Questions about the Credibility of the Gospel in a Pluralistic World

SHAWN P. BEHAN

☙PICKWICK *Publications* • Eugene, Oregon

THE CONGREGATION AS HERMENEUTIC OF THE GOSPEL
Investigating Lesslie Newbigin's Answer to Questions about the Credibility of the Gospel in a Pluralistic World

American Society of Missiology Monograph Series

Copyright © 2024 Shawn P. Behan. All rights reserved. Except for brief quotations in critical publications or reviews, no part of this book may be reproduced in any manner without prior written permission from the publisher. Write: Permissions, Wipf and Stock Publishers, 199 W. 8th Ave., Suite 3, Eugene, OR 97401.

Pickwick Publications
An Imprint of Wipf and Stock Publishers
199 W. 8th Ave., Suite 3
Eugene, OR 97401

www.wipfandstock.com

PAPERBACK ISBN: 979-8-3852-1109-8
HARDCOVER ISBN: 979-8-3852-1110-4
EBOOK ISBN: 979-8-3852-1111-1

Cataloguing-in-Publication data:

Names: Behan, Shawn P. [author].

Title: The congregation as hermeneutic of the gospel : investigating Lesslie Newbigin's answer to questions about the credibility of the gospel in a pluralistic world / Shawn P. Behan.

Description: Eugene, OR: Pickwick Publications, 2024 | Series: American Society of Missiology Monograph Series | Includes bibliographical references.

Identifiers: ISBN 979-8-3852-1109-8 (paperback) | ISBN 979-8-3852-1110-4 (hardcover) | ISBN 979-8-3852-1111-1 (ebook)

Subjects: LCSH: Newbigin, Lesslie. | Missions—Theory. | Mission of the church. | Church.

Classification: BV2063 B44 2024 (print) | BV2063 (ebook)

To my grandmothers, Hope and Verdie, who were my biggest cheerleaders and advocates throughout my education. To my mother, Bev, who has been the biggest supporter of all of my endeavors. Without these amazing women helping to raise me and support me, I would not be where I am today.

And to my father, Mike, who always beamed with pride when I talked about my research, even when he didn't understand exactly what I was researching.

Contents

Acknowledgments ix
Abbreviations xi

1. The Reason for Studying the Congregation as Hermeneutic of the Gospel 1
2. Newbigin and the Nature of the Church 27
3. Constituted by the Holy Spirit 53
4. Representing the Kingdom of God 88
5. Living by the Gospel 117
6. So What? 144

Bibliography 157

Acknowledgments

I WAS FIRST EXPOSED to the work of Lesslie Newbigin during my graduate studies in 2008, and I reread his writings often while working in ministry and non-profits after seminary. Newbigin emerged as a major conversation partner when I returned to academia and began the pursuit of my doctorate in 2014. When I had to make my final decision about what I would research for that doctorate, Newbigin was a natural selection. While I may have started as a master's student impressed by Newbigin's ideas, I have become a scholar who has been largely formed in the prophetic and scriptural heritage of Bishop James Edward Lesslie Newbigin.

As I developed and refined my study of Newbigin, many helped me along the way, through conversations, critiques, editing, or asking insightful questions. While I cannot name everyone who has aided during this journey, a few do stand out: Dr. Charles Van Engen introduced me to mission theology and also provided a unique perspective on the subjects I have studied; Dr. Robert L. Gallagher has been a tremendous friend and confidant as I learn to navigate the academic world; Dr. Lalsangkima Pachuau gave me the first support I needed to pursue studying Newbigin for my dissertation; Dr. Paul Weston, who's introductions at the University of Cambridge, even if only digitally, granted me access to libraries across their campus; Dr. Philip Saunders, Archivist at the Cambridge Centre for Christianity Worldwide, who hosted me in at the Centre during my week there and helped me understand the intricacies of the British university library system; Ms. Helen Weller, Archivist at Westminster College, Cambridge, who granted me access to their library and tracked down a solitary master's thesis I sought from their archives; the staff of the Orchard Learning Resource Centre at the University of Birmingham for all of their help finding and photocopying books/chapters; Ms. Susanah Hanson, Library Director at Trinity School of Ministry, who helped me track down and then sold

Acknowledgments

and mailed me a copy of the *Trinity Journal for Theology and Ministry*; Dr. George R. Hunsberger has been a tremendous conversation partner on all things Newbigin, who's opinion and insight has helped shape my Newbigin scholarship and who's guidance in my rewrites is appreciated beyond what words can express; Dr. Gregg Okesson, besides providing tremendous leadership as my dean (and now Provost), has supported me, advocated for me, challenged me, and refined my scholarship throughout my time at Asbury; and most importantly, Dr. A. Sue Russell, my mentor, who has spent the last seven years helping form me into a scholar, a writer, and a teacher, without her helpful guidance, there is no way I would have finished this program. I also would be remiss not to mention my fellow PhD students, especially those who participated in the Dissertation Writing Group, who have been incredibly helpful and spurred me on towards the completion of this dissertation. But I wish to single out Danny and Lisa Hunter, Amanda Allen, and Geoff and Kris Whiteman, you all have become more than friends, you are family, and I can't wait to see what God does through each of you.

Abbreviations

ASM	American Society of Missiology
CSI	Church of South India
CWME	Commission on World Mission and Evangelism (of the WCC)
DWME	Division of World Mission and Evangelism (of the WCC)
GOCN	The Gospel and Our Culture Network (North America)
GPS	*The Gospel in a Pluralist Society*
IMC	International Missionary Council
SCM	Student Christian Movement
WCC	World Council of Churches

1

The Reason for Studying the Congregation as Hermeneutic of the Gospel

INTRODUCING THE TOPIC

IN THE FALL OF 2008, I was assigned to read Lesslie Newbigin's *The Gospel in a Pluralist Society* (*GPS*)[1] as part of my studies for the Master of Arts in Leadership degree at Denver Seminary. While I was not excited about the book when I bought it, reading Newbigin's eminent discussion of the interaction between gospel, church, and culture forever changed my understanding of church and ministry. In particular, Newbigin's concept of the local congregation as the hermeneutic of the gospel was radically different from my experience of churches at that point in my life. Since then, I have returned to *GPS*, particularly to re-read Newbigin's concept of the local congregation functioning as *the hermeneutic of the gospel*, to gain a deeper understanding of his view of the church and try to translate this view into my context. During my Master of Theology in Intercultural Studies program at Fuller Theological Seminary, I was assigned *GPS* again. While at Fuller, I attended the 2014 Fuller School of Intercultural Studies (SIS) Missiology Lectures on the twenty-fifth anniversary of *GPS*, which discussed the impact that Newbigin's work has had upon the church, particularly in North America. In the SIS lectures, Wilbert Shenk remarked, "The fact that *The Gospel in a Pluralist Society* continues to resonate and reverberate with a wide range of people, twenty-five years on, surely owes

1. Throughout this monograph, the first time *The Gospel in a Pluralist Society* appears in a chapter, it will have its full title. After that, I will use the abbreviation *GPS* to signify this book.

a good deal to the provenance offered by that Glasgow classroom."[2] These lectures, along with my course assignments, showed me that *GPS* is continually impacting the church, which drove me back to Newbigin to read further into his discussion of ecclesiology from throughout his life in order to gain a fuller understanding of the congregation as hermeneutic of the gospel.

My interest in *GPS* and the congregation as hermeneutic of the gospel expanded to include reviewing relevant interpretations of the concept[3] during my doctoral coursework at Asbury Theological Seminary. This led to my assessment that in the congregation as hermeneutic of the gospel, Newbigin is declaring "the local congregation 'to be in its own life an enacted interpretation of and witness to the good news that in Christ God is making all things new.'"[4] These interactions with Newbigin's concept led me to focused research upon his intended meaning, its relation to his ecclesiology, and its implications for the twenty-first century North American Church. Thus, in this study, I will argue for the congregation as hermeneutic of the gospel as Newbigin's understanding of the nature of the church, as a response to questions about the credibility of the gospel as public truth in Western society.

THESIS AND ARGUMENTATION

This research has taken me through the terrain of Newbigin's life and work, showing me the complexity of Newbigin's ecclesiology and the essentialness of this ecclesiology to many other topics he addressed throughout his life. It is in mapping this complexity that I have developed an understanding of the congregation as hermeneutic of the gospel as a key component to Newbigin's ecclesiology and missiology. My understanding of Newbigin's concept of the congregation as hermeneutic of the gospel will best be explained in my thesis, the structure of my argument in support of that thesis, and the ultimate goal that this thesis and argumentation will achieve.

---

2. Shenk, "Newbigin in His Time," 47.

3. I refer to 'the congregation as hermeneutic of the gospel' as a concept due to its wide range of components, most notably its six characteristics, its focus as the answer to the question of the credibility of the gospel as public truth, and its connections to Newbigin's ecclesial writings from the 1940s to the 1990s. All these things will be discussed throughout this study. As well, Newbigin provides an overview of this concept, which makes it more than an idea, but he also leaves a lot of room for further discussion, which leaves it partially concrete and partially abstract. Thus, referring to the congregation as hermeneutic of the gospel as a concept attests to Newbigin's comprehensive thought on the topic while allowing room for further discussion.

4. Behan, "Hermeneutical Congregation," 113–14.

The Reason for Studying the Congregation

Thesis

Having read Newbigin's many different discussions of ecclesiology throughout his life, I believe that the congregation as hermeneutic of the gospel serves a very specific role within his ecclesiology. *Newbigin's concept of the congregation as the hermeneutic of the gospel voices a vision for local congregations that are constituted by the Holy Spirit, represent the Kingdom of God, and live by the gospel, as evidence of the credibility of Jesus Christ as the last word for all human affairs.* There is a continuity between these three elements, they all build upon and support each other. But they also deserve their own specific attention because they depict different aspects of the same missionary nature of the church. This understanding of the nature of the church persists throughout Newbigin's life (as I will show later), but it is specifically in his consideration of re-missioning the West that the linguistic form of the local congregation as the hermeneutic of the gospel is expressed. Specifically, this language of the congregation as the hermeneutic of the gospel comes in response to questions about the credibility of the gospel in Western culture. Newbigin viewed the West as a society that dismisses all claims to public truth by religious or ideological worldviews that are based on revelation rather than the scientific method. In this context, Newbigin is arguing for the local congregation to serve as a witness to the gospel through their actions and words in society. The type of witness that Newbigin is advocating calls for the local congregation to model a new social order for society, based upon a biblical plausibility structure.[5] I will support this thesis through a specific argumentation.

Structure of Argument

In support of my thesis, the argumentation of this study will take a very specific pathway, which will be reflected in the individual chapters to follow. The congregation as hermeneutic of the gospel language is a specific expression of Newbigin's understanding of the nature of the local congregation. Thus, chapter 2 will look at the context of Newbigin's usage of the congregation as hermeneutic of the gospel concept. Chapter 3 will address the constituting presence of the Holy Spirit in the local congregation as it is seen in the characteristics Newbigin lists in *GPS*, pointing to the credibility of Jesus Christ as the last word in human affairs. Chapter 4 will address the role of representing the kingdom of God within the congregation as hermeneutic of the gospel concept. The local congregation representing the kingdom of God attests to

---

5. Newbigin did not provide or seek a singular biblical plausibility structure, but rather one that embraces the plurality of biblical interpretations. This is an important distinction and one that deserves further research, but it is beyond the scope of this study.

the credibility of Jesus Christ by being the sign, instrument, and foretaste of the kingdom in the world. Chapter 5 will address how a local congregation living by the gospel (through their shared life together) is a sign of the credibility of Jesus Christ by expressing their knowledge and belief in the gospel through actions and words throughout the society they inhabit. Finally, chapter 6 will address the implications of Newbigin's vision of the congregation as the hermeneutic of the gospel and other areas of research relevant to this vision. This thesis and argumentation coalesce into a central goal.

Goal

Throughout this study, in support of my stated thesis and through the structure of my argument for that thesis, the central goal is to show that my interpretation of Newbigin's concept of the congregation as the hermeneutic of the gospel will provide a fuller and more robust vision of the missionary nature of the church. This is vitally important for the North American Church to recover its missionary identity. Other authors have picked up on Newbigin's vision, but they also point to a need for a deeper understanding of this vision.

MAJOR CONVERSATION PARTNERS

Newbigin is the primary conversation partner for this study, and while I will interact with many of his writings throughout, it is necessary to give a brief overview of his life in order to provide some context for his writings.[6] James Edward Lesslie Newbigin was born on December 8, 1909 in northern England. While he grew up in a Christian home, it was through the Student Christian Movement (SCM) at the University of Cambridge that Newbigin really embraced his faith and received his call to ministry. This call took him to work for the SCM at the University of Glasgow, where he met his wife, and then to India as a missionary of the Church of Scotland (Presbyterian) in 1937. In India, Newbigin became deeply involved in the unification scheme of the Church of South India (CSI) and was elected as a founding bishop in 1947. Newbigin first served as bishop in Madurai from 1947–58, then he received permission to take the assignment of General Secretary at the International Missionary Council (IMC) in London and oversee its integration with the World Council of Churches (WCC) in Geneva. After nearly six years based in Europe and traveling the world with the IMC and WCC, Newbigin returned to India as Bishop of Madras and Deputy Moderator of the CSI. He continued

---

6. While many have developed biographies of various length on Newbigin within their works, this overview is primarily based upon Weston, "Introdction," 1–13; and Newbigin *Unfinished Agenda*.

in this post until his retirement in 1974, when he moved to Birmingham, England. In retirement, Newbigin taught, served as a part-time pastor, was the Moderator of the United Reformed Church (URC), traveled internationally as a sought-after speaker, and wrote extensively. This later period of Newbigin's life produced many of the books that he is most known for, including *GPS*. Newbigin passed away in London, England on January 30, 1998 from heart failure.

There are a plethora of scholars, missionaries, and pastors that have utilized Newbigin's concept of the congregation as hermeneutic of the gospel as they discuss the current state of the church, particularly in the English-speaking Western world (United States, Canada, United Kingdom, Australia, etc.). I am picking up from their valuable evaluations and insights with respect to Newbigin's work to help further the conversation about the nature of the church in the West. Of the many possible partners for furthering this conversation, the following eight authors stand out as foundational partners for my thesis.

Murray Rae

The book, *Theology in Missionary Perspective*,[7] is a collection of essays that address Newbigin's legacy through discussions on his contributions to theology, Western theology, and global theology in the twenty-first century. Murry Rae's essay, which explores Newbigin's influence on theology in the Western context, looks at the congregation as hermeneutic as a challenge that Newbigin left to the Western Church in the twenty-first century. According to Rae, "He (Newbigin) calls the church, by which he means, first of all, the local congregation, to be a hermeneutic of the gospel, to be in its own life an enacted interpretation of and witness to the good news that in Christ God is making all things new."[8] This challenge, Rae asserts, is to be a visible community of Christ,[9] which provides a model of a new order of life.[10] Therefore, the church must reconsider its form in the post-Christendom West by becoming the

---

7. See Laing and Weston, *Theology in Missionary Perspective*. In this book, "the congregation as hermeneutic" is quoted in Kärkkäinen, "Church in the Post-Christian Society," 125; Wainwright, "Contemporary Ecumenical Challenges," 282; Weng, "Going Public with Lesslie Newbigin," 293–94; referenced in Weston, "Ecclesiology in Eschatological Perspective," 75; discussed in Schuster, "Clue to History," 44, and Rae, "Congregation as Hermeneutic of the Gospel," 189–201.

8. Rae, "Congregation as Hermeneutic of the Gospel," 190.

9. Rae, "Congregation as Hermeneutic of the Gospel," 190–92.

10. Rae, "Congregation as Hermeneutic of the Gospel," 192–93.

place where people believe and live the gospel before the watching world.[11] In being a visible community, Rae calls on each local congregation being identified by and with the gospel.[12] Rae goes on to argue that to answer this challenge, the local congregation must gather together under biblical preaching and practicing the liturgy, baptism, and the Lord's Supper as its regular way of life.[13] The congregation then is sent, in the benediction, to enact and proclaim the gospel in the world throughout their daily lives.[14] Such a congregation will have embraced and be living its missionary identity.

Rae connects these ideas to some of Newbigin's other writings as well. This is an important locating of the congregation as hermeneutic as a component of Newbigin's discussions of ecclesiology throughout his life. Yet, as John G. Flett points out, Rae's analysis and application of the congregation as hermeneutic does not fully agree with Newbigin's ecclesial writings. Flett's critique of Rae develops across his foundational understanding of the church within a Christendom mindset,[15] and his assertion that the local congregation being the hermeneutic of the gospel is part of God's self-presentation.[16] Flett explicitly denies this last point as a possible meaning for Newbigin, since it would make the church an end in itself (as part of God's self-presentation) and Newbigin saw the church as existing and pointing to something beyond itself.[17] Flett's view is that Newbigin holds the church in tension between valuing itself and understanding its identity which lies beyond itself.[18] Flett's critique is that this tension is missing in Rae. While Rae provides the starting interpretation of the congregation as hermeneutic of the gospel being associated with the local congregation as the visible community of Christ, Flett digs deeper into the nuance of Newbigin's argument.

John G. Flett

Flett's discussion of the congregation as hermeneutic, "What Does It Mean for a Congregation to Be a Hermeneutic?" comes from his presentation at the 2014 Fuller SIS Missiology Lectures on the legacy of *GPS*, published a

---

11. Rae, "Congregation as Hermeneutic of the Gospel," 193–95.
12. Rae, "Congregation as Hermeneutic of the Gospel," 189–91.
13. Rae, "Congregation as Hermeneutic of the Gospel," 195–200.
14. Rae, "Congregation as Hermeneutic of the Gospel," 195–200.
15. Flett, "What Does It Mean for a Congregation to Be a Hermeneutic?," 198–203.
16. Flett, "What Does It Mean for a Congregation to Be a Hermeneutic?," 203–6.
17. Flett, "What Does It Mean for a Congregation to Be a Hermeneutic?," 203–6.
18. Flett, "What Does It Mean for a Congregation to Be a Hermeneutic?," 202–3.

year later as *The Gospel and Pluralism Today*.[19] Within this discussion, Flett locates the congregation as hermeneutic within Newbigin's discussion of the credibility of the gospel as public truth in a pluralist culture.[20] Flett notes that Newbigin's answer comes in a dialectic between the visible and invisible church.[21] Building upon Rae's discussion of the church as a visible community, Flett states that the resurrection is an invisible revelation of God, while the Cross is a visible revelation and part of human history, but both are made known in the church by the presence of the Holy Spirit leading the congregation in cruciform living.[22] Thus, the local congregation is the hermeneutic of the gospel when it is filled with the presence of the Holy Spirit and lives out the visible and invisible revelation of God. Flett points out the tension between the visible and invisible, which exists within Newbigin's six characteristics of the congregation as hermeneutic of the gospel.[23]

Another important part of Flett's analysis of the congregation as hermeneutic of the gospel is the dual direction Newbigin utilizes whereby the local congregation is formed by the gospel, but it is also the active agent for making the gospel credible in a pluralist society.[24] Flett writes,

> Notable here is the direction of the hermeneutic: living in the gospel, the congregation develops a way of interpreting the world. . . . As soon as he makes this point, however, Newbigin inverts the direction: in answer to the question of how the church might claim the gospel as public truth . . . he states that "the only hermeneutic of the gospel is a congregation of men and women who believe it and live by it."[25]

So, the local congregation, by indwelling the gospel, develops a way of viewing the world, but it also lives out the gospel as a credible witness to the viability of the gospel as public truth. By indwelling the story of Jesus Christ—His birth,

---

19. Flett's is the only reference, quote, or discussion of the congregation as hermeneutic of the gospel in this book.

20. Flett, "What Does It Mean for a Congregation to Be a Hermeneutic?," 196–98.

21. Flett, "What Does It Mean for a Congregation to Be a Hermeneutic?," 198–203.

22. Flett, "What Does It Mean for a Congregation to Be a Hermeneutic?," 203–6. Flett draws a connection, through Barth, between the visibility of the Church and the actions of God in history. The resurrection, though historical fact as Flett argues, is not visible to anyone to whom God has not revealed it. Meanwhile, the Cross is visible as a recorded act of history acknowledged outside of the Christian community. Thus, Flett asserts that for the church to live the visible reality of the resurrection, it must live a cruciform life.

23. Flett, "What Does It Mean for a Congregation to Be a Hermeneutic?," 210–12.

24. Flett, "What Does It Mean for a Congregation to Be a Hermeneutic?," 196–98.

25. Flett, "What Does It Mean for a Congregation to Be a Hermeneutic?," 198.

life, crucifixion, resurrection, and ascension—"the community claims no control over history, but witnesses to its 'real meaning and goal.'"[26] Thus, the local congregation takes on a cruciform life,[27] whereby Jesus serves as the center of human history and the church as His agent of witness in human history. Flett goes on to point out that the local congregation, by indwelling the gospel, is the locus of mission and a learning community journeying towards the completion of history.[28] Ultimately, Flett is arguing from Newbigin's congregation as hermeneutic of the gospel, that "The Church represents God's reign not because it has a technique but because it is a body of people shaped by the gospel," and thus it is "the endpoint to which his argument has been developing" throughout *GPS*.[29] Flett believes that Newbigin is arguing that being formed by and in the gospel, the local congregation serves as God's representative, His hermeneutic, and His method of interpreting revelation to the world.

Flett does an excellent job of discussing some of the most important elements in Newbigin's chapter on the congregation as hermeneutic of the gospel. He even connects this chapter to earlier parts of *GPS* and some of Newbigin's other writings to highlight its place in Newbigin's discussions of the presence of the Holy Spirit within the church, indwelling the gospel, the kingdom of God, and the imagery of the local congregation as the sign, instrument, and foretaste of God's present and future kingdom. Building upon Rae's work on the congregation as hermeneutic as the foundation of the visible community of the church, and combining it with Barth's understanding of the cruciform life of the church in the invisible resurrection of Christ through the visible Cross, Flett provides a thickening texture to Newbigin's idea, which gives it context both within Newbigin's writings and other ecclesial conversations of the twentieth century. The dual purpose Flett addresses is that the congregation is formed by the gospel, and in turn shares the gospel as public truth to the world. This public truth element is important for Flett's analysis of the congregation as hermeneutic because without the mission of the congregation bearing witness to the gospel as public truth, then the congregation as hermeneutic of the gospel remains insular and only forms the congregation in a gospel-shape, but fails to live it out. Witness as public truth drives the congregation to be the hermeneutic of the gospel for others, most often its immediate neighbors. Thus, the public witness of the gospel as truth for all of

---

26. Flett, "What Does It Mean for a Congregation to Be a Hermeneutic?," 208.

27. Flett, "What Does It Mean for a Congregation to Be a Hermeneutic?," 203–6. Flett connects this to the Barthian understanding of cruciformity, whereby the Church is living in the resurrection of Christ through the Cross.

28. Flett, "What Does It Mean for a Congregation to Be a Hermeneutic?," 208–10.

29. Flett, "What Does It Mean for a Congregation to Be a Hermeneutic?," 198, 210.

society is an integral part of the congregation as hermeneutic of the gospel. Flett's description of this dual purpose, especially the purpose of the witness of the gospel as public truth, builds upon the discussion of credibility and supports my thesis of the congregation as hermeneutic speaking to the credibility of the gospel as public truth.

Shawn P. Behan

My article, "A Hermeneutical Congregation," published in the *Asbury Journal* in 2017, builds upon both Flett and Rae in discussing the congregation as hermeneutic as Newbigin's answer to questions about the local congregation making the gospel credible as public truth. Understanding the congregation as the visible representation of the Cross and resurrection serves as the foundation for my exploration of the six characteristics Newbigin lists for the local congregation as the hermeneutic of the gospel.[30] In summarizing my exploration of these characteristics across multiple subsections of this article, I review what Newbigin says about the characteristics of such a congregation in *GPS*, and then expand upon them with evidence from other theologians or missiologists, and insights from the lived experience of churches or church movements.[31] I conclude by pointing out that local congregations should want to be the hermeneutic of the gospel because, "It is the role of the church, in seeking to follow the Holy Spirit, to reach out to its surrounding community with the arms of Christ and interpreting the words of the Father, Son, and Holy Spirit in proclamation and action, for the glory of God and the living out of the Kingdom on earth as it is in Heaven."[32] Thus, the church, which is established and sustained by the Holy Spirit, must be the church which functions as the hermeneutic of the gospel for its surrounding community. I go on to provide a shortlist of how local congregations can start functioning as the hermeneutic of the gospel. In this list, I include being daily immersed in scripture reading, preaching the whole Bible, having open dialogue within the congregation about itself (strengths, weaknesses, need for repentance), individualized discipleship, deep engagement with its surrounding community, contextualized evangelism, and being the constant reminder of the hope of Jesus Christ.[33]

This article provides a unique expansion upon the study of the congregation as hermeneutic by connecting it to other theological discussions and

---

30. Behan, "Hermeneutical Congregation," 114.
31. Behan, "Hermeneutical Congregation," 113–22.
32. Behan, "Hermeneutical Congregation," 123.
33. Behan, "Hermeneutical Congregation," 122.

in the lived reality of churches and church movements. I firmly connect to the discussion of the congregation as hermeneutic as a solution to Newbigin's question of the credibility of the gospel as public truth, which Flett addressed. As well, my article connects Newbigin's discussion with other theologians, missiologists, and pastors, showing the relevance and importance of Newbigin's work today. Yet, it leaves open the possibility that the congregation as hermeneutic could be seen as a program of a church, rather than the way of being for all congregations.

Adam Dodds

In "Newbigin's Trinitarian Missiology," Adam Dodds's contribution to the *International Review of Mission* in 2010, Dodds investigates Newbigin's doctrine of the Trinity as a central component for his understanding of the gospel and evangelism, which he then applies to Newbigin's missionary encounter with the West. Dodds shows that the gospel reveals the actions and nature of the Triune God through the person of Jesus Christ. Therefore, speaking of the gospel of Jesus Christ requires a discussion of the Trinity.[34] In agreement with Newbigin, Dodds takes a full section of this article to explain how evangelism must begin with describing the Triune God, and that means there is an irreducible link between the gospel and the Trinity.[35] Exploring this idea within Newbigin, Dodds addresses three key topics. First, is a theological anthropology based on trinitarian theology that influences the rest of Newbigin's missiology and ecclesiology. Here, Dodds references the congregation as hermeneutic of the gospel when discussing the mutual responsibility of the relationality of humanity derived from the Trinity within Newbigin's understanding of *imago Dei*.[36] Dodds brings this point back to a genesis within Newbigin's doctrine of election, which is his second topic.[37] Lastly, Dodds discusses the practical implications of this connection between evangelism and the Trinity. Dodds clearly states that "The church is called to be a sign, instrument, and foretaste" of God's community on earth, and that it is continually being redefined to look more and more like its head, Christ, rather than its members.[38] This redefinition is, "so she (the Church) can become what Newbigin famously called the hermeneutic of the gospel."[39] In being the hermeneutic of the gospel, "Newbigin suggests that the gospel becomes credible to the world when there

34. Dodds, "Newbigin's Trinitarian Missiology," 69–70.
35. Dodds, "Newbigin's Trinitarian Missiology," 70–76.
36. Dodds, "Newbigin's Trinitarian Missiology," 77–79.
37. Dodds, "Newbigin's Trinitarian Missiology," 79–82.
38. Dodds, "Newbigin's Trinitarian Missiology," 82–84.
39. Dodds, "Newbigin's Trinitarian Missiology," 82.

is a congregation of people who believe it and live it."[40] Thus, Dodds is clearly stating that the local congregation being the hermeneutic of the gospel is what makes the gospel credible in the world which that congregation inhabits. The credibility of the gospel connects to the Trinity through Dodds' gospel-Trinity link discussed earlier in his article.

Dodds expertly builds links between trinitarian theology, evangelism, theological anthropology, election, and the role of the missionary church within Newbigin. For Dodds, the congregation as hermeneutic becomes a result of the coalescing of all of these various conversations. As well, he builds a connection to Newbigin's use of sign, instrument, and foretaste, all of which serves to make the gospel credible in the world through the local congregation. Dodds is another that connects the congregation as hermeneutic of the gospel to the credibility of the gospel in society, adding to this an understanding of Newbigin's trinitarian missiology. Dodds' connection between the gospel and the Trinity shows the necessity of understanding Newbigin's view of the Trinity and its influence on the congregation as hermeneutic of the gospel concept.

George R. Hunsberger

George R. Hunsberger, being a Newbigin scholar, has utilized the congregation as hermeneutic of the gospel concept more than any other author here. And in those uses, he has provided important contributions to interpreting, understanding, and applying the concept to the North American Church. Generally, his understanding of the congregation as hermeneutic of the gospel is that "The church is the interpretive lens through which the gospel will be known in any society, in conversation with any human language or culture."[41] Thus, he calls forth Newbigin's concept upon the church as the interpretive lens of the gospel for culture. While this does provide an overview of Hunsberger's understanding of the congregation as hermeneutic of the gospel concept, it is necessary to look at the many ways that he utilizes this concept and how they further advance the discussion of it today.

In "The Newbigin Gauntlet," Hunsberger engages with the congregation as hermeneutic, highlighting its role in challenging the Western Church to indwell the gospel, believe it, and testify to it before the world.[42] Hunsberger first lays out the problem of identity within the church in the West, which does not see its need or even a place for evangelism within its own context.[43]

---

40. Dodds, "Newbigin's Trinitarian Missiology," 83–84.
41. Hunsberger, "Mission of Public Theology," 321.
42. Hunsberger, "Newbigin Gauntlet," 6.
43. Hunsberger, "Newbigin Gauntlet," 15.

Hunsberger then takes an expanded look at grasping a renewed identity of cultural exiles. He asserts that, like the exilic Israel, the church in the West must see itself as cultural exiles and live as an alternative community, which both accepts and challenges culture.[44]

In Hunsberger's contribution to *A Scandalous Prophet*,[45] "The Church in the Postmodern Transition," he focuses on Newbigin's engagement of the postmodern critique within his consideration of a needed missionary encounter with Western culture.[46] In this discussion, Newbigin applies the congregation as hermeneutic of the gospel in the missional relationship of the Church to its surrounding community. In doing this, he concludes that the church's "very being is the lens through which people view and comprehend the gospel."[47] The church, as the hermeneutic of the gospel, is the interpretive lens through which the world comes to know and understand the gospel. In this missional relationship, Hunsberger envisions the community of Christ speaking the truth of the gospel into the postmodern shift currently taking place in culture.

In "Renewing Faith During the Postmodern Transition," Hunsberger explores Newbigin's focus on mission to the West, and specifically its influence on the topic of preaching. Hunsberger charts four main ways Newbigin cultivated the missionary encounter with the West that are helpful for the current transition from modern to postmodern—of believing, witnessing, being a community, and hope.[48] Within those ways, the way of being a community highlights the congregation as hermeneutic as vital for understanding the rationale and authority for the church both to exist and to witness. "The presence of the Christian community functions as a hermeneutical key, an interpretive lens through which onlookers gain a view of the gospel in the living colours of common life."[49] Thus, the church exists and witnesses because it is the hermeneutic of the gospel for society. This existence and witness help the Christian community to alleviate the growing identity crisis for churches experiencing the transition from modern to postmodern culture.[50] And this

---

44. Hunsberger, "Newbigin Gauntlet," 16–19.

45. See Foust et al., *Scandalous Prophet*. "The congregation as hermeneutic of the gospel" is referenced in Cruchley-Jones, "Entering Exile," 24; Goheen, "Missional Calling of Believers in the World," 45, 48, 53; and quoted by Hunsberger, "Church in the Postmodern Transition," 103.

46. Hunsberger, "Church in the Postmodern Transition," 95. Another relevant article on the postmodern transition that references, though does not engage with, "the congregation as hermeneutic of the gospel" is Van Engen, "Mission Theology," 437–61.

47. Hunsberger, "Church in the Postmodern Transition," 103.

48. Hunsberger, "Renewing Faith during the Postmodern Transition," 11–13.

49. Hunsberger, "Renewing Faith during the Postmodern Transition," 13.

50. Hunsberger, "Renewing Faith during the Postmodern Transition," 12–13.

identity, Hunsberger argues, is shaped by biblical preaching that faithfully roots and recreates the church's identity in the gospel.[51]

The Story That Chooses Us[52] is a collection of Hunsberger's essays, articles, and chapters on the topic of missional theology from over twenty years of his discussion of it within the Gospel and Our Culture Network in North America (GOCN). Throughout these essays, Hunsberger addresses the implications of the congregation as hermeneutic of the gospel on multiple topics, including Newbigin's challenge to view North America as a mission field,[53] congregations embracing the missionary posture,[54] what it means to be a sent community of the Great Commission,[55] the integrity of word and deed in evangelism,[56] and having the authority to witness by being a place where the gospel is visibly present, believed, and followed.[57] While all of these address different implications of the congregation as hermeneutic of the gospel concept, they all follow one simple understanding of the concept, that the local congregation in "its very being is the lens through which people view and comprehend the gospel."[58] This understanding is consistent throughout Hunsberger's utilization of the concept in this book.

Hunsberger's 2006 *Missiology* article, "The Missional Voice and Posture of Public Theologizing" addresses what he sees as a necessary connection for post-Christendom North America between missional church and public theologizing. He argues that public theologizing is an essential activity of the church and will include five key features: a spirit of companionship,[59] humility in Truth-telling,[60] particularity in discourse,[61] courage in public action,[62] and an eye on the horizon.[63] It is in his discussion of a spirit of companionship that Hunsberger discusses the congregation as hermeneutic of the gospel. He asserts that the church sits on both sides of the gospel-culture encounter, which

51. Hunsberger, "Renewing Faith during the Postmodern Transition," 13.

52. Hunsberger, *Story That Chooses Us*. Throughout Hunsberger either references, quotes, or discusses "the congregation as hermeneutic" on pp. 14, 18, 20, 28, 82, 99, 108, 158.

53. Hunsberger, *Story That Chooses Us*, chap. 2, "Challenge."

54. Hunsberger, *Story That Chooses Us*, 82–85.

55. Hunsberger, *Story That Chooses Us*, 99–100.

56. Hunsberger, *Story That Chooses Us*, chap. 7, "Encounter."

57. Hunsberger, *Story That Chooses Us*, 158–59.

58. Hunsberger, *Story That Chooses Us*, 82.

59. Hunsberger, "Missional Voice and Posture of Public Theology," 20–22.

60. Hunsberger, "Missional Voice and Posture of Public Theology," 22–23.

61. Hunsberger, "Missional Voice and Posture of Public Theology," 23–24.

62. Hunsberger, "Missional Voice and Posture of Public Theology," 25–26.

63. Hunsberger, "Missional Voice and Posture of Public Theology," 26–27.

leads the church to a continuing conversion from the cultural worldview to the biblical worldview.[64] In sitting on both sides of this encounter, Hunsberger argues that the church functions as "the 'hermeneutic' of the gospel by which they (society) see it (the gospel) taking shape within their own culture."[65] It is in this function that the gospel is proclaimed as public truth for society. Hunsberger then connects this understanding with the congregational evangelism strategy of Raymond Fung in *The Isaiah Vision*. In this combination, Hunsberger advocates for individual churches working with others for things God wants in the world, inviting those others they work with to join them in worshiping God, and finally inviting those who join worship into discipleship to Jesus Christ.[66]

Hunsberger's 2005 article for *Swedish Missiological Themes*, "The Mission of Public Theology" provides an overview of the mission of public theology, which is deeply grounded in Newbigin. Hunsberger first establishes the need for theologizing in the public square, but then turns the majority of his argument onto the topic of the church encountering culture with both acceptance and challenge.[67] Hunsberger believes this encounter will include a gracious comradeship, a humble epistemology, a courageous particularity, risk-taking proposals and actions, and a hope-filled horizon.[68] If this list seems familiar, it is because it has a lot of similarities with Hunsberger's list from "The Missional Voice and Posture of Public Theology," both of which speak to the necessary components of public theologizing. In his discussion of the public encounter between church and culture in which public theologizing happens, Hunsberger utilizes the congregation as hermeneutic of the gospel as a foundational building block for this encounter; an encounter that believes and expressly proclaims the gospel as public truth. Hunsberger shows that because of the congregation being the hermeneutic of the gospel, the gospel will change the church and how it engages culture.[69] Hunsberger argues that through the local congregation believing and living the gospel, that culture is encountered, accepts and is accepted, is challenged, and is changed by the gospel.

Throughout decades of writing about Newbigin, missional church/theology, and public engagement by the gospel, Hunsberger has routinely applied the congregation as hermeneutic of the gospel as an essential component to all those conversations. In "The Newbigin Gauntlet," Hunsberger's view of

---

64. Hunsberger, "Missional Voice and Posture of Public Theology," 21.

65. Hunsberger, "Missional Voice and Posture of Public Theology," 21.

66. Hunsberger, "Missional Voice and Posture of Public Theology," 21–22.

67. Hunsberger, "Mission of Public Theology," 317–19.

68. Hunsberger, "Mission of Public Theology," 322–24.

69. Hunsberger, "Mission of Public Theology," 321.

The Reason for Studying the Congregation

the congregation as hermeneutic of the gospel is a challenge to the Western Church to indwell, believe, and testify to the gospel.[70] "The Church in the Postmodern Transition" discusses the implications of the congregation as hermeneutic as the foundation for the missional relationship between church and culture whereby culture comes to know the gospel. In "Renewing Faith During the Postmodern Transition," Hunsberger utilizes the congregation as hermeneutic of the gospel concept for answering questions about the authority of the church to exist and preach the gospel in society. Hunsberger's multiple uses of the congregation as hermeneutic of the gospel in *The Story That Chooses Us* reveals the impact of the congregation as hermeneutic concept upon discussions of witness, evangelism, the Great Commission, encountering culture, reclaiming the missionary nature of the church, a missionary encounter with the West, truth, authority, history, the presence of the Holy Spirit, and the local congregation. In "The Missional Voice and Posture of Public Theologizing," Hunsberger's application of the congregation as hermeneutic within his discussion of a spirit of comradeship shows a very practical implication of the concept, calling for the church to partner with members of the community in building towards God's purposes in society.[71] Lastly, "The Mission of Public Theology" argues that the local congregation is the interpretive device for the world to see and understand the gospel, utilizing the congregation as hermeneutic of the gospel as an important bridge between the public theology and missiology conversations. In all these many uses of the congregation as hermeneutic of the gospel concept, Hunsberger has stayed consistent to his understanding of this concept and applied it to many different conversations—the identity of the church in North America, the postmodern transition in Western culture, missional theology, and public engagement/theologizing. Thus, Hunsberger has shown the vast implications of Newbigin's concept and begun using it in discussions for the contemporary North American Church, and is an essential building block for any investigation of the concept.

Jeppe Bach Nikolajsen

Jeppe Bach Nikolajsen's *The Distinctive Identity of the Church*[72] focuses on identity, while also arguing for a new social order from Newbigin's work. Nikolajsen's book studies the ecclesiologies of Newbigin and John Howard

---

70. Hunsberger, "Newbigin Gauntlet," 6.

71. This idea can be found spread throughout Newbigin's writings in part or in total, but some of the most coherent are Newbigin, "What Kind of Britain?"; Newbigin, "Leading Off," 4, 18; Newbigin, "Can a Modern Society Be Christian?," 95–108.

72. Nikolajsen, *Distinctive Identity of the Church*. Nikolajsen references "the congregation as hermeneutic" on 32, and quotes it on 63, 66, 76, 87–88, 178.

The Congregation as Hermeneutic of the Gospel

Yoder, putting them in conversation with each other for the purpose of understanding the distinctive identity of the church in the post-Christendom West. Nikolajsen begins by charting his way through Newbigin's missionary ecclesiology, in which he comes across the congregation as hermeneutic multiple times. But his most significant interaction with it comes in his discussion of Newbigin's understanding of the church as a new social ethic for society. Nikolajsen starts his point here by saying, "Newbigin states that the Christian community must believe, embody and proclaim the gospel. Hence, the gospel is not announced as a disembodied gospel, but rather, a community which represents the gospel."[73] He argues that Newbigin views the gospel as embedded in the community of Christ, from which it is made known to the world. This community, in representing the gospel, is the hermeneutic of the gospel to society. As such, Nikolajsen argues that it must establish a new social order in society, what he calls the new social ethic for public engagement.[74] He says that for Newbigin, this new social order is modeled by Christians who are active agents of God's kingdom, and the church, which is part of this new eschatological reality, was inaugurated by Christ.[75] Thus, this new social order that is established by the congregation being the hermeneutic of the gospel forms (at least in part)[76] the distinctive identity of the church. Nikolajsen concludes that Newbigin "clearly believes that the church's way of life is distinct."[77] This new social order comes directly out of the centrality of Christ for the congregation, whereby "Christ is the new fact, the new datum, from which Christian ethics spring."[78] Thus Christology is centrally important to the congregation living out its distinctive identity as the hermeneutic of the gospel for society, as the example of the Christian order and ethic.

Nikolajsen's charting and summarizing of Newbigin's ecclesiology is very well done, and he effectively argues its meaning for understanding the distinctive identity of the church through Newbigin. His focus on the congregation as hermeneutic of the gospel as central to understanding Newbigin's view of the church as a new social order is important because it links between the alternative community and missionary identity of the church. Though, the

---

73. Nikolajsen, *Distinctive Identity of the Church*, 62.

74. Nikolajsen, *Distinctive Identity of the Church*, 62–67.

75. Nikolajsen, *Distinctive Identity of the Church*, 66.

76. Nikolajsen, *Distinctive Identity of the Church*, 176–80. Nikolajsen will later argue for combining this identity of new social order in Newbigin with Yoder's identity of the Church as a distinctive people living a distinct way of life grounded in an eschatological reality, as the full distinctive identity of the Church.

77. Nikolajsen, *Distinctive Identity of the Church*, 176–80.

78. Nikolajsen, *Distinctive Identity of the Church*, 176–80.

new social order that arises from Newbigin's concept of the congregation as hermeneutic of the gospel only partially explains Newbigin's use of this concept as an expression of the missionary nature of the church.

Paul Weston

Paul Weston is another Newbigin scholar who has utilized the congregation as hermeneutic of the gospel within his writings. From those uses, two stand out for their deep and critical engagement with the concept. First, in Weston's dissertation from King's College, University of London, entitled *Mission and Cultural Change*,[79] he provides a critical reading of Newbigin's post-1974 writings in light of their influence from scientist and philosopher Michael Polanyi. Weston argues that understanding Polanyi is key to interpreting Newbigin in relation to his discussion of the epistemological shift from modern to postmodern in Western society. Within his argument, Weston has an extended discussion about the congregation as hermeneutic of the gospel as an essential part (along with indwelling the gospel story) of understanding Newbigin's reflections upon Western culture. Weston argues that the tacit knowledge of God comes through the indwelling of the gospel story by the local congregation, which then makes this indwelling public to the community through being the hermeneutic of the gospel.[80] Weston notes that the congregation as hermeneutic is the answer to the question of the credibility of the gospel in a culture that no longer accepts the truth of God's existence.[81] Thus, the church must reorient itself scripturally through indwelling the gospel, so that they may live out a fresh plausibility structure in culture as an alternative community.[82] This, Weston credits, comes from Newbigin's understanding of Polanyi's claimed "crisis of the hour," the changing plausibility structure of Western culture.[83] Weston says that Newbigin saw this as a dual problem, requiring a fresh epistemological starting point for culture, and doing so from within culture itself so that it will become the lived reality for all of culture.[84] According to Weston, "Newbigin's response to this dual challenge is that it is through the church's 'indwelling' of the gospel—as the only possible 'hermeneutic'—that both needs are addressed."[85] Weston is saying that Newbigin believed the local

---

79. Weston, *Mission and Cultural Change*. "The congregation as hermeneutic" is referenced/quoted on 253, 274, 317, and 320 and is discussed at length on 116–19.
80. Weston, *Mission and Cultural Change*, 116.
81. Weston, *Mission and Cultural Change*, 118.
82. Weston, *Mission and Cultural Change*, 118.
83. Weston, *Mission and Cultural Change*, 118.
84. Weston, *Mission and Cultural Change*, 118.
85. Weston, *Mission and Cultural Change*, 119.

congregation indwelling the gospel and living as its hermeneutic in society provides both the fresh epistemological starting point for cultural renewal, and that it does so from within contemporary culture. Later, Weston connects the congregation as hermeneutic of the gospel with the overlap of Newbigin, Polanyi, and missionary theology through the topics of witness and apologetics.

Second is Weston's 2015 *Journal of Missional Practice* article, "Lesslie Newbigin: Looking Forward in Retrospect," reflecting upon the impact of Newbigin's work. In this, he asserts that Newbigin's discussion of the necessary missionary encounter with the West stands the test of time as a prophetic word to the church of today.[86] Weston points out that Newbigin has a unique way of articulating the most important questions with "missionary passion, cultural questioning, and theological weight."[87] He then goes on to specifically talk about three main points of Newbigin's discussion of the missionary encounter with the West and their continued importance for today. First, Weston discusses the dynamic relationship between community and witness. "What Newbigin stressed was that the only way in which the outlandish message about a crucified saviour and reigning Lord could truly be understood and experienced was through the complex of caring, praising, confessing, and forgiving relationships that we know as the local congregation."[88] Weston, building upon the congregation as hermeneutic, relates that the relationship between the community of Christ (established and sustained by the personal and relational love of God) and witness is foundational to the missionary encounter with the West.[89] Weston's second point shows the need to heed Newbigin's call to subvert the stranglehold on apologetics by the Enlightenment ideals and plausibility structure.[90] And Weston's final point is that, also in countering the Enlightenment plausibility structure, Newbigin calls for a humble but confident witness by the local congregation in the public square (based on Newbigin's assumption of the gospel as public truth because it is public fact).[91]

In both examples, Weston is utilizing the congregation as hermeneutic of the gospel as a centerpiece to his arguments about Newbigin's view of engagement with Western culture and legacy for today, respectively. Weston's dissertation takes a very philosophical stance on the congregation as hermeneutic, as the lived starting point for culture in the midst of epistemological change.

---

86. Weston, "Lesslie Newbigin," 2.
87. Weston, "Lesslie Newbigin," 3.
88. Weston, "Lesslie Newbigin," 4.
89. Weston, "Lesslie Newbigin," 3–5.
90. Weston, "Lesslie Newbigin," 5–7.
91. Weston, "Lesslie Newbigin," 7–9.

The Reason for Studying the Congregation

This view sees the congregation as hermeneutic of the gospel as essential for both individual witness and public witness. It is in living out the indwelling of the gospel that congregations witness to society and act as an alternative community calling on the culture to change. This change, Weston is assuming, is not only inevitable but is already happening. He is arguing that Newbigin's perspective provides a mechanism for the church to speak into and guide that change towards a biblical plausibility structure. All of which is predicated upon the congregation as hermeneutic of the gospel as the answer to the question of the credibility of the gospel in Western culture. Later, in Weston's article about Newbigin's legacy, his engagement with the congregation as hermeneutic is essential to Newbigin's call for a missionary encounter with the West specifically looking at its role within the public witness of local congregations. Weston ties together two key components of Newbigin's thought—the personal and relational love of God, and the visible community of Christ as the sign, instrument, and foretaste of that love in the world—through the congregation as hermeneutic of the gospel. But more importantly, Weston's connection between the community of Christ and witness is foundational to understanding Newbigin's view of the missionary encounter with the West. It is in Newbigin's application of his missionary ecclesiology to the Western context that the congregation as hermeneutic concept developed its linguistic form. And it is through this form that Weston builds a bridge between witness and the corporate Christian community. Thus, to Weston, there is a clear connection between witness and each member of every congregation, so that in living as the hermeneutic of the gospel they are bearing witness to the message of salvation in Jesus Christ. With Newbigin having already stated that the nature of the church is bound to its bearing witness to the present and future salvation of Jesus Christ,[92] Weston is providing a way of this nature shaping each local congregation in the West through the congregation as hermeneutic of the gospel concept. Respectively, Weston takes a philosophical and historical look at the congregation as hermeneutic of the gospel concept, both of which are important for understanding the concept and discussing its meaning. While I do believe that these perspectives on the congregation as hermeneutic of the gospel provide valuable insight into understanding Newbigin's concept, I would push Weston to go beyond the historical and philosophical to think about the implications that this concept has for the Western Church today.

---

92. Newbigin, *Household of God*, 108.

The Congregation as Hermeneutic of the Gospel

Michael W. Goheen

Michael W. Goheen is also a Newbigin scholar who has often quoted or referenced the congregation as hermeneutic of the gospel within his works. Similar to Weston, there are two of Goheen's books that have a more robust engagement with the congregation as hermeneutic of the gospel concept and are necessary reading for any investigation of the concept.

Goheen's dissertation, *"As the Father Has Sent Me, I Am Sending You"*[93] is the seminal text on Newbigin's missionary ecclesiology, charting its location across the entire corpus of Newbigin's works. Goheen also places Newbigin's missionary ecclesiology in conversation with other twentieth-century ecclesiologies, locating it within the context in which Newbigin would have been thinking and discussing the church. Throughout, Goheen quotes, references, and discusses the congregation as hermeneutic of the gospel multiple times, but it serves as a primary piece of two of his arguments. First, Goheen notes the role of the congregation as hermeneutic of the gospel in Newbigin's understanding of the missionary character of the church, specifically discussing the church's witnessing to and participating in the Kingdom of God. Goheen then highlights in Newbigin the important elements of election, sign, instrument, and foretaste, the provisional incorporation of humankind into Christ, and lastly the congregation as hermeneutic. Within this discussion, Goheen notes that it is the Holy Spirit which "is both the real presence now and the future promise of the kingdom," and thus the church, which is inhabited by the presence of the Spirit, "is the community that has begun to experience the presence of the kingdom."[94] This, Goheen notes from Newbigin, is what makes the local congregation the hermeneutic of the gospel, "the living reality of a community who has a foretaste of the kingdom and is a faithful preview of its future consummation."[95] He goes on to point out that as the hermeneutic of the gospel, the local congregation "is privileged and called to seek justice, freedom and peace, to share in the sufferings of an encounter with evil, to exhibit solidarity with the oppressed, and to share the assurance, hope, and joy of the victory of the kingdom."[96] This serves as the foundation for Goheen's understanding of the congregation as hermeneutic, which he applies to other parts of Newbigin's missionary ecclesiology.

---

93. Goheen, *"As the Father Has Sent Me, I Am Sending You."* In this book, Goheen quotes "the congregation as hermeneutic" on 107, 111, 224, 303, 367, 372, 373, 378; references it on 166, 231, 239, 140, 244, 263, 273, 373, 378, 389; and discusses it on 175–76, 406–9.

94. Goheen, *"As the Father Has Sent Me, I Am Sending You,"* 176.

95. Goheen, *"As the Father Has Sent Me, I Am Sending You,"* 176.

96. Goheen, *"As the Father Has Sent Me, I Am Sending You,"* 176.

The Reason for Studying the Congregation

The second major argument of his dissertation where Goheen utilizes the congregation as hermeneutic of the gospel is within his discussion of Newbigin's writings on a missionary encounter with Western culture. Here, Goheen notes that the congregation as hermeneutic is essential for making the Cross known and relevant in the world. Specifically, Goheen addresses the vision of the church as an alternative community, to which he says, "Newbigin outlines the salient features of such a community."[97] The first expression of this community that Goheen highlights from Newbigin is the congregation as hermeneutic of the gospel. Goheen builds this idea off of his brief synopsis of the six characteristics that Newbigin lists in *GPS*, noting, "In these six characteristics Newbigin is concerned to nurture a church that stands as an alternative community over against the idolatries that are destroying western culture."[98] Thus, Goheen sees these characteristics as an outline of the form of an alternative community actively engaged with its society. He breaks down this form into three requisite pieces, "The church is a community that lives by a different light than the dominant culture. . . . [A] missiological understanding of culture is essential to this task" and "this call involves both a communal embodiment and individual responsibility of each believer in his or her calling in culture."[99] Here, Goheen shows that the alternative community the church is called to model requires a new worldview or plausibility structure, a missiological understanding of culture, and both personal and communal responsibility to live missionally within culture.

Nearly twenty years after his dissertation, Goheen's continued research, reflection, and application of Newbigin brought about *The Church and Its Vocation*,[100] specifically dealing with the impact and legacy of Newbigin's missionary ecclesiology. In this book, Goheen retraces his dissertation argument about Newbigin's missionary ecclesiology, combining it with twenty years of further research on Newbigin and missionary churches to provide a clear theological vision of Newbigin's ecclesiology.[101] Goheen recapitulates his dissertation argument, highlighting the differences between Newbigin's ecclesiology and other twentieth-century ecclesiologies. In explaining these differences, Goheen notes that the congregation as hermeneutic impacts many of Newbigin's points, such as the missionary nature of the church,[102] the public

---

97. Goheen, *"As the Father Has Sent Me, I Am Sending You,"* 406.

98. Goheen, *"As the Father Has Sent Me, I Am Sending You,"* 408.

99. Goheen, *"As the Father Has Sent Me, I Am Sending You,"* 408–9.

100. Goheen, *Church and Its Vocation*. Goheen quotes "the congregation as hermeneutic" on 114, 128 and references it on 81, 86, 125, 128, 143, 187, 206.

101. Goheen, *Church and Its Vocation*, xiv.

102. Goheen, *Church and Its Vocation*, 81, 86.

witness of the church,[103] discipleship and fellowship,[104] and the role of the laity in ministry.[105] Within these, Goheen points to Newbigin's understanding of the congregation as hermeneutic of the gospel as indicative of its role as a distinct community. Goheen writes, "A community that lives like this will be a 'foretaste of a different social order.'"[106] By being the congregation as hermeneutic of the gospel, which Goheen noted in his original dissertation only happens by the presence of the Holy Spirit in the congregation, local congregations will be shaped by and live out of the gospel, and as such will model a new social order. Goheen also mentions that Newbigin notes that the activities of the church only have meaning and power as they point back to a believing congregation.[107] Thus, believing and living the gospel is essential for the congregation being the hermeneutic of the gospel, through which they model a new reality for society in which God has placed them and called them to minister.

These two books of Goheen clearly outline his understanding of the congregation as hermeneutic of the gospel as a key component to Newbigin's missionary ecclesiology, and as a calling upon local congregations to be the living embodiment of the gospel as an alternative community in society. In his dissertation, Goheen masterfully charts Newbigin's missionary ecclesiology and particularly the many places where the congregation as hermeneutic functions as an essential component of that ecclesiology. His connection of the congregation as hermeneutic to Newbigin's discussion of the missionary nature of the church and the identity of the church as an alternative community provides clues as to how the concept should be read and interpreted within all Newbigin's work. For any study that engages Newbigin's congregation as hermeneutic of the gospel and its place within his missionary ecclesiology, Goheen's dissertation is the starting point. Goheen's later expansion upon his dissertation within a discussion of Newbigin's legacy, more firmly establishes that the local congregation that knows, believes, and lives the gospel due to the presence of the Holy Spirit within it, functions as the hermeneutic of the gospel and models an alternative community for society. These two books provide an overview of Goheen's understanding and usage of the congregation as hermeneutic of the gospel concept, and deeply connect it to Newbigin's missionary ecclesiology and his calling on congregations to be an alternative community for their society. I appreciate Goheen's locating of the

---

103. Goheen, *Church and Its Vocation*, 143, 187.
104. Goheen, *Church and Its Vocation*, 114, 125, 128.
105. Goheen, *Church and Its Vocation*, 206.
106. Goheen, *Church and Its Vocation*, 81.
107. Goheen, *Church and Its Vocation*, 81.

congregation as hermeneutic of the gospel concept within Newbigin's missionary ecclesiology, but I would also expand that location to his trinitarian missiology since both are impacted by this concept.

The authors addressed here provide an overview of the major ways in which scholars and practitioners are interpreting and discussing Newbigin's concept of the local congregation as the hermeneutic of the gospel. These ways speak to the credibility of the gospel as public truth, the gospel engagement of the public by the church, the postmodern transition in society, the church as an alternative community, and Newbigin's trinitarian missiology lived out in the church. They also provide a group of conversation partners with whom my thesis can agree, critique, and build upon to further the understanding and usage of Newbigin's concept for the church in North America. These authors also influenced the parameters within which my research took place. And while each of these authors has provided a thorough interpretation and application of the congregation as hermeneutic of the gospel concept, what I am doing with this research is identifying the major elements of Newbigin's thinking that are involved with this concept. These major elements—being constituted by the Holy Spirit, representing the Kingdom of God, and living by the gospel—help to provide a fuller understanding of the congregation as hermeneutic concept. By investigating each of these elements, I am expanding our understanding of Newbigin's congregation as hermeneutic concept in support of these author's interpretations and applications of the concept.

METHODOLOGY AND SCOPE

All academic research functions within a certain set of parameters and utilizes a methodology for gathering and analyzing the data that it addresses. Within this study, the methodology and scope of research provide the foundation for understanding the approach I used in investigating the congregation as hermeneutic of the gospel, which led to the stated thesis, argumentation, and goal, as well as the authors selected in the section above.

Methodology

This research combines the systematizing approach of Goheen,[108] the qualitative analysis of theological literature approach of Schuster,[109] and the historical contextualization of Hunsberger.[110] It is systematizing in that I am bringing together multiple locations where Newbigin discusses ecclesiology and

---

108. Goheen, *"As the Father Has Sent Me, I Am Sending You,"* 6–7.
109. Schuster, "Significance of the Kingdom of God," 53.
110. Hunsberger, "Biography as Missiology," 524.

mapping their connections with one of his central expressions of ecclesiology—the congregation as hermeneutic of the gospel. It is qualitative in that I am deeply engaging and reflecting upon both published and unpublished writings of Newbigin. And it is historical because throughout I acknowledge markers of significant events in Newbigin's life which influence his utilizing of the linguistic form of the congregation as hermeneutic of the gospel to express his understanding of the missionary nature of the church. In doing this, my reflections upon Newbigin's work incorporates theology of mission, ecclesiology, and missiology.

I began my research with a review of a comprehensive Newbigin bibliography that is provided in *A Scandalous Prophet*[111] to determine the most relevant materials. From this bibliography, I began reviewing relevant resources from my own personal library of Newbigin materials, newbiginresources.org, and libraries at the University of Cambridge (Centre for Christianity Worldwide, Westminster College, and University Library), the University of Birmingham (Main Library and Orchard Learning Resource Centre), Wheaton College (Buswell Library and The Billy Graham Center Archives), Concordia Theological Seminary—St. Louis, the Trinity School of Ministry (Ambridge, PA), and Asbury Theological Seminary.

From this review of Newbigin's writings, I mapped his various discussions about ecclesiology, noting the places where his discussion overlapped. I then narrowed in on sixteen of Newbigin's articles, chapters, or books that gave his most detailed discussion of ecclesiology, along with his autobiography. By reading Newbigin's autobiography alongside these other writings, I was able to place Newbigin's work within the context of his life. I then read these materials a second time, focusing on the major pieces of his ecclesiological argument in each. In this reading I reflected theologically and missiologically upon Newbigin's writings, attempting to observe their biblical fidelity and missiological meaning. From this reading and mapping, two key points guided my writing: (1) there is a connection between the context of the church in the West and Newbigin's expression of the congregation as hermeneutic of the gospel, (2) there are three elements[112] of Newbigin's life-long discussion of ecclesiology that are essential for understanding this expression.

---

111. Foust and Hunsberger, "Bishop J. E. Lesslie Newbigin," 249–305.

112. The three things that I will be discussing throughout this study can be expressed as elements, pieces, aspects, dimensions, components, major themes, features, or a plethora of other terms. I have chosen to use the term element because I believe it provides a permeable structure in which to discuss these three ideas, and because these three pieces have become key for my understanding of the congregation as hermeneutic of the gospel concept. Thus, I contend that they are essential for understanding this concept and should be present in our minds any time we think about or discuss this concept.

The Reason for Studying the Congregation

First, there is a connection between the context of the church in the West, which Newbigin is specifically addressing in *GPS*, and his expression of the congregation as hermeneutic of the gospel. This expression itself is one of many Newbigin uses about the missionary nature of the church, but it is the context of the Western Church, which in his opinion has abdicated its position in society, that elicits this expression from Newbigin. This expression is Newbigin's explicit call upon the Western Church to regain its missionary identity, and he does this by directing the local congregation to answer the question about what makes the gospel credible to a pluralist society. The answer is congregations full of men and women who believe the truth of the gospel and live that truth in every aspect of their life, every day.

Second, I identified three elements that are essential to understanding the congregation as hermeneutic of the gospel, as Newbigin expresses it. The first element is being constituted by the Holy Spirit.[113] The second element is representing the kingdom of God.[114] The third element is living by the gospel.[115] I am addressing these three elements because I have found them to be especially important in understanding and discussing the concept of the congregation as hermeneutic of the gospel. These elements, while discussed distinctly, are interwoven with each other and should be seen as parts of a whole.

I have selected each of these elements for very distinct reasons. First, being constituted by the Holy Spirit and representing the kingdom of God are parts of Newbigin's missionary ecclesiology that are always present. He continually discusses these ideas, in different forms and with various focus, throughout his lifetime of writing about ecclesiology. Thus, to understand the congregation as hermeneutic of the gospel it is important to also understand these two elements. The third element, living by the gospel, is uniquely attached to the congregation as hermeneutic of the gospel expression.[116] Newbigin saw in the Western, plural context that there was a credibility gap, the culture no longer viewed the gospel as a credible source of truth about the world. Thus, in recalling the local congregation in the West to its missionary identity, Newbigin explicitly says that the church must believe and live by the gospel (two ideas that he implies the church in the West is no longer doing). In the chapters that expound upon each of these elements, there will be a focus on certain dynamics of the life of the missionary congregation that is the hermeneutic of the gospel. When I discuss these three elements, I place constituted

---

113. Derived from Newbigin, *Household of God*.
114. Derived from Newbigin, *Sign of the Kingdom*.
115. Derived from Newbigin, *Gospel in a Pluralist Society*.
116. Newbigin, *Gospel in a Pluralist Society*, 227.

by the Holy Spirit and representing the kingdom of God first, because they were always present in Newbigin's ecclesiology, and living by the gospel third because it is something new Newbigin has added for the Western Church he is specifically addressing in *GPS*. As well, I believe that being constituted by the Holy Spirit should be first because it is from the active presence of the Holy Spirit that representing the kingdom of God and living by the gospel flow.

Because these three elements are three pieces of one whole which fluidly interweave with each other, it can be difficult to distinguish them from each other. One of the ways that I have found helpful to distinguish them from each other is to think of the relationship of primary focus. There are three relationships that the church must nurture—with God, with the world, and within itself—and in each of these elements one of these relationships is the primary focus. Being constituted by the Holy Spirit focuses on the relationship between the church and God, and in this relationship God's purpose of forming the followers of Jesus in to the Body of Christ is enacted. Representing the kingdom of God focuses on the relationship between the church as the world, and in this relationship of God's purpose of sending the Body of Christ to fulfill God's mission is enacted. Living by the gospel focuses on the relationship of the church within itself (both within individual congregations and between congregations), and in this relationship God's purpose of unifying and sanctifying the Body of Christ is enacted. All three of these elements are responding to Newbigin's question, "How can the Church be fully open to the needs of the world and yet have its eyes fixed always on God?"[117] Yet, each element expresses this in its own way.

Scope

Research within Newbigin required that I limit myself first to his published works and those unpublished works that have been made publicly available. As well, I focused my search on Newbigin's materials that discussed ecclesiology or one of the six characteristics he lists in *GPS*. Due to the wide array of possible conversation partners on Newbigin, I have specifically chosen to focus primarily on the academic conversations of Newbigin scholarship, The Gospel and Our Culture Network in North America (GOCN), the public missiology group of the American Society of Missiology (ASM), and a few representative digital sources. From these conversations, I have focused on those who provide a critical substantial engagement with, or meaningful use of the congregation as hermeneutic of the gospel. These parameters guided my research. With these parameters in mind, I can now move to the results of this research.

---

117. Newbigin, *Gospel in a Pluralist Society*, 226.

2

Newbigin and the Nature of the Church

INTRODUCTION

THE CONGREGATION AS HERMENEUTIC of the gospel is a specific expression of Newbigin's understanding of the missionary nature of the church. This understanding is expressed in many ways throughout Newbigin's life, which Michael W. Goheen has summarized as Newbigin's missionary ecclesiology.[1] This vision of the missionary nature of the church, while present throughout Newbigin's lifetime of ecclesial discussions, takes on the specific expression of the hermeneutic of the gospel in his retirement. It is part of Newbigin's continual discussion of missionary ecclesiology which has caught the attention of many who utilized it in discussing ecclesiology today (particularly those addressing re-missioning the West). By calling each local congregation the hermeneutic of the gospel, Newbigin is explicitly stating that each congregation is the interpretive body through which the gospel is seen as credible in the world. Thus, to fully comprehend Newbigin's expression of the congregation as hermeneutic of the gospel as part of his complex understanding of the missionary nature of the church, it is necessary to study its use within *The Gospel in a Pluralist Society* (*GPS*), Newbigin's other reflections upon the missionary nature of the church, and the experiences which shaped Newbigin's ecclesial reflections—in particular those that influenced his retirement writings on the subject.

---

1. Goheen, *"As the Father Has Sent Me, I Am Sending You."*

THE CONGREGATION AS HERMENEUTIC OF THE GOSPEL

Newbigin's description of the local congregation as the hermeneutic of the gospel expresses his understanding of each congregation providing an interpretive lens for the world to see the gospel and the gospel to see the world. Thus, every local congregation is an interpretive body that functions as God's instrument for making the gospel known and credible in society. As the hermeneutic, Newbigin envisions the local congregation as the community that provides their society with an embodied interpretation for seeing and understanding the gospel. But to understand Newbigin's meaning of the congregation as hermeneutic of the gospel, it is necessary to unpack both where and how Newbigin expresses this specific vision of the missionary nature of the church. In this section, I will provide a detailed exegesis of the chapter where Newbigin expresses the congregation as hermeneutic of the gospel concept, a discussion of Newbigin's use of the term 'hermeneutic,' and finally an overview of *GPS*.

Chapter 18—"The Congregation as Hermeneutic of the Gospel"

How is it possible that the gospel should be credible, that people should come to

> believe that the power which has the last word in human affairs is represented by a man hanging on a cross? I am suggesting that the only answer, the only hermeneutic of the gospel, is a congregation of men and women who believe it and live by it.[2]

Having worked through the epistemological foundations for Christian belief, the historicity of the gospel, the need for Christian missions, and aspects of the encounter of the gospel and Western culture earlier in *GPS* (see chapter 1 of *GPS*), Newbigin focuses on the role of the church within a pluralist society in chapter 18. That role, Newbigin notes, is for every local congregation to be the interpretive body of the gospel for culture—the hermeneutic of the gospel. Being a community, which serves as the interpretive lens of the gospel, means that local congregations are the visible and verbal presentation of the gospel to their society. They are the way in which the gospel is made known and seen as credible in the world.

At the beginning of chapter 18, Newbigin shows that the early church was a martyr church, preaching a public truth that often got its members persecuted and killed.[3] Yet, when the Roman structure of society collapsed, it

---

2. Newbigin, *Gospel in a Pluralist Society*, 227.
3. Newbigin, *Gospel in a Pluralist Society*, 222–24.

turned to the church to reorder society, due to its centuries of both preaching and living as a counterculture.[4] This reordering put Western society on a path for over a millennium where the gospel became the shaper of the public truth and worldview; a path that corrupted the church at times and itself had begun to crumble in recent centuries.[5] In our contemporary context, the church must work at rediscovering its missionary nature in a new era, and reestablishing the gospel as the foundation of public truth.

Retracing some of his previous arguments, Newbigin leans on the sovereignty of God to argue that the responsibility for transforming culture falls upon God alone. The role of Christians, then, is to emulate Christ in service to God and service to the world. Using John 6, Newbigin points to the fact that Jesus resisted what was expected of Him and instead preached a message that was countercultural, Kingdom focused, and hard to accept.[6] Newbigin argues that in serving God, the church will serve the world. In serving God and the world Newbigin uses the language of the congregation as hermeneutic of the gospel. Newbigin starts this argument with a particularly poignant question, "How is it possible that the gospel should be credible, that people should come to believe that the power which has the last word in human affairs is represented by a man hanging on a cross?"[7] Newbigin asks how the story of Jesus Christ can make sense to a culture whose plausibility structure is based on the dogma[8] of the scientific method. Newbigin's answer, the only answer he envisions, is individual communities of people who know, believe, and live by the gospel every day of their lives.

After laying out the foundational questions and his answer to how the church serves both God and the world, Newbigin provides six characteristics of this hermeneutical congregation. These characteristics are given as a way of identifying and evaluating the presence of the Holy Spirit within the local congregation, leading them to be the hermeneutic of the gospel.[9] Newbigin does not indicate whether these characteristics are given in any particular order, or

---

4. Newbigin, *Gospel in a Pluralist Society*, 222–24.
5. Newbigin, *Gospel in a Pluralist Society*, 222–24.
6. Newbigin, *Gospel in a Pluralist Society*, 224–26.
7. Newbigin, *Gospel in a Pluralist Society*, 227.
8. Generally, when Newbigin uses the terminology of dogma, he is discussing the collection of assumed beliefs that undergird a plausibility structure. His usage and understanding of dogma are much more nuanced and detailed, and I do not have the space to cover it here, but this general understanding will serve as a starting point for any references to dogma throughout this study.
9. These characteristics will be investigated more in-depth in chapter 3.

whether or not they are exclusive, but rather that these are the characteristics he thinks the congregation will have.[10] These characteristics are:

1. It will be a community of praise—serving a dual purpose of countering the prevalent hermeneutic of suspicion and giving gratitude to the only worthy receiver of that gratitude (the forgiving, merciful God),[11]

2. It will be a community of truth—providing a healthy skepticism about culture and rehearsing the gospel story of Truth,[12]

3. It will be a community that does not live for itself but is deeply involved in the concerns of its neighborhood—"it is God's embassy in a specific place," thus it both belongs to God and exists in a particular place and time,[13]

4. It will be a community where men and women are prepared for and sustained in the exercise of the priesthood in the world—calls all members to the priesthood of every believer; "The office of a priest is to stand before God on behalf of people and to stand before people on behalf of God,"[14]

5. It will be a community of mutual responsibility—providing a new social order that is accountable to and for each other, thus serving as a foretaste of the Kingdom of God,[15]

6. It will be a community of hope—is so immersed in the gospel story that it becomes the new plausibility structure for the members, spurring them to eagerly and actively waiting for and witnessing to the coming reign of God.[16]

These six characteristics are how a congregation will be able to tell if the Holy Spirit is present within the community, leading it to be the hermeneutic of the gospel. They do not dictate specific activities or programs, nor are they goals that a congregation should strive to do; rather, they outline the character of the congregation; it's about who the congregation is, not what they do.

Being the congregation as hermeneutic of the gospel as evidenced by the above six characteristics is only possible for the community of Christ

---

10. Newbigin, *Gospel in a Pluralist Society*, 227.
11. Newbigin, *Gospel in a Pluralist Society*, 227–28.
12. Newbigin, *Gospel in a Pluralist Society*, 228–29.
13. Newbigin, *Gospel in a Pluralist Society*, 229.
14. Newbigin, *Gospel in a Pluralist Society*, 229–31.
15. Newbigin, *Gospel in a Pluralist Society*, 231–32.
16. Newbigin, *Gospel in a Pluralist Society*, 232.

followers that exists in the presence of the Holy Spirit, and indwells the gospel. Christ left behind followers, it was the Holy Spirit that organized them into the church, and it is the Holy Spirit that continues to form, transform, lead, and guide the church into being the hermeneutic of the gospel. Krishna Kandiah states, "It is as the congregation functions as this community of the Spirit that it becomes a hermeneutic of the gospel. . . . [I]t is precisely as the congregation is understood as a pneumatological community that it functions as the hermeneutic of the gospel."[17] Kandiah's dissertation about the doctrine of revelation in Newbigin specifically states here that he sees in Newbigin a connection between the presence of the Holy Spirit and the congregation as hermeneutic of the gospel. In its pneumatological foundation and relationship, the local congregation is both enabled to be the hermeneutic of the gospel and lives as this hermeneutic in society. The characteristics that Newbigin lists serve as markers for determining the health of the relationship of the local congregation with the Holy Spirit; much like the Fruit of the Spirit in Gal. 5, Newbigin provides what I propose to call a congregational fruit of the Spirit.[18] But one of the things that stands out in this expression of the missionary nature of the church is Newbigin's use of the word *hermeneutic*.

Newbigin's Use of Hermeneutic

The term hermeneutic is one Newbigin used sparingly but intentionally throughout his lifetime of writings, which makes its use in *GPS* stand out. In *GPS*, Newbigin uses the term hermeneutic in a slightly different way than the typical biblical sense—as a way of interpreting scripture. By calling local congregations the hermeneutic of the gospel, Newbigin is making a specific expression of the missionary nature of the church. He is reminding the church that each individual congregation is the interpretive body through which the gospel is made known and credible in its society. Within this discussion of Newbigin's use of the word hermeneutic, the elements of representing the Kingdom and living by the gospel arise, both in association with what Newbigin means for the congregation to be the hermeneutic of the gospel. Newbigin's expression of the congregation as hermeneutic of the gospel is an explicit identification of local congregations as the way that the message of the gospel is seen as credible, is the only public truth, for all of society. Others have addressed Newbigin's use of hermeneutics here as well.

---

17. Kandiah, "Towards a Theology of Evangelism for Late-Modern Cultures," 300, 299.

18. This idea will receive more thorough discussion in chapter 3.

The Congregation as Hermeneutic of the Gospel

John G. Flett's consideration of the congregation as hermeneutic of the gospel for today specifically addresses Newbigin's use of the term hermeneutic. Flett states,

> A hermeneutic, simply stated, is a set of rules that assist the faithful interpretation of a text. Hermeneutics examines how human beings communicate, investigates the conditions of symbolic interaction, observes the ground of all thought within a cultural and historical context, and recognizes the effect social structures, political institutions and economic order have on the reading of a text. As a hermeneutic, in other words, the congregation is the method of the gospel's interpretation.[19]

What Flett is saying here is that at its core, the word "hermeneutic" is about the way a text is interpreted. He goes on to argue that Newbigin uses hermeneutic to mean the gospel is interpreted, made known, and seen as credible in public society through the visible presence of the church in the public square.[20] This is a similar understanding of Newbigin's use of hermeneutic found in Duncan B. Forrester, quoting from *Truth to Tell*, "The missionary action of the church is the exegesis of the gospel."[21] This quote, while not using the word hermeneutic, embodies the idea that local congregations are the community where the gospel is made known in society. Forrester supports this idea with a story from *Honest Religion for Secular Man*, where Newbigin shows that in Indian villages the credibility and relevance of the gospel message preached by the church is witnessed by others through Christians who live by the gospel in their active participation in the villages.[22] Forrester concludes from Newbigin that, "The message of the gospel is public truth which cannot be separated from the actual, day-to-day life of the community of faith. The life and nature of that community is a hermeneutic of the gospel."[23] Thus, Forrester is showing that Newbigin's use of hermeneutic is explicitly linked to his understanding of the church as the locus for making the gospel known and credible in the world. In doing this, the church fulfills part of Newbigin's goal of providing a new social order for society. According to Newbigin, "The most important contribution which the Church can make to a new social order is to be itself a

---

19. Flett, "What Does It Mean for a Congregation to Be a Hermeneutic?," 195–96.
20. Flett, "What Does It Mean for a Congregation to Be a Hermeneutic?," 198–203.
21. Newbigin, *Truth to Tell*, 35.
22. Forrester, "Lesslie Newbigin as Public Theologian," 10–11, quoting Newbigin, *Honest Religion for Secular Man*, 108–9.
23. Forrester, "Lesslie Newbigin as Public Theologian," 11.

new social order."²⁴ Newbigin is calling the church, especially in the context of cultural change that is taking place in the West (both in the 1980s and today), to be a new social order for a society based upon a biblical worldview.

While Forrester expresses the heart of Newbigin's concept of the congregation as hermeneutic of the gospel, in quoting *Truth to Tell* and referencing *Honest Religion for Secular Man*, his focus is upon the publicness of the gospel coming through the church. Flett, meanwhile, addresses the interpretive nature of the congregation as hermeneutic of the gospel concept, ultimately coming to a similar conclusion as Forrester, but through the discussion of the church as the visible interpretation of the gospel in society. By calling the local congregation the hermeneutic of the gospel, Newbigin is saying that every congregation is the interpretive body through which the gospel is visibly presented to the world and the body through which the gospel is shown to be credible as public truth. The local congregation serves as the interpretive lens through which the gospel is presented to society as a new way of seeing and understanding the world, and organizing society. Thus, the local congregation is the model of the new society, grounded in the gospel and led by the Holy Spirit, for the rest of the world to witness the relevance and credibility of the gospel.

The Gospel in a Pluralist Society

Newbigin's 1988 Alexander Robertson Lecturer series at the University of Glasgow was turned into the book *GPS*. Having given lecture series' before, Newbigin was surprised when he arrived in Glasgow and was informed that he would be presenting these lectures to a course over the entirety of the semester.²⁵ This caused Newbigin to re-organize and expand his material, and that material also was likely enhanced by the diverse group of students in the class, with whom Newbigin met weekly in small groups.²⁶ These lectures focused on addressing the issues of the witness of the gospel by the church within a plural society. Ultimately, Newbigin provides a vision of a missionary ecclesiology as the identity of the local congregation.

While Ch. 18 of *GPS* provides the lens through which I am reading the rest of Newbigin's missionary ecclesiology, this chapter comes within the context of Newbigin's discussion about a specific topic. Goheen has suggested that Newbigin's missionary ecclesiology "is revealed in the structure of the book wherein the entire argument climaxes in a call for the congregation to be a

---

24. Newbigin, *Truth to Tell*, 85.
25. Shenk, "Newbigin in His Time," 47.
26. Shenk, "Newbigin in His Time," 47.

hermeneutic of the gospel."[27] This explanation draws the conclusion that Newbigin was intentionally building to this point. But Newbigin's argument in *GPS* discusses different aspects of considering the role of the gospel in a pluralist society. Newbigin's begins this discussion by addressing the epistemological reasoning for Christian faith in chapters 1–5. He then moves on to discuss human history in chapters 6–9, specifically addressing the place of the gospel within that history. Chapter 10–13 is Newbigin's discussion of Christian missions grounded in and presenting the gospel around the world. Here, Newbigin outlines a firm trinitarian foundation for missions, which is present in many of his other discussions of Christian mission.[28] Then in chapters 14–17[29] Newbigin specifically addresses the cultural context of the West and the role of the gospel both in forming Western society and in Western society today. Lastly, in chapters 18–20 Newbigin addresses the role of the church within this conversation. All of this points to Newbigin's triangulation between gospel, church, and culture, which guided much of his conversation about the missionary encounter with the West.[30] It is within this discussion of the role of the church in gospel-culture encounter in the West which Newbigin's expression of his understanding of the missionary nature of the church—the congregation as hermeneutic of the gospel—appears in its most developed form.[31]

27. Goheen, *"As the Father Has Sent Me, I Am Sending You,"* 244.

28. Newbigin's trinitarian missiology includes being sent by the Father, bearing witness to the redemption of the Son, by the power of the Holy Spirit—which is similar to the perspective of *missio Dei*. While Newbigin seldom uses that term, his inclusion in the conversations of trinitarian missiology, especially at Willingen in 1952 alludes to his understanding and use of trinitarian missiology along similar lines to *missio Dei*. There are many great discussions of *missio Dei*, but those that are most aligned with its use here would be: Vicedom, *Mission of God*; Bosch, *Transforming Mission*; Bosch, *Witness to the World*; Blauw, *Missionary Nature of the Church*. For discussions specifically of Newbigin's trinitarian missiology, see Hutton, "Rooting the Practice of Evangelical Protestant Church Planting," 216–29; Dodds, "Newbigin's Trinitarian Missiology," 69–85.

29. Some may connect chapter 14, "Gospel and the Religions" with Newbigin's discussion of mission. I group it with cultural context because he is specifically talking about the religiously plural situation of Western society as the context for his discussion of encountering other religions.

30. A very concise overview of Newbigin's triangulation of gospel, church, and culture can be found in Hunsberger, "Newbigin Gauntlet," 7–10.

31. As shown later, Newbigin used this expression before *GPS*, but it is in its most developed form as a full chapter in *GPS*.

NEWBIGIN'S OTHER WRITINGS ON THE NATURE OF THE CHURCH

Newbigin, from very early on, had a vision of the church as missionary by nature, which is expressed in many different ways throughout his lifetime of writings. Paul Weston notes,

> The understanding of the Church as a "missionary" community is not in itself a new idea for Newbigin. From his earliest writings, he had articulated an essentially "missionary" ecclesiology which had found classic expression in such books as *The Household of God* published in 1953, and in later studies which emphasised the Trinitarian aspects of mission and their implications for ecclesiology. Nonetheless, with Newbigin's more specific reflections on the question of what would be involved in a "missionary engagement" with Western culture, the development of this missionary ecclesiology is now brought much more closely into line with what—in his reading of Polanyi—Newbigin had come to consider as the need of the hour.[32]

Weston clearly sees Newbigin's missionary ecclesiology, which he states has always existed within Newbigin's writings, beginning with *The Household of God*. From this ecclesiology, Newbigin specifically expresses the congregation as hermeneutic of the gospel in *GPS* for the encounter of the gospel, church, and Western culture. Weston also notes that this specific expression began to be seen in *Your Kingdom Come*[33] and was expressed in "Evangelism in the City" along with *GPS*.[34] It is specifically in Newbigin's return to England that he vocalizes this expression of the missionary nature of the church. Unlike in India, when Newbigin returned to England he more readily spoke to the issues of culture, taking stances more as a public theologian than he did in India.[35] Forrester notes that while in India, "he was, as an alien, somewhat reticent at that time on political and economic matters," but that in his return to England he was much more willing to engage with those issues.[36] Forrester states, "Mission, unity, and ecclesiology were still major themes, but Newbigin felt able, as he had not in India, to engage as a theologian in political

---

32. Weston, *Mission and Cultural Change*, 118.

33. *Your Kingdom Come* is the British title of this book. In the United States, this book is titled *Sign of the Kingdom*. The version I will be using is Lesslie Newbigin, *Sign of the Kingdom* (Grand Rapids: Eerdmans, 1980).

34. Weston, *Mission and Cultural Change*, 116–18.

35. Forrester, "Lesslie Newbigin as Public Theologian," 5–6.

36. Forrester, "Lesslie Newbigin as Public Theologian," 5.

controversy."[37] Thus, Forrester is pointing out that Newbigin, in his retirement and return to his native England, was much more vocal as a public theologian in that society. It is in confronting the issues of the church in the West, particularly in England, that Newbigin utilizes the language of the congregation as hermeneutic of the gospel as a way of expressing his view of the missionary nature of the church. But this expression is only one way that Newbigin discusses the missionary nature of the church throughout his life. To look at Newbigin's ecclesial writings, it is helpful to break them down chronologically within three major periods of his life—during his time in India, London, and Geneva, during the 1970s and 1980s in England, and after *GPS*. In this section, I will review the various ways Newbigin discusses his missionary ecclesiology within each of these periods of his life.

From India, London, and Geneva

Newbigin spent a significant period of his life (1937–74) as a missionary, pastor, and bishop in southeast India, first as foreign missionary of the Church of Scotland, than as bishop with the Church of South India (CSI), and for a short period (1959–65) as an ecumenical leader in London with the International Missionary Council (IMC), and Geneva with the World Council of Churches (WCC). Throughout this time period, Newbigin traveled frequently, to international conferences and on furlough, as an apologist for the unification scheme of the CSI, and in leading the IMC into its merger with the WCC, then as director of the WCC's Division of World Mission and Evangelism. During this period of his life, Newbigin learned the reality of living as a church missionary. His pastoral and theological reflections and actions during this period solidified his understanding of the missionary nature of the church. During this time, there are several of Newbigin's writings which voice different perspectives or aspects of his missionary ecclesiology.

The first publication that discusses Newbigin's missionary ecclesiology can be seen in his letter to the editor for *The Christian News-Letter*—"Some Thoughts on Britain from Abroad." This letter, written during his trip back to India after a year-long furlough in England, expresses Newbigin's impressions about British society in the late 1940s. In particular, Newbigin highlights the Christian foundation of British society, and then notes the growing evils that are occurring in a society grounded in Christian principles but devoid of God.[38] Newbigin's response is the living out of Christian faith, which he states is "the only faith which can sustain a society of free and responsible

---

37. Forrester, "Lesslie Newbigin as Public Theologian," 5.
38. Newbigin, "Some Thoughts on Britain from Abroad," 8–10.

men and women."[39] In this article, Newbigin is already showing the critical analysis of the change in British society that would become prominent in his post-retirement writings and provides the answer of living by the Christian gospel. This idea of living by the gospel is one of the central tenets of Newbigin's ecclesiology.

Newbigin's first extensive investigation of the nature of the church comes from his 1952 Kerr Lectures at Trinity College, Glasgow, which was later published as *The Household of God*. With the starting point of the CSI constitution that states that the church is a pilgrim people, Newbigin calls on the church to recover its eschatological identity, in the power of the Holy Spirit, "hastening to the ends of the earth to beseech all men to be reconciled to God, and hastening to the end of time to meet its Lord."[40] In this evaluation, Newbigin calls out the strengths and weaknesses of the Protestant tradition (hearing and believing the gospel, but broken historically from the past),[41] the Catholic tradition (the historical participation in the sacraments, but over institutionalized),[42] and the Pentecostal/Charismatic tradition (receiving and abiding in the Holy Spirit, but tending towards experientialism and extemporaneous expression).[43] For the church, which is God's visible community founded in Christ, all three of these traditions are held together in eschatology, for God's purpose of witnessing to the world.[44] Newbigin writes, "The Church's life in Christ is thus a unique supernatural life which, from the point of view of our human language, must be described in paradoxical terms: dying with Him in order to live with Him; being in Him, yet hoping for His appearing; a life of which we must say both 'He lives in me' and 'I live by faith in Him.'"[45] Newbigin describes the church as a paradox where it is both living in Christ's presence and hoping for Christ's return. In this paradox, the church is commissioned to spread the good news of God's redemption throughout the world until the time when Christ returns.[46] Within this discussion of the nature of the church, Newbigin explicitly describes it as a missionary nature. "The Church has its existence in relation to the salvation which has been wrought at Christ's coming into the world and is to be consummated at His coming again. Since that consummation concerns the whole world, the

39. Newbigin, "Some Thoughts on Britain from Abroad," 10–11.
40. Newbigin, *Household of God*, 25–26.
41. Newbigin, *Household of God*, chap. 2.
42. Newbigin, *Household of God*, chap. 3.
43. Newbigin, *Household of God*, chap. 4.
44. Newbigin, *Household of God*, 111.
45. Newbigin, *Household of God*, 126.
46. Newbigin, *Household of God*, 136–39.

Church's existence is in the act of being the bearer of that salvation to the whole world. 'The Church exists by mission as fire exists by burning.'[47] While this book highlights Newbigin's view of the nature of the church, this Emil Brunner quote affirms that this nature is missionary. Thus, in *The Household of God* Newbigin expresses his ecclesiology from an eschatological and missiological perspective.

A few years later, Newbigin expressed in two different publications the role of the church in making the gospel of Jesus Christ known to the world. This role stems directly from the missionary nature of the church which Newbigin has already established. In the English translation of a training book of basic Christian doctrine and catechesis in Tamil India,[48] *Sin and Salvation*, Newbigin explicitly names the role of the church. In discussing how salvation comes to individuals, Newbigin notes that Jesus left behind a community and that through that community others come to know the gospel and join in discipleship to Jesus.

> When we look at the record, what strikes us is that the story of Jesus has reached us through a group of men and women who were so closely bound to Him that their life could almost be spoken of as an extension of His life. . . . Thus, we can give the first and simplest answer to the question: "How does what Christ has done for men become mine?" by saying this: "It becomes mine when I become part of this society, this fellowship, He left behind Him to be the continuation of His life on earth."[49]

Here, Newbigin is saying that the salvation that is given to the world by Jesus Christ is made known through a community of devoted followers. He highlights that in the biblical record, this community of devoted followers is so closely bound to Christ that their lives can be seen as an extension of His life. The implication of this is that Christlikeness is an essential part of the gospel being made known in the world. Later that same year in "Witnessing to Jesus Christ," Newbigin expresses the essential role of the Holy Spirit in the lives of Christians and in their witness to Jesus Christ in India.[50] Both of these writings provide different expressions of Newbigin's missionary ecclesiology as he is addressing different topics which need a clear ecclesiological answer. In *Sin and Salvation*, Newbigin is discussing issues of catechesis in the village

---

47. Newbigin, *Household of God*, 142. The quote within this quote is attributed to Emil Brunner within Newbigin's text.

48. Newbigin, *Sin and Salvation*, 7–10.

49. Newbigin, *Sin and Salvation*, 92–93.

50. Newbigin, "Witnessing to Jesus Christ," 59.

churches of his Madurai diocese. In "Witnessing to Jesus Christ," Newbigin is discussing issues of the witness of Christians to the good news of Jesus Christ in society through the power and presence of the Holy Spirit.

After Newbigin had taken his leave from the CSI to become the head of the IMC and begin the process of integrating it within the WCC, he published a small booklet discussing the nature of the church. This booklet, *One Body, One Gospel, One World*, began as a paper to IMC officials, was reformatted for a three-day conference of IMC staff and consultants, and ultimately updated from that discussion for publication.[51] This paper turned publication was meant to stir discussion and action to evaluate the current state of global missions, return to the gospel source of missions, seek the leading of the Holy Spirit for this new age of missions, and refocus the church upon the mission of Christ by the whole church for the whole world.[52] To do this, Newbigin challenges the church to re-merge with missions, seeing that the work of missions happens through the laity on Monday-Saturday, and Sunday is meant as a day of spiritual renewal for these lay missionaries.[53] The laity is involved in various spheres of public life throughout the week, and it is in those spheres that they are to engage in Christ's mission in the world. "Only those who are actually engaged in these various spheres of work . . . can make clear what are the issues upon which Christians can speak a relevant word, or take an action which will bear witness to the Lordship of Christ."[54] Thus, Newbigin is pointing out that only the laity that works and lives in these public spheres know how to bring Christ into these spheres. This means that the church must seek the leading of the Holy Spirit in mission.

> As the community of the Holy Spirit, the Church is related to the mission in these three ways: a. It is the place where the fruit of Christ's mission is already present in foretaste and as an earnest of that which is to come. . . . b. It is the place where the powers of the Holy Spirit are available to serve men in all their needs, as they were available to Christ. . . . c. It is the place where witness is borne to that which is above and beyond the Church, namely to the mercy and judgement of God Himself in Jesus Christ.[55]

Newbigin's point is that the church is linked to Jesus' mission through the presence and leading of the Holy Spirit. In this book, the presence of the Holy

---

51. Newbigin, *One Body, One Gospel, One World*, 7–8.
52. Newbigin, *One Body, One Gospel, One World*, 7–8.
53. Newbigin, *One Body, One Gospel, One World*, 16–17.
54. Newbigin, "Work of the Holy Spirit in the Life of the Asian Church," 32.
55. Newbigin, *One Body, One Gospel, One World*, 19–20.

Spirit and the idea of the mission of the whole church to the whole world are present. Newbigin continued discussing these ideas about mission and the church throughout the IMC/WCC integration.

In *The Relevance of Trinitarian Doctrine for Today's Mission*, Newbigin investigates what he believes are the most important questions surrounding missions at that time, addressing them from a trinitarian perspective.[56] Newbigin charts, through the twentieth-century global mission conferences, the move from Kingdom-minded mission to church-centric mission to world-centric mission, but he comes back to the need for a trinitarian foundation for mission.[57] Newbigin then goes on to discuss three questions for the current (1960s) state of missions to illustrate the relationship "between what is happening in the world and what God is doing through the missionary work of the Church"—the relation of missions to world history, missions and the secularization of society, and the failure of modern missions to advance as expected.[58] Newbigin's response to all three of these issues is a recovery of the trinitarian foundation of mission. "We may sum this up by saying that the Church's mission to all the nations is a participation in the work of the triune God."[59] Newbigin's summation is that mission is participating in the work of the triune God in the world. Newbigin is expressing a key element for mission, which can be found throughout his missionary ecclesiology, that mission is a participation in the activity of the Trinity on earth.

Each publication on the missionary nature of the church from Newbigin's career as a missionary and ecumenical leader shows different dimensions of his ecclesiology. They point to the consistency of his perspective of the missionary nature of the church, a nature that would begin to find new forms of expression upon Newbigin's retirement and return to England.

The 1970s and 1980s

Confronted with a very different England than the one he had left in 1937, Newbigin's return after nearly 40 years as a missionary in India surprised him.[60] His initial assessment pointed to a passive and reluctant church facing many challenges in a new society. "There seemed to be so much timidity in commending the Gospel to the unconverted people of Britain."[61] Newbigin

---

56. Newbigin, *Relevance of Trinitarian Doctrine for Today's Mission*, 9.
57. Newbigin, *Relevance of Trinitarian Doctrine for Today's Mission*, 22–24.
58. Newbigin, *Relevance of Trinitarian Doctrine for Today's Mission*, 28–30.
59. Newbigin, *Relevance of Trinitarian Doctrine for Today's Mission*, 50.
60. Newbigin, *Unfinished Agenda*, 230–32.
61. Newbigin, *Unfinished Agenda*, 230.

saw the Church in England as a tertiary observer of society, rather than an active participant in it. This timidity, as Newbigin saw it, was connected to two issues challenging the Church in England in the mid-1970s—the belief that the church must tailor the gospel to the modern scientific worldview, and the increase in people from other religions.[62] There were three major influences early in this time period that influenced Newbigin's reflections. First, during their 1974 trip home, the Newbigin's took the overland route and were forced to worship alone in Cappadocia.[63] Once a great center of Christian thinking and missions, Newbigin was struck by the profound lack of churches and Christian community in this now Turkish city.[64] This experience drove home the reality of how easily the church can disappear when it is disconnected—by choice or by force—from its missionary nature. "This had a profound effect upon Lesslie and helped to energize his later reflections on European culture, for it brought home just how completely a once-strong Christian heritage could all but disappear."[65] Having seen the disappearance of the church in Cappadocia, Newbigin feared that Europe was on its way to losing its Christian heritage, and this energized him to ask questions about the revitalization of the church in the West. The second experience was the months that Newbigin spent reading Barth's *Church Dogmatics*, which he said, "was an immensely rewarding experience" and a "needed preparation for the much more difficult missionary experience which (as I did not then realize) lay ahead."[66] This missionary experience would cover the rest of his life as he sought the missionary encounter between gospel, church, and Western culture as a teacher, speaker, writer, and pastor. The third important experience came at an international conference in 1975 when Newbigin happened to be sitting next to Indonesian General T. B. Simatupang, who mumbled under his breath, "can the West be converted?"[67] This question provided the shape to Newbigin's retirement considerations of "a deep preoccupation of his since the 1930s with the relationship between Christianity and the modern Western civilization."[68] These experiences paved the way for Newbigin considering the re-evangelizing of the West and the role of the church in this re-evangelization, from a trinitarian perspective. It is in this context that Newbigin began teaching mission and ecumenics at the Selly Oak Colleges, and continued writing and speaking around England and

62. Newbigin, *Unfinished Agenda*, 230–31.
63. Weston, "Introduction," to Newbigin, *Unfinished Agenda*, 12.
64. Weston, "Introduction," 12.
65. Weston, "Introduction," 12.
66. Newbigin, *Unfinished Agenda*, 229.
67. Newbigin, "Can the West be Converted?," 25.
68. Wainwright, *Lesslie Newbigin*, 14.

continental Europe.[69] Teaching, writing, and speaking provided Newbigin many opportunities to address the nature of the church from different perspectives, one of which is the congregation as hermeneutic of the gospel.

One significant discussion of the missionary nature of the church happened in Newbigin's book concerning the theology of mission, *The Open Secret*.[70] The ideas of this book, primarily the trinitarian foundation of mission, were originally embodied during his time at the IMC/WCC in *The Relevance of Trinitarian Doctrine for Today's Mission*, and was expanded while teaching at the Selly Oak Colleges and at a 1977 Princeton Theological Seminary summer course.[71] Newbigin begins this book by discussing the history of Christian mission[72] and the current context and questions that mission must address.[73] Ultimately, he concludes that "The Christian mission is thus to act out in the whole life of the whole world the confession that Jesus is Lord of all."[74] Newbigin's point is that mission requires every Christian living by the gospel in every arena and sphere of their lives. Newbigin then ventures into discussing the Trinity as the foundation of Christian mission. "The fundamental belief is embodied in the affirmation that God has revealed himself as Father, Son, and Spirit."[75] It is from the fundamental belief that Newbigin spends the rest of this book discussing current issues in missions from a trinitarian perspective, such as the universality and particularity of Christian mission,[76] the false dichotomy of social justice and evangelism,[77] the encounter of gospel/church/culture,[78] and interaction with other religions.[79] Throughout this discussion, various elements of Newbigin's missionary ecclesiology are expressed. Elements such as witnessing to power, the patient-eager hope, the truth of the gospel, engaging with the public square, caring for your neighbors, binding together social action and evangelism, being rooted in a believing community, and the universal nature of the gospel. The presence of these elements points

---

69. Newbigin, *Unfinished Agenda*, 230–31.

70. While the original version of *The Open Secret* was published in 1978, I will use the updated version from 1995. The updates of this version were primarily on issues of style and grammar which were appropriate for 1995.

71. Newbigin, *Open Secret*, vii–viii.

72. Newbigin, *Open Secret*, chap. 1.

73. Newbigin, *Open Secret*, chap. 2.

74. Newbigin, *Open Secret*, 17.

75. Newbigin, *Open Secret*, 29.

76. Newbigin, *Open Secret*, chap. 7.

77. Newbigin, *Open Secret*, chap. 8.

78. Newbigin, *Open Secret*, chap. 9.

79. Newbigin, *Open Secret*, chap. 10.

to the essential binding of church and mission within Newbigin. Even when Newbigin is focused on mission he includes discussions of the church, because his ecclesiology is firmly planted in the missionary nature of the church.

In *Sign of the Kingdom*,[80] Newbigin discusses the topic of the Kingdom of God as it pertains to contemporary issues of the church and missions. This book, originally presented at the Theological Seminary of the Swedish Covenant Church, specifically addresses the relevance of the Kingdom of God to contemporary conversations about the split between purely spiritual faith and faith that necessitates action, questions about the proper form of leadership for the present church, and issues that have arisen from the confrontation of Western Christendom and Islam.[81] Newbigin addresses the Kingdom of God from a historical, a biblical, and a contemporary perspective, which makes up the three chapters of this book. Ultimately, Newbigin's assessment is that "The Church is its proper self, and is a sign of the Kingdom, only insofar as it continually points men and women beyond itself to Jesus and invites them to personal conversion and commitment to him."[82] Thus, the presence of the kingdom in and through the church comes only when that church is functioning as a missionary body in society.

Newbigin makes significant use of the congregation as hermeneutic of the gospel as an expression of the missionary nature of the church in *Sign of the Kingdom*. He states,

> From the beginning the announcement of the Kingdom led to a summons to follow and so to the formation of a community. It is the community which has begun to taste (even only in foretaste) the reality of the Kingdom which can alone provide the hermeneutic of the message. In a recent article on the theme of the Kingdom, Raymond Fung of the Urban Industrial Mission team in Hong Kong has written: "I believe the Kingdom of God suggests that Christian Mission should take the form of community, in an environment in which God's rule is recognized, whereby the values of justice, peace and love operate." Without the hermeneutic of such a living community, the message of the Kingdom can only become—once again—an ideology and a programme; it will not be the gospel.[83]

---

80. This is the name of the American title. It was published in England as *Your Kingdom Come*.
81. Newbigin, *Sign of the Kingdom*, viii–ix.
82. Newbigin, *Sign of the Kingdom*, 69.
83. Newbigin, *Sign of the Kingdom*, 19.

Here, Newbigin explicitly states that the community of Christ followers has begun to experience the reality of the kingdom, and thus they alone are the hermeneutic of the gospel message in their society. But this is not the only thing Newbigin has to say about the church as the hermeneutic of the gospel message of the kingdom. Later, Newbigin remarks that "the only hermeneutic of the message of the Kingdom is the presence of a community in which the foretaste of the kingdom, the Spirit, is already present."[84] Newbigin is showing that through the presence of the Spirit in the Christian community, the Spirit utilizes the church to be the hermeneutic of the message of the kingdom in the world. He later returns to this idea and goes on to describe that message more fully:

> On the other hand, apart from a living community in which there is already a foretaste of the reality of the Kingdom, a present experience of its joy and freedom, the preaching of the kingdom becomes mere ideology. . . . The *content* of the preaching of the Kingdom can never be any such concepts; it can only be Jesus himself, incarnate, crucified and risen. The *hermeneutic* can only be the living reality of a community which the first fruits of the Kingdom are already being enjoyed and shared. . . . Such a community will be the living hermeneutic of the message of the Kingdom which it preaches.[85]

Newbigin here has reinforced the importance of the presence of the Holy Spirit in the church, and the church living by that presence in enjoying and sharing the gifts of the kingdom of God both within its body and within its society. Newbigin is stressing that knowing, believing, and living the gospel, through the presence of the Holy Spirit, is what makes the Christian community the hermeneutic of the gospel message it preaches to the world. Newbigin also includes the fact that "It is the Church as a whole which has to be the hermeneutic of the Gospel."[86] Newbigin believes that being the hermeneutic of the gospel requires the whole church (every member and tradition), and that any missionary endeavor of the church must consider its faithfulness to living out the kingdom in the world.[87] Throughout *Sign of the Kingdom*, Newbigin is making his most explicit point to date that the church is the hermeneutic of the gospel through the presence of the Holy Spirit being the foretaste of the kingdom of God; and that foretaste bearing the first fruits of the kingdom in

---

84. Newbigin, *Sign of the Kingdom*, 42.
85. Newbigin, *Sign of the Kingdom*, 42–43.
86. Newbigin, *Sign of the Kingdom*, 63.
87. Newbigin, *Sign of the Kingdom*, 64.

the church for and in the world. Besides *GPS*, *Sign of the Kingdom* is the place where Newbigin most clearly builds the elements of being constituted by the Holy Spirit, representing the kingdom, and living by the gospel as for his missionary ecclesiology.

In the early 1980s, the British Council of Churches, through a series of conversations decided to sponsor a conference in 1984 discussing the direction of the British Church.[88] Newbigin was invited onto the planning committee for this conference, and as the planning moved forward he expressed his discomfort that it did not seem to address the underlying issues that the British Church must address.[89] Newbigin was then invited to write a pamphlet that would raise the necessary questions the conference needed to address, and that pamphlet was published as *The Other Side of 1984*.[90] Newbigin's analysis starts with an assessment of the current situation of British culture. "The totality of all observable phenomena is 'Nature.' 'Nature' in effect replaces the concept of God, which is no longer necessary."[91] Newbigin is pointing to the fact that the rise of the scientific method and Enlightenment ideals that have attempted to replace God with nature. The result of this is removing any sense of hope from culture. "In the subsequent years of ministry in England I have often been asked: 'What is the greatest difficulty you face in moving from India to England?' I have always answered: 'The disappearance of hope.'"[92] This failure to provide meaning has shown cracks in Enlightenment culture, cracks which are slowly crumbling away the foundation of this culture.[93] Thus, Newbigin argues that the church is in need of a post-critical philosophy that expresses the dogma of gospel as public truth.[94] This philosophy will have to address three key questions: (1) how is the proper use of dogma to be presented in light of its negative perception, (2) how would this not revert to a Christendom era, and (3) how does scripture warrant Christian judgements and actions in the public sphere?[95] Newbigin believes it is the responsibility of the church to answer these questions and provide a new vision for understanding the world.[96] The contemporary church must "offer to our dying culture the framework of understanding that has its base in the work of Jesus and to

88. Newbigin, *Unfinished Agenda*, 251–52.
89. Newbigin, *Unfinished Agenda*, 252.
90. Newbigin, *Unfinished Agenda*, 252.
91. Newbigin, *Other Side of 1984*, 11.
92. Newbigin, *Other Side of 1984*, 1.
93. Newbigin, *Other Side of 1984*, 12–16.
94. Newbigin, *Other Side of 1984*, 12–16.
95. Newbigin, *Other Side of 1984*, 28.
96. Newbigin, *Other Side of 1984*, 55–56.

invite our contemporaries to join with us in a vigorous attempt to understand and deal with our experience afresh in the light and power of that name."[97] Newbigin's analysis is of a culture in transition, and he sees the church as being able to facilitate this transition through speaking the truth of the gospel into it. This treating of the gospel as public truth and the public witness of that truth, both point to the public proclamation of the kingdom of God.

Newbigin was brought to Princeton Theological Seminary to present the Warfield Lectures in 1984, where he developed some of the issues from *The Other Side of 1984* to express more fully what he saw as the needed missionary encounter with Western culture.[98] These lectures were turned into the book *Foolishness to the Greeks*. Newbigin begins by addressing the question, "What would be involved in a missionary encounter between the gospel and this whole way of perceiving, thinking, and living that we call 'modern Western culture'?"[99] He determines that scripture must be announced publicly and tested by the same rigorous standards of any truth-claim, only then can it possibly provide an alternative plausibility structure for society.[100] Newbigin's evaluation of current Western culture is that the Enlightenment is: privatizing faith,[101] making society more mechanized,[102] making society more urbanized,[103] absolutizing science,[104] and placing everything into a market-economy.[105] Thus, the church exists to introduce God to society and help society hear its purpose, which only the Creator can provide. This witness of introduction will include a recovery of true eschatology,[106] a doctrine of freedom,[107] a declericalizing of theology,[108] a radical critique of denominationalism,[109] witness of the whole ecumenical family,[110] and confidence and perseverance in faith,[111] all of which

---

97. Newbigin, *Other Side of 1984*, 63.
98. Newbigin, *Foolishness to the Greeks*, iv.
99. Newbigin, *Foolishness to the Greeks*, 1.
100. Newbigin, *Foolishness to the Greeks*, 18–20.
101. Newbigin, *Foolishness to the Greeks*, 31.
102. Newbigin, *Foolishness to the Greeks*, 32–33.
103. Newbigin, *Foolishness to the Greeks*, 32.
104. Newbigin, *Foolishness to the Greeks*, 33–35.
105. Newbigin, *Foolishness to the Greeks*, 29–31.
106. Newbigin, *Foolishness to the Greeks*, 134–37.
107. Newbigin, *Foolishness to the Greeks*, 137–41.
108. Newbigin, *Foolishness to the Greeks*, 141–44.
109. Newbigin, *Foolishness to the Greeks*, 144–46.
110. Newbigin, *Foolishness to the Greeks*, 146–48.
111. Newbigin, *Foolishness to the Greeks*, 148–49.

comes from an overflow of praise.[112] The argument of this book provides the foundations for understanding a missionary engagement with the West.

"On Being the Church for the World" is Newbigin's contribution to the book *The Parish Church*. While this book is discussing the connection between the church and the world, Newbigin is taking the perspective that the church exists to provide a vision and experience of the kingdom for a specific time and place. "The Church exists because God has revealed himself in the story of Israel, in the ministry and death and resurrection of Jesus Christ, and we are in the world as the bearers of a revelation of God's purpose for creation, and that is the only criterion, ultimately, by which we have to be guided."[113] Newbigin is saying that it is God's revelation to the church, which the church is meant to share with the rest of the world. This sharing is based upon the specific place (and time) in which the church exists, thus the using of the title *ekklēsia* for the first assembly of Christ followers.[114] "There can be other possible definitions of 'place,' but it is the very essence of the church that it is *for* that place, for the section of the world for which it has been made responsible."[115] Newbigin is explicitly calling out the church as responsible for the place and time in which God has positioned it. Newbigin then affirms that it is only when the church is operating on the frontiers of the world, "where the reign of God challenges the rulers of this world," that it bears the marks of the Passion of Jesus, and lives in the power of the resurrection.[116] The church living on the frontiers of society becomes the sign, instrument, and foretaste of the kingdom for a specific place: (1) foretaste in that it is filled by the Holy Spirit as the down payment of the coming kingdom;[117] (2) instrument in being God's tool for bringing His justice, peace, and freedom into the world;[118] (3) a sign by "pointing people to a reality which is beyond what we can see."[119]

These examples show Newbigin's focus on the missionary nature of the church and the missionary encounter with the West in his retirement years. It is the combination of these two topics that elicited the language of the hermeneutic of the gospel as an expression of that combination in *GPS*. This language continues to occur in Newbigin's writings on these topics throughout the rest of his life.

112. Newbigin, *Foolishness to the Greeks*, 149–50.
113. Newbigin, "On Being the Church for the World," 28–29.
114. Newbigin, "On Being the Church for the World," 28–31.
115. Newbigin, "On Being the Church for the World," 31.
116. Newbigin, "On Being the Church for the World," 34–35.
117. Newbigin, "On Being the Church for the World," 37–39.
118. Newbigin, "On Being the Church for the World," 39–40.
119. Newbigin, "On Being the Church for the World," 40–41.

After GPS

The last decade of the Twentieth Century was a time of transition, and in the field of missiology this was especially true. In Dana Robert's retrospective on forty years of the American Society of Missiology (ASM), she notes that after decades of establishing itself and mission studies as an academic field, the "founding phase of the ASM ended around 1989 to 1991."[120] She goes on to identify four influential publications in this time period that signaled this transition, one of which was *GPS*. Robert notes that in *GPS*, "By identifying the secular West as a mission field, Newbigin's work launched multiple movements to consider the meaning of the Gospel in Western culture."[121] The shift that Robert notes from *GPS* to considering the West as a mission field is one of the major transitions of this time period, one which would launch several church renewal movements in the West. For Newbigin, the 1990s continued his global travels, presenting, teaching, and writing, very often on the issues of re-missioning the West. From *GPS* until his passing, Newbigin continued to discuss his missionary ecclesiology, and these discussions connecting to the congregation as hermeneutic of the gospel concept are important for grasping the fullness of his ecclesiology and the place in it of this concept.

After *GPS*, Newbigin frequently discussed the topics of the missionary nature of the church and the needed missionary encounter with the West. *Truth to Tell* began as the Osterhaven Lectures at Western Theological Seminary (Holland, MI) and focused primarily on the gospel as public truth. Newbigin begins by providing a framework for his argument, that (1) every human has a responsibility to seek truth and share it with society,[122] (2) the truth of the gospel is incomprehensible to those whose mind has not already been changed by the gospel (and the Holy Spirit),[123] and (3) the church affirming the gospel as public truth is a challenge of reorientation to society away from its Enlightenment grounding and toward the reality of God.[124] Newbigin makes an important connection between seeing the gospel as public truth and the missionary ecclesiology espoused in *GPS*. "So mission is not a one-way promotion but a two-way encounter in which we learn more of what the gospel means. We are learning as we go. That is the only way we affirm that the gospel is not just 'true for us' but true for all. The missionary action of the

---

120. Robert, "Forty Years of the American Society of Missiology," 15.
121. Robert, "Forty Years of the American Society of Missiology," 16.
122. Newbigin, *Truth to Tell*, 1–5.
123. Newbigin, *Truth to Tell*, 6–10.
124. Newbigin, *Truth to Tell*, 10–13.

Church is the exegesis of the gospel."[125] What Newbigin is saying here is that mission is about engagement with culture—an engagement that will also help Christians learn more about the gospel. Working this idea out using a Polanyian model, Newbigin calls for Christians to indwell scripture and live fully in the language of the tradition of scripture in order to encounter culture with a new lens for interpreting the world.[126] This model of the Polanyian sense of knowing within a tradition, necessitates a committed pluralism.[127] This type of tradition happens only in the local congregation committed to the gospel and training its members in the Christian plausibility structure.[128]

A few years later, a collection of previously unpublished Newbigin works on the topic of mission was compiled and published as *A Word in Season*. Within these works, there are two that stand out for their ecclesial discussions. First, "The Cultural Captivity of Western Christianity as a Challenge to a Missionary Church," addresses two important lessons Newbigin learned on the mission field. The first is that missionaries are constantly faced with wandering either toward syncretism or irrelevancy.[129] The second is that Christians need the religious other and Christians from other parts of the world to help them see and eliminate the syncretism they brought with them into the faith.[130] Both of these are lessons that he brings to the discussion of re-missioning the West through his missionary ecclesiology. Second, "Evangelism in the Context of Secularization," begins with rehearsing Newbigin's arguments about the Enlightenment shape of culture and the role of dogma.[131] His response to this situation is that evangelism takes place in the congregation that knows the gospel and lives by it, "a certain kind of shared life," for all of society to witness—garnering questions about the faith that is modeled by this congregation, which leads to the verbal proclamation of the gospel.[132] In the shared life of the community, Newbigin notes that, "Such a community is the primary hermeneutic of the gospel."[133] Thus, Newbigin is saying that the shared life of the local congregation living by the gospel is the primary hermeneutical lens of the gospel to society. This vision of the shared life of

---

125. Newbigin, *Truth to Tell*, 35.
126. Newbigin, *Truth to Tell*, 45–50.
127. Newbigin, *Truth to Tell*, 60–64.
128. Newbigin, *Truth to Tell*, 65–73.
129. Newbigin, *Word in Season*, 67.
130. Newbigin, *Word in Season*, 67.
131. Newbigin, *Word in Season*, 148–50.
132. Newbigin, *Word in Season*, 151–55.
133. Newbigin, *Word in Season*, 155.

the community is essential to his missionary ecclesiology and in particular the congregation as hermeneutic of the gospel expression of that ecclesiology.

Newbigin's Hickman Lectures at Duke Divinity School in the fall of 1994 focus on the topic of "The Gospel in the Public Square." These lectures remained unpublished until 2010, when the *Trinity Journal for Theology and Ministry* published them, along with responses from a colloquium held at the University of Leeds in 1996 where a group of the neo-Calvinist school of thought discussed Newbigin's works (with Newbigin).[134] The first lecture, "The Gospel as Truth," seeks to answer the question about the place of the gospel within the public square.[135] "All knowing depends, as I have said, upon a tradition of learning, a tradition of knowing, and the Christian church embodies that tradition which takes as its *datum*, as its starting point, in faith, that in Jesus Christ, Almighty God was present, to bear and bear away the sin of the world, and which uses the concepts, the models, the language of the Bible to develop this tradition."[136] Newbigin is stating that the church functions as a tradition that is grounded in the gospel, seeing it as public truth. This foundation of the gospel as public truth is interwoven with his understanding of the missionary nature of the church. The second lecture, "Scripture as the Locus of Truth," seeks to understand the role of scripture in determining truth for the public square.[137] Newbigin asserts that the confession of the incarnation, life, death, and resurrection of Jesus Christ provides the hermeneutical key to the whole Bible; and thus in the hierarchy of levels of knowledge, theology has a primacy over all other traditions of knowledge because it is the only one that can explain all the other levels.[138] This explanation of the role of scripture in establishing public truth is an expansion upon Newbigin's view of Christianity as a tradition, and it shows how Christianity as a tradition interacts with other traditions of understanding. The third lecture, "What Kind of Society?," addresses the public square where Christians are to speak the truth of the gospel.[139] In this article, Newbigin provides a vision of a Christian society[140] in the manner that he sees it, which includes: (a) it must remember

---

134. LeMarquard, "Editorial," 5–7.
135. Newbigin, "Gospel as True," 22–23.
136. Newbigin, "Gospel as True," 34.
137. Newbigin, "Scripture as the Locus of Truth," 35.
138. Newbigin, "Scripture as the Locus of Truth," 43–48.
139. Newbigin, "What Kind of Society?," 49.
140. Newbigin's use of the term "Christian society" is further discussed in the upcoming chapter on the subject by Hunsberger "Lesslie Newbigin's Idea of a Christian Society." Prepublication copy used with author's permission.

the good and bad history of Christendom,[141] (b) it must safeguard religious freedoms because the heart of the Cross is toleration of untruth in the face of truth,[142] (c) the church must believe in revelation as the authority for the public square,[143] (d) there must be a sufficient amount of witnessing Christians to influence the public square (but not control it),[144] (e) there needs to be structures of lay theologizing in every sector of society,[145] and (f) the church must be evangelizing in word and deed.[146] This vision for a Christian society is the implication of the church living out Newbigin's missionary ecclesiology. Throughout these lectures, Newbigin is painting a picture of the society that is strongly influenced and led by Christians who are living the gospel in every area of their lives.

In the mid-1990s, Newbigin was enlisted by the Institute of Mennonite Studies for a contribution to their book series—Christian Mission and Modern Culture,[147] which became *Truth and Authority in Modernity*. Newbigin begins his argument by showing that Jesus teaches as one with authority and that Christians are to internalize this authority in order to live in authority in a world that is largely built upon doubt, which is more fully discussed in chapter 1, "Divine Authority."[148] Within this chapter, Newbigin shows that God, in His grace, has redeemed creation through Jesus Christ, and this grace must be accepted on faith by Christians as the authority of the message of the gospel.[149] "He (Jesus) chose, called, and prepared a company of people; he entrusted to them his teaching; and he promised them the gift of the Holy Spirit of God to guide them in matters that were beyond their present horizons."[150] Newbigin here is calling out that the authority of the message of Christ is made known in the world through the church, which is guided by the presence and leading of the Holy Spirit. In chapter 2, "The Mediation of Divine Authority," Newbigin notes that the way the church discusses this authority is in scripture, tradition, reason, and experience.[151] Finally, Newbigin discusses how Christianity tells the story of God's interaction with human history as the sole divine authority

---

141. Newbigin, "What Kind of Society?," 57.
142. Newbigin, "What Kind of Society?," 57–58.
143. Newbigin, "What Kind of Society?," 58–59.
144. Newbigin, "What Kind of Society?," 59–60.
145. Newbigin, "What Kind of Society?," 60.
146. Newbigin, "What Kind of Society?," 60–61.
147. Newbigin, *Truth and Authority in Modernity*, vii–ix.
148. Newbigin, *Truth and Authority in Modernity*, 1–24.
149. Newbigin, *Truth and Authority in Modernity*, 1–24.
150. Newbigin, *Truth and Authority in Modernity*, 27.
151. Newbigin, *Truth and Authority in Modernity*, 32–63.

The Congregation as Hermeneutic of the Gospel

for all of creation in chapter 3, "Witnessing to Divine Authority in the Context of Modernity."[152] This book provides another perspective on Newbigin's missionary ecclesiology in the context of the authority of the church to live and preach gospel truth in society.

Throughout his life, Newbigin held a consistent view of the missionary nature of the church, which he sees as the way the gospel becomes relevant and credible in society. This understanding of the nature of the church found many different expressions throughout his life, but Newbigin's use of the congregation as hermeneutic of the gospel is one expression with vibrance that has caught the attention of the Western world for the last thirty years.

SUMMARY

The congregation as hermeneutic of the gospel is a specific expression of Newbigin's missionary ecclesiology. It arose linguistically within Newbigin's retirement considerations about re-missioning the West, but it was always part of his missionary ecclesiology. Thus, seeing this concept within its context, with an understanding of the uniqueness of Newbigin's use of hermeneutic, provides a fuller picture of the congregation as hermeneutic concept. But it is also necessary to see how this concept fits within Newbigin's larger scheme of missionary ecclesiology. Throughout Newbigin's lifetime of writing about ecclesiology he builds upon three fundamental elements of this ecclesiology—that the church is constituted by the Holy Spirit, represents the kingdom of God, and lives by the gospel. These elements, while at times can be more or less prominent in Newbigin's ecclesial writings, are always present in some form or fashion. Thus, in order to understand Newbigin's missionary ecclesiology, and particularly the congregation as hermeneutic concept, it is necessary to understand each of these elements.

---

152. Newbigin, *Truth and Authority in Modernity*, 64–83.

3

Constituted by the Holy Spirit

INTRODUCTION

ECCLESIOLOGY IS ONE OF Newbigin's most common topics of discussion throughout his lifetime of speaking and writing, and in that lifetime Newbigin highlighted the relationship between the church and the Holy Spirit. "The Church is, in the most exact sense, a *koinonia*, a common sharing in the Holy Spirit," and this is because it "is truly known only to faith, because it is constituted by the Holy Spirit. But it is a visible congregation."[1] Newbigin states that the church is constituted by the Holy Spirit, and therefore is the visible community of the Spirit, who makes each congregation the hermeneutic of the gospel within their society. This constituting presence of the Holy Spirit is one of the key elements of Newbigin's missionary ecclesiology, and is essential to study in connection with the congregation as hermeneutic of the gospel. The element of being constituted by the Holy Spirit is essential because it speaks directly to the relationship between God and the church, a relationship that is foundational for the other elements of Newbigin's missionary ecclesiology. The constituting presence of the Holy Spirit in the local congregation functioning as the hermeneutic of the gospel is evidenced by the characteristics Newbigin mentions, all of which point to the credibility of Jesus Christ as the last word in human affairs. These characteristics form a congregational fruit of the Spirit, in the same manner as the characteristics Paul mentions as Fruit of the Spirit in Gal 5:13–26. In this chapter, I will establish what Newbigin means by saying the church is constituted by the Holy

---

1. Newbigin, *Household of God*, 90, 26.

Spirit, investigate Newbigin's ecclesial characteristics (with particular focus on the characteristics of the congregation as hermeneutic of the gospel concept), and argue for the characteristics of the hermeneutic of the gospel concept to be seen as congregational fruit of the Spirit.

THE CONGREGATION BEING CONSTITUTED BY THE HOLY SPIRIT

> Suddenly a sound like the blowing of a violent wind came from heaven and filled the whole house where they were sitting. They saw what seemed to be tongues of fire that separated and came to rest on each of them. All of them were filled with the Holy Spirit and began to speak in other tongues as the Spirit enabled them. (Acts 2:2–4 NIV)

At Pentecost, Jesus' promise for the gift of the baptism of the Holy Spirit from the Father (Acts 1:4) is fulfilled. In this gift, the followers of Christ were incorporated into the church through the presence, power, and guidance of the Holy Spirit. The early chapters of Acts recount the amazing ministry and gospel witness that happened in those early years of the church—all of which took place by the power and leading of the Holy Spirit within the Christian community. Newbigin, throughout his ecclesiology, specifically addresses the presence of the Holy Spirit as the essential establishing and sustaining fact of each congregation. Thus, when he expresses his understanding of the missionary nature of the church as the congregation as hermeneutic of the gospel, Newbigin does so with a firm understanding of the presence of the Holy Spirit as constituting for their existence and continuation of Christ's mission. Here, I will provide a brief overview of Newbigin's pneumatology and its connection to his ecclesiology, in particular, the congregation as hermeneutic of the gospel.

Newbigin very clearly understood the importance of the Pentecostal movement for reminding all of Christianity about the role and importance of the Holy Spirit in the life of the church and every Christian. Newbigin categorically stated in *The Household of God* that, "The Holy Spirit is the Church's life."[2] The rest of the chapter of *The Household of God* that discusses the Holy Spirit describes the connections between the Holy Spirit and the church, and what this means for understanding the missionary nature of the church.[3] Later, Newbigin would assert that the Holy Spirit is the *arrabon*, or the first fruit

---

2. Newbigin, *Household of God*, 89–90.
3. Newbigin, *Household of God*, 90–110.

and foretaste of the kingdom, found in the church, and from which the church is to share that foretaste with the world.[4] Thus, it is by having the presence of the Holy Spirit within itself that the church becomes the sign, instrument, and foretaste of the kingdom of God in the world.[5] Finally, in describing the role of Christians as the royal priesthood of God, Newbigin notes, "Jesus is himself the one High Priest who alone can fulfill and has fulfilled this office. The church is sent into the world to continue that which he came to do, in the power of the same Spirit, reconciling people to God (John 20:19–23)."[6] Here, Newbigin is calling out each Christian to be a royal priest,[7] in the model of Christ, and with the power of the Holy Spirit which dwells within them as part of the church in that place and time. All these connections point to Newbigin's understanding of the church as constituted by and the dwelling place of the Holy Spirit, from which the presence and power of the Spirit enables each local congregation to be the hermeneutic of the gospel for that place and time. Thus, the ability of the local congregation to be the hermeneutic of the gospel for their society is derived directly from the presence of the Holy Spirit in that congregation, leading it into a living out of the gospel in service to that society. The pneumatological influence on Newbigin's ecclesiology and specifically its connections to the congregation as hermeneutic of the gospel is highlighted by some Newbigin scholars as well.

Krishna Kandiah's 2005 dissertation from King's College, entitled "Towards a Theology of Evangelism for Late-Modern Cultures," addresses Newbigin's pneumatology, specifically in connection to his ecclesiology by way of the congregation as hermeneutic of the gospel concept. Kandiah enters a discussion about the relationship between the gospel and the congregation in which he establishes a view from Newbigin of the church as a pneumatological community, and from this view, the congregation as hermeneutic concept emerges. Kandiah clearly states this twice, first saying, "it is precisely as the congregation is understood as a pneumatological community that it functions as the hermeneutic of the gospel." Later he reinforces this idea, stating, "It is as the congregation functions as a community of the Spirit that it becomes a hermeneutic of the gospel."[8] Kandiah has picked up the pneumatological

---

4. Newbigin, *Sign of the Kingdom*, 37–38.

5. Sign, instrument, and foretaste are important themes for Newbigin, which will be discussed further in chapter 4.

6. Newbigin, *Gospel in a Pluralist Society*, 230.

7. Newbigin defines this as, "The office of a priest is to stand before God on behalf of people and to stand before people on behalf of God." Newbigin, *Gospel in a Pluralist Society*, 230.

8. Kandiah, "Towards a Theology of Evangelism for Late-Modern Cultures," 299, 300.

foundation for the congregation as hermeneutic of the gospel and then applies this idea to the rest of his analysis of the concept. Kandiah focuses on the importance of the local congregation as "the primary missionary entity,"[9] the centrality of revelation,[10] and ultimately that the only way the congregation can be the hermeneutic of the gospel is through the empowering of the Holy Spirit.[11] He states, "It is only as the Spirit-empowered community that the congregation can be the hermeneutic of the gospel. . . . [T]he congregation is to be both an active participator in God's mission and yet this participation is only possible due to the presence of the Spirit in the congregation as 'empowering presence.'"[12] Here, Kandiah is making his point that for Newbigin, the local congregation is both "a pneumatological and hermeneutical community."[13] Kandiah then notes the implications of this pneumatological idea for the congregation as hermeneutic concept—that it is an alternative community, that it is enabled to be "the hermeneutic" by the presence of the Holy Spirit, and that there is an inextricable link between the gospel and local congregations.[14] Kandiah's integration of eschatological foretaste, missional community, and united body through a pneumatological hermeneutic within Newbigin helps to provide an overarching understanding of the interconnection of gospel, culture, and congregation, which guides much of Newbigin's post-retirement writings.

Similarly, Robert Hughes's 2014 dissertation from Asbury Theological Seminary, "Lesslie Newbigin's Understanding of the Holy Spirit and the Church in Mission," also examines Newbigin's discussions of the Holy Spirit throughout his ecclesial writings. Hughes marks the importance of the congregation as hermeneutic of the gospel within Newbigin's missiological and ecclesial writings and expressly connects this concept with the Spirit's witness in the world.[15] Hughes takes a different approach from Kandiah to understand the role of the Holy Spirit in Newbigin's ecclesiology, focusing on the witness of the Spirit through the church. And when it comes to the congregation as hermeneutic, Hughes focuses on the characteristic of the corporate community of Christ as part of the witness of the Spirit in the world. For Hughes then, the Holy Spirit is the forming and guiding presence of God within local congregations, enabling them to be the hermeneutic of the gospel in society.

9. Kandiah, "Towards a Theology of Evangelism for Late-Modern Cultures," 301.
10. Kandiah, "Towards a Theology of Evangelism for Late-Modern Cultures," 302.
11. Kandiah, "Towards a Theology of Evangelism for Late-Modern Cultures," 303–4.
12. Kandiah, "Towards a Theology of Evangelism for Late-Modern Cultures," 303–4.
13. Kandiah, "Towards a Theology of Evangelism for Late-Modern Cultures," 304.
14. Kandiah, "Towards a Theology of Evangelism for Late-Modern Cultures," 309.
15. Hughes, "Lesslie Newbigin's Understanding of the Holy Spirit," 214.

These two examples point to the relevance of the Holy Spirit for understanding the congregation as hermeneutic of the gospel concept, and firmly establish that the presence of the Holy Spirit is what makes the congregation the hermeneutic of the gospel.

While there are many other places where Newbigin discusses the Holy Spirit, the examples above and the connections that Kandiah and Hughes build between Newbigin's pneumatology and the congregation as hermeneutic of the gospel show the integral relationship between the two. For Newbigin, the Holy Spirit is the gift of God for the church, meant to guide the church into continuing the mission of God in the world as it was taught and modeled by Jesus Christ. Thus, each local congregation formed by the Holy Spirit to be the hermeneutic of the gospel for its place and time is also participating in a relationship with the Trinity, which shares the message of the salvation of Jesus Christ for all the world to see and hear. This requires local congregations to live the gospel, and when asked, preach the gospel as an explanation for their different way of living in the world. Being the hermeneutic of the gospel comes from being a community that is formed around Christ, by the Holy Spirit, continuing the ministry of the Father. Newbigin says the evidence of this formation and presence by the Holy Spirit is seen in the characteristics of the congregation as hermeneutic of the gospel.

ECCLESIAL CHARACTERISTICS

Newbigin often used lists to unpack the meaning and implications of the arguments that he has made, and this is especially true of his ecclesial discussions, where his lists provide insight into the implications he foresaw for his understanding of the missionary nature of the church. Throughout these lists, Newbigin has many overlapping topics which he addresses, but each list also provides a different perspective on his understanding of the missionary nature of the church. When he came to express the missionary nature of the church as the congregation as hermeneutic of the gospel, Newbigin developed an ecclesial list that was slightly different from the others but still deeply connected to them. This list focuses on the character of the congregation, which is formed and led by the Holy Spirit to be the hermeneutic of the gospel for their society. In studying Newbigin's list of characteristics of the congregation as hermeneutic of the gospel, it is necessary to also understand his other ecclesial lists as they provide context to his understanding of the missionary nature of the church. From these lists, there are five that are of particular note because of their overlap and connection with the congregation as hermeneutic of the gospel. Thus, in this section, I will provide a brief overview of the other five lists of note and their context for understanding Newbigin's ecclesiology and then take a deeper look at the characteristics Newbigin lists with the congregation as hermeneutic of the gospel in *The Gospel in a Pluralist Society* (GPS).

Newbigin's Other Ecclesial Lists

Throughout Newbigin's ecclesial writings he made lists of elements, questions, components, and the authority of Christians to preach the gospel all in association with his understanding of the missionary nature of the church. But what differentiates the list of the congregation as hermeneutic of the gospel concept and these lists is that within the congregation as hermeneutic concept, Newbigin is describing characteristics of who the church is, while these lists address the particular ecclesial issue he writing about. These lists provide context for Newbigin's missionary ecclesiology, and at times overlap with his characteristics of the congregation as hermeneutic of the gospel.

Newbigin's theology of mission book, *The Open Secret*, provides an exploration of his trinitarian foundations for missions. In his discussion of the authority of the church to preach the gospel, Newbigin states that this authority is based in the faith of the church in their confession of Jesus as Lord, that the church lives out this confession in its daily life, and that the church does this because it has been laid hold of by the Holy Spirit as witnesses to the gospel.[16] Newbigin extends this list of the authority that the church has to preach the gospel to each individual Christian (adding a second list that includes acting in accordance with the gospel they believe, treating others with the love and mercy they have received from Christ, and living and proclaiming the gospel in deed and word),[17] noting that Christians are to act in accordance with the gospel that they believe, that this gospel is verified by their preaching which explains their actions, that they are to treat others with love, grace, and mercy, and that they are to live by and proclaim the gospel in deeds and words throughout their everyday life.[18] Between these two lists, Newbigin has provided a similar purpose for the church and for Christians to preach the gospel to the world in everything they do and say as each goes about their life in the world.

The second list comes from *Sign of the Kingdom*. This book investigates the topic of the kingdom of God, looking at it from historical, biblical, and contemporary mission perspectives. While addressing the kingdom of God from the perspective of contemporary (late-1970s) mission, Newbigin first uses the expression the hermeneutic of the gospel for the local congregation.

---

16. Newbigin, *Open Secret*, 15–17.
17. Newbigin, *Open Secret*, 17–18.
18. Newbigin, *Open Secret*, 15–17.

"It is the Church as a whole which has to be the hermeneutic of the Gospel, and the question which has to be asked about these and other movements of fresh outreach into the world is whether they contribute to the renewal and reshaping of the life of the ordinary local congregation in every place."[19] Here, Newbigin is specifically labeling the church as the hermeneutic of the gospel and poses the question about whether this perspective and understanding of the church is beneficial for local congregations living out the gospel within their contexts. Newbigin goes on to ask whether this understanding of the church within local congregations makes them "a credible sign of God's reign in justice and mercy over the whole of life ... whether its common life is recognisable as a foretaste of the blessing which God intends for the whole human family."[20] Being a place where the presence of the Holy Spirit brings the foretaste of the kingdom of God into reality, Newbigin sees local congregations only being the hermeneutic of the gospel by making that reality present in the world in which God has placed them. Within this discussion, Newbigin shares what he sees as the key markers of such a congregation, describing what he saw as the evidence of local congregations being the hermeneutic of the gospel. First, Newbigin states, "that the development of this kind of congregational life will call for congregations which are related to the different sectors of the secular world as well as those which are related to the geographical areas of residence."[21] Newbigin is calling for local congregations to be actively engaged with, ministering to, partnering with, and serving the geographical and relational locals that intersect with that congregation. Second, Newbigin calls for a more flexible and varied style of ministry. This variation comes from a congregation that is neighborly (engaged with and caring for their neighbor), but also that is compassionately and actively living out a different worldview within their society.[22] Third, Newbigin calls on the leadership of these congregations and their ministries to be developed from within the congregation and community.[23] Fourth, Newbigin stresses the importance of maintaining faithfulness to gospel truth in the midst of this new openness and engagement with the world.[24]

In *Foolishness to the Greeks*, Newbigin approaches the topic of the missionary encounter between gospel and culture through the lens of his missionary experience, and his theological reflections upon the current state of the

19. Newbigin, *Sign of the Kingdom*, 63–64.
20. Newbigin, *Sign of the Kingdom*, 64.
21. Newbigin, *Sign of the Kingdom*, 64.
22. Newbigin, *Sign of the Kingdom*, 51–57.
23. Newbigin, *Sign of the Kingdom*, 66.
24. Newbigin, *Sign of the Kingdom*, 68–70.

church in the West. Within this discussion, Newbigin asserts that the church is to be "the bearer to all the nations of a gospel that announces the kingdom, the reign, and the sovereignty of God."[25] Newbigin's call on the church to bear this witness to all the nations leads him to provide a list about the essentials he sees for the church challenging culture with the gospel. First on Newbigin's list is a recovery and firm grasp of the doctrine of eschatology. "The curtain of death shuts off our view. But Jesus has gone before us through the curtain ... Jesus has gone down there before us and has appeared victorious on the other side. He is himself the path, the way that goes through death to life."[26] Second, Newbigin says that it is necessary for the church to provide a thorough doctrine of freedom. "True freedom is a gift of grace given by the one who is in fact Lord: that gift, freely given, can only be received in freedom."[27] This freedom is the freedom from the bonds of sin and death, and the freedom to choose, even choosing to reject the truth of Jesus Christ.[28] Third, Newbigin says that these congregations must declericalize theology and ministry. Newbigin asserts that theology must be developed in the world by people who are fully participating in that world, a lay theology by lay Christians active in the world.[29] Fourth, Newbigin believes that this type of church will provide a radical critique of denominationalism. While only a collection of like-minded individuals, denominations, Newbigin argues, cannot confront society with Truth and must be challenged and deconstructed by local congregations that are grounded in the Truth.[30] Fifth, Newbigin calls for unity in diversity across the entire global Body of Christ. "We need the witness of the whole ecumenical family if we are to be authentic witnesses of Christ to our own culture."[31] Sixth, Newbigin calls on the Christians of these churches to be bold and confident in holding to their faith, which will only be proven true at the end of human history.[32] Seventh, Newbigin includes the fact that all of these things come out of the congregation that is grounded in praise.[33] "The church's

---

25. Newbigin, *Foolishness to the Greeks*, 124.
26. Newbigin, *Foolishness to the Greeks*, 136.
27. Newbigin, *Foolishness to the Greeks*, 141.
28. Newbigin, *Foolishness to the Greeks*, 137–41.
29. Newbigin, *Foolishness to the Greeks*, 141–44.
30. Newbigin, *Foolishness to the Greeks*, 144–46.
31. Newbigin, *Foolishness to the Greeks*, 146.
32. Newbigin, *Foolishness to the Greeks*, 148–49.
33. It is notable that in Newbigin's Warfield Lectures at Princeton Theological Seminary ("Post-Enlightenment Culture as a Missionary Problem: Can the West Be Converted?"), from which *Foolishness to the Greeks* was written, there were originally only six essentials noted. In the writing of *Foolishness to the Greeks*, he added praise as a seventh essential. Thanks to George R. Hunsberger for drawing my attention to this fact.

witness among the nations is at heart the overflow of a gift. The boldness and the expectancy are marks of those who have been surprised by joy and know that there are still surprises to come, because God is great."[34] Newbigin points out that all ministry comes from an overflow of praise for God, who loves His creation more than they know.

Newbigin's next ecclesial list comes from the 1994 publication, *A Word in Season*, which is a collection of previously unpublished materials concerning different topics of global missions. Within this book, the chapter "Evangelism in the Context of Secularization" (originally published in Dutch in 1990) has two lists that discuss different aspects of Newbigin's understanding of the missionary nature of the church. Newbigin begins by showing that evangelism should be in response to questions about how a local congregation is living out the gospel, in the leading and power of the Holy Spirit, within the public life of the society.[35] Newbigin notes that living out the gospel in this way only happens in congregations that live "by a certain kind of shared life, by actions, and by words that interpret the actions."[36] This is Newbigin's first ecclesial list in this chapter, and he explains that the shared life is one formed around praise,[37] that the actions (such as healing, deliverance, service, etc.) come out of the community living out the new reality of the presence of the Holy Spirit (as first fruit of the kingdom) in the world,[38] and that words attest to and explain the actions of the congregation living out this new reality in the world.[39] Newbigin then continues to say that in light of this shared life of the new reality, the church must rethink evangelism in a secular society in five distinct ways: (1) evangelism must be about sharing the Good News of God's reign both now and in the future,[40] (2) evangelism must be grounded in the local congregation believing and living out the gospel,[41] (3) these congregations must train and enable members to be agents of the kingdom in the sectors of public life that they inhabit,[42] (4) members of these congregations must be taught how to enter into dialogue with the religious/ideological other and faithfully explain the Christian story,[43] and (5) evangelism is a movement of Christians achiev-

34. Newbigin, *Foolishness to the Greeks*, 150.
35. Newbigin, *Word in Season*, 151–52.
36. Newbigin, *Word in Season*, 152.
37. Newbigin, *Word in Season*, 152–53.
38. Newbigin, *Word in Season*, 153–54.
39. Newbigin, *Word in Season*, 154–55.
40. Newbigin, *Word in Season*, 155.
41. Newbigin, *Word in Season*, 155–56.
42. Newbigin, *Word in Season*, 156.
43. Newbigin, *Word in Season*, 157.

ing the highest standards of excellence in every area of public life and leading society into being reshaped by the Christian story.[44]

In Newbigin's 1994 Hickman Lectures at Duke Divinity School, "The Gospel in the Public Square," he again provides a list of his understanding of the missionary nature of the church, from yet another perspective. Throughout these lectures, Newbigin discussed the truth of the gospel and its place within public society, particularly focusing on the pluralist society of Western Europe and North America. Within the third lecture of this series, Newbigin provides a Christian vision for society. Newbigin asks what would be required for a Christian society to work, from which he envisions six key points.[45] First, Newbigin argues that any sort of Christian society must learn from history, remembering both the good and the bad lessons from Christendom.[46] Second, Newbigin believes that a Christian society must vehemently protect religious freedom (for all peoples of all religions), because he argues that the heart of the Cross is tolerating untruth in the face of Truth.[47] Third, Newbigin believes that the church in this society must be "a church which has the courage to believe in its own gospel and to proclaim that gospel as truth because God has revealed it as so."[48] Fourth, Newbigin believes that a Christian society will come about not by Christian control on society, but by a sufficient number of witnessing Christians influencing the public square.[49] Fifth, "A Christian society would be one where there were agencies which made it possible for Christian lay men and women in all the different sectors of public life . . . to explore and explicate the implications of the Christian faith for that particular area of public life."[50] Newbigin is arguing for structures of discipleship and theologizing throughout the public sectors of life, where Christians can theologize in ways that are "primarily concerned with the elucidation of the implications of the gospel for that particular sector in which they work."[51] Sixth, Newbigin calls on the church to always be evangelizing, in deed and word, in all that it says and does, every day.[52] Connecting this list to Newbigin's congregation as hermeneutic of the gospel concept, these six points provide an overview of

---

44. Newbigin, *Word in Season*, 157.
45. Newbigin, "What Kind of Society," 56–57.
46. Newbigin, "What Kind of Society," 57.
47. Newbigin, "What Kind of Society," 57–58.
48. Newbigin, "What Kind of Society," 59.
49. Newbigin, "What Kind of Society," 59–60.
50. Newbigin, "What Kind of Society," 60.
51. Newbigin, "What Kind of Society," 60.
52. Newbigin, "What Kind of Society," 60–61.

what Newbigin sees as the results of congregations living as the hermeneutic of the gospel and influencing society with the Christian story.

In all these lists, Newbigin provides different (though often overlapping) perspectives on his understanding of the missionary nature of the church. They also provide further insight into Newbigin's missionary ecclesiology, but the list of characteristics of the congregation as hermeneutic of the gospel speaks directly to the nature, identity, and being of the church. This nature is given to the church by the constituting and active presence of the Holy Spirit, leading it to be the Body of Christ in the world. Thus, the characteristics of the congregation as hermeneutic concept, while they may overlap with some of the other ecclesial lists, deserve extra attention as they are imparted by and evidence of the Holy Spirit in the local congregation.

The Characteristics of "The Congregation as Hermeneutic of the Gospel" in GPS

In his chapter on the topic, Newbigin, having laid out the primary question he is attempting to address (the credibility of the gospel in a pluralist society), and his answer (the congregation as hermeneutic of the gospel), goes on to explain what he envisions this congregation will look like.[53]

> Jesus, as I said earlier, did not write a book but formed a community. This community has at its heart the remembering and rehearsing of his words and deeds. . . . [I]t becomes the place where men and women and children find that the gospel gives them the framework of understanding, the 'lenses' through which they are able to understand and cope with the world.[54]

Newbigin points to the church as the place where men and women come into a fuller understanding and practicing of their faith, providing them the worldview they need to address the world. Christians are enabled to this fuller understanding and practice of their faith through the presence of the Holy Spirit, forming and leading the congregation. From this vision of the church, Newbigin goes on to say, "Insofar as it is true to its calling, this community will have, I think, the following six characteristics,"[55] from which he enters into a discussion of the six characteristics he believes will be evident in the congregation, which is the hermeneutic of the gospel for their society. It needs to be noted, that each of these characteristics is prefaced by the phrase, "it will

---

53. Newbigin, *Gospel in a Pluralist Society*, 227.
54. Newbigin, *Gospel in a Pluralist Society*, 227.
55. Newbigin, *Gospel in a Pluralist Society*, 227.

be a community of/that/where," indicating these characteristics of the congregation are derived from the Holy Spirit.

It Will Be a Community of Praise

For a congregation filled by the presence of the Holy Spirit and functioning as the hermeneutic of the gospel, Newbigin says, "It will be a community of praise. This is, perhaps, its most distinctive character."[56] Newbigin's understanding of praise[57] is that it can take on many forms, all of which are subsequent to what praise is—an act of reverence and thanksgiving to the merciful Creator who draws all of creation back into an intimate relationship with Himself. Newbigin states the fact that reverence and thanksgiving happen within the context of weekly worship. But he also points out that it takes place within the activity of the local congregation every other day of the week as they interact with the society which the congregation and its members inhabit. Newbigin also shows that praise results in being both the place of unity for all Christians and the first public witness of the church to the watching world.

Having spent time debating the structure of weekly worship and the issues of ecclesial authority while working on the unification scheme that became the Church of South India (CSI),[58] Newbigin did not spend much time working on specifics of a worship service. Instead, Newbigin's focus on worship looks more at the nature of worship. In focusing on the nature of worship, Newbigin developed two key elements of praise within *GPS*.[59] Newbigin's first element about the nature of praise is its role in providing reverence towards God. "Reverence, the attitude which looks up in admiration and love to one who is greater and better than oneself, is generally regarded as something unworthy of those who have 'come of age' and who claim that equality is essential to human dignity. With such presuppositions, of course, the very idea of God is ruled out."[60] Newbigin is arguing here that in a plural society like England, which is focused on equality, giving reverence is not something that is viewed as appropriate; yet, the local congregation is called to be a place of reverence to the God who gives it life. Reverence, Newbigin argues, is part of what marks

---

56. Newbigin, *Gospel in a Pluralist Society*, 227.

57. It should be noted that throughout his life, Newbigin often used praise and worship interchangeably. Thus, within this study, I will follow Newbigin's lead of using them interchangeably in discussing Newbigin's thought on the subject.

58. Newbigin, *Unfinished Agenda*, 79–92.

59. The nature of praise is also clearly discussed by Newbigin in *A South India Diary*, *The Holy Spirit and the Church*, *The Good Shepherd*, and "Human Flourishing in Faith, Fact, and Fantasy."

60. Newbigin, *Gospel in a Pluralist Society*, 227–28.

out the church and all of its members from the rest of society. "The Christian congregation, by contrast, is a place where people find their true freedom, their true dignity, and their true equality in reverence to One who is worthy of all the praise that we can offer."[61] Newbigin believes that in the congregation, the praise of reverence becomes the common ground on which freedom and equality exist amongst all of humanity.

While reverence is key for Newbigin's understanding of the nature of praise, he also saw praise as an act of thanksgiving to God. In the age of suspicion, which is how Newbigin saw England specifically and the West generally upon his return from India,[62] it is hard for modern men and women to give thanksgiving. Yet, Newbigin argues that when humanity is faced with the Creator and Sustainer of life, the only justice that they deserve is death; their rights are meaningless in comparison to the right of the Creator to seek justice for sins committed against Him and His creation.[63] God is merciful and by the "charity" of His grace humans are forgiven for their sins and given life.[64] Thus, the praise of the local congregation, for Newbigin, is also a thanksgiving for the grace they have received, and a reminder that they are to share that grace in service to their neighbor. "In Christian worship we acknowledge that if we had received justice instead of charity we would be on our way to perdition. A Christian congregation is thus a body of people with gratitude to spare, a gratitude that can spill over into care for the neighbor."[65] Praise, as Newbigin shows, draws the Christian community back to gratitude for the mercy they have received by the grace of God in their salvation. Thus, Newbigin determines that the praise of the local congregation is one of reverence and thanksgiving, which are to mark the Christian community as a counterculture to that of the world in which it lives.

While Newbigin's understanding of praise focuses on its nature, he also discusses the results of praise, which include unity and mission.[66] Newbigin believed that praise should be a place of union for the Body of Christ, both within a single congregation and within the larger ecumenical movement. Newbigin shows that praise is a place of unity for the church. In his experience

---

61. Newbigin, *Gospel in a Pluralist Society*, 227–28.
62. Newbigin, *Gospel in a Pluralist Society*, 227–28.
63. Newbigin, *Gospel in a Pluralist Society*, 227–28.
64. Newbigin, *Gospel in a Pluralist Society*, 227–28.
65. Newbigin, *Gospel in a Pluralist Society*, 227–28.
66. The results of praise are also clearly discussed in Newbigin's works: "The Christian Layman in the World and in the Church," *The Mission and Unity of the Church*, *The Holy Spirit and the Church*, *Christian Witness in a Pluralist Society*, "Integration—Some Personal Reflections 1981," and "Human Flourishing in Faith, Fact, and Fantasy."

with the CSI, Newbigin would highlight the unity he witnessed in the first worship service of the newly constituted denomination.[67] As well, Newbigin points to the unity that happens in the action of praise when all those who claim to follow Jesus Christ come together to worship as one Body of Christ.[68] It is in this action that praise also becomes a witness to the watching world. Building off Christ's assurance of His presence when His followers are gathered (Matt 18:20), Newbigin points to the missionary nature of the Holy Spirit and how that nature spills over into the congregation during the act of praise.[69] Newbigin reiterates this point by showing that praise becomes the grounding for evangelism and engagement with those of other religions or ideologies.[70]

The nature and results of praise provide an overview of Newbigin's understanding of praise. For Newbigin, the nature of praise is identified in the reverence and thanksgiving of God by His People. But in giving this reverence and thanksgiving, Christians are bound together in unity and bear witness to the world. Thus, the results of this nature of praise are physically manifested in the Body of Christ active in the world. Thus, praise is an expression of the presence of the Holy Spirit, leading the congregation to be the hermeneutic of the gospel.

It Will Be a Community of Truth

Newbigin claims that all society is formed around a plausibility structure and that this structure within the modern Western culture is antithetical to Christianity.[71] Thus, the congregation that is the hermeneutic of the gospel must be one of truth, gospel truth. This truth must exude from everything that they say and do. "And, if the congregation is to function effectively as a community of truth, its manner of speaking the truth must not be aligned to the techniques of modern propaganda, but must have the modesty, the sobriety, and the realism which are proper to a disciple of Jesus."[72] Newbigin is calling on the local congregation to witness to gospel truth in honesty, integrity, and authenticity within society, not in the ways of marketing and publicity campaigns by consumer products. This calling for the congregation to be a community of truth speaks to Newbigin's deeper understanding of truth.

67. Newbigin, *South India Diary*, 6.

68. Newbigin, *Mission and Unity of the Church*, 3; Newbigin, "Christian Layman in the World and in the Church," 185.

69. Newbigin, *Holy Spirit and the Church*, 15.

70. Newbigin, *Good Shepherd: Meditations on Christian Ministry in Today's World*, 29–30; Newbigin, *Christian Witness in a Plural Society*; Newbigin, "Integration," 251–52.

71. Newbigin, *Gospel in a Pluralist Society*, 228–29.

72. Newbigin, *Gospel in a Pluralist Society*, 229.

Newbigin discusses truth as truth in, of, or as the gospel of Jesus Christ.[73] For Newbigin, gospel truth forms the foundation for belief and how to understand and interpret reality. Newbigin believes "that all human thinking takes place within a 'plausibility structure' which determines what beliefs are reasonable and what are not."[74] This plausibility structure, Newbigin mentions, is the lens through which humans see and interpret the world. The Christian plausibility structure, Newbigin states, is one that is built solidly upon the foundation of the truth within the gospel. Newbigin shows the gospel as the foundation for Christian understanding and message of truth, which has not changed or wavered throughout the course of human history.[75] This unchangingness of the gospel that Newbigin speaks of is that it is a record of historical happenings which cannot unhappen, therefore the gospel itself is unchangeable.[76] This foundation, which the church receives from the Holy Spirit,[77] prepares the local congregation to become a counterculture. Truth for Newbigin, then, is found exclusively within the gospel, thus he talks about the truth in, of, or as the gospel of Jesus Christ.

Newbigin also discusses truth in the context of the church bearing witness to gospel truth in the public square. As Newbigin points out in *Sign of the Kingdom*, the church is the representative of God's kingdom in the world. As well, Newbigin shows in *Truth to Tell* that the public nature of the gospel necessitates that the church shares the gospel in the public square as public truth. To fulfill these points, Newbigin believes that the Christian community must learn how to inhabit the plausibility structure of Christ to share the truth of the gospel with their society. "A Christian congregation is a community in which, through the constant remembering and rehearsing of the true story of human nature and destiny, an attitude of healthy scepticism can be sustained, a scepticism which enables one to take part in the life of society without being bemused and deluded by its own beliefs about itself."[78] Thus, in the acts of studying, living, and repeating the truth of the gospel, the congregation can critically engage with its society. This critical engagement calls for the church to challenge the false narratives and plausibility structures of modern society,

73. Some important discussions of this perspective of truth from Newbigin can be found in "Witness to Jesus Christ," *The Mission and the Unity of the Church*, "Mission in an Ecumenical Perspective," "Mission in the 1980s," and "The Bible and Our Contemporary Mission."

74. Newbigin, *Gospel in a Pluralist Society*, 228.

75. Newbigin, "Bible and Our Contemporary Mission," 15–16.

76. Newbigin's idea of the unchangeability of the gospel should not be confused with many contemporary conversations about the gospel being unchangeable.

77. Newbigin, "Witnessing to Jesus Christ," 57, 58; Newbigin, *Good Shepherd*, 120.

78. Newbigin, *Gospel in a Pluralist Society*, 229.

and share the true story of humanity found in Jesus Christ. This critical engagement calls for the constant and regular remembering and rehearsing of the gospel for the Christian community as a counter-narrative to that of society.[79] Thus, the local congregation that functions as the hermeneutic of the gospel will regularly engage with the truth of the gospel to be prepared to provide a countering narrative to society. Through their understanding of gospel truth, the local congregation provides a counterculture to society.

Newbigin's understanding of truth always connects back to the gospel—Jesus is the Truth and the gospel testifies to Jesus. In the congregation which functions as the hermeneutic of the gospel in society, they are the interpretive lens of gospel truth in the world. And they are only this because the Holy Spirit dwells within the local congregation, enabling and leading them to be the interpretation of the gospel truth. Thus, being a community of truth is evidence of the presence of the Holy Spirit within the local congregation living out their missionary identity as the hermeneutic of the gospel truth for all the world to witness.

It Will Be a Community That Does Not Live for Itself but Is Deeply Involved in the Concerns of Its Neighborhood

Newbigin believed that the church is always focused on others. He states that "it is God's embassy in a specific place."[80] This gives the church a twofold constituency, God and the society it inhabits. "It will be the church for the specific place where it lives, not the church for those who wish to be members of it—or, rather, it will be for them insofar as they are willing to be *for* the wider community."[81] Newbigin is expressing his view of the local congregation being focused on serving its community, and that the care of its own members even comes through its ministry to society. Newbigin's characteristic of being a community that is involved in its neighborhood, or neighborliness, is built primarily through scripture and experience.

Multiple times throughout his writings, Newbigin references specific scripture to show the necessity of neighborliness for the church.[82] He connects this scriptural foundation for neighborliness in *Behold, I Make All Things New* using 1 John 2:7–17, and in *The Good Shepherd* using James 2. As well, Newbigin found the model of biblical servanthood as seen in Jesus

---

79. Newbigin, *Gospel in a Pluralist Society*, 228–29.

80. Newbigin, *Gospel in a Pluralist Society*, 229.

81. Newbigin, *Gospel in a Pluralist Society*, 229.

82. Newbigin, *Behold, I Make All Things New*; Lesslie Newbigin, *Christ Our Eternal Contemporary*, 74, 89; Newbigin, *Good Shepherd*, 91–95.

Christ and expanded upon it to show that such servanthood is meant for the whole church to utilize in its engagement with the world, most notably their immediate neighbors.[83]

The scriptural grounding for Newbigin's understanding of neighborliness comes from his reading of the New Testament term *ekklēsia* and his theological understanding of that word, both of which are outlined in "On Being the Church for the World" and *GPS*. Referencing the use of *ekklēsia*, Newbigin notes that the only two qualifications of the term within the New Testament are to the congregation as the Church of God or of Christ, and to the church of a specific place.[84] The local congregation is to be defined by these relationships, first to God and second to a specific place. As Newbigin puts it, "it is God's embassy in a specific place."[85] His meaning is that the church is meant to be the visible location of God's presence in a specific place. Newbigin's use of *ekklēsia* is foundational for understanding how he sees the church in the world.[86]

This role of place in Newbigin's thought is picked up and expanded upon in the work of David Porter. Porter's ThD dissertation from Duke Divinity School, "The Predicament of Place," develops a missionary theology of place, which he then tests against the life and writings of Newbigin. Porter, after establishing the need for a missionary theology of place, develops a three-fold typology for his missionary theology of place, using sacred creation, sacred journey, and sacred construction. Within sacred construction, Porter notes that in the congregation as hermeneutic of the gospel, Newbigin "contends that the most important interpretation of the gospel is not a logical proof or polished argument but the gospel's demonstration in the lives of a transformed community who live what they believe."[87] Thus, the transformed community of those who believe and live the gospel serves as a building block for the sacred construction of a missionary theology of place for Porter. It is also important to note, Porter does specifically address Newbigin's investigations of *ekklēsia Theou*, as discussed above.[88] But in Porter's analysis of Newbigin's view of the local congregation as the church for a specific place, he notes that this commitment to place: "(1) prioritizes service over self-fulfillment,

---

83. Newbigin, "Church as a Servant Community," 258; Newbigin, "Human Flourishing in Faith, Fact, and Fantasy," 411.

84. Newbigin, *Gospel in a Pluralist Society*, 229.

85. Newbigin, *Gospel in a Pluralist Society*, 229.

86. Newbigin, "On Being the Church for the World," 25.

87. Porter, *Predicament of Place*, 319.

88. These discussions can be specifically found in: Newbigin, *Gospel in a Pluralist Society*, 229; Newbigin, "On Being the Church for the World," 25.

(2) takes responsibility for the community, (3) identifies with its immediate neighborhood, (4) welcomes anyone who shares its mission, and (5) positions itself publicly as a community *for* others."[89] This list depicts the necessary components of a congregational commitment to place. Ultimately, Porter concludes that "Newbigin's construction suggests that a congregational commitment to place is synonymous with a missionary commitment to place."[90] Thus, Porter finds in Newbigin an interlocutor who helps him prove the necessity and role of a missionary theology of place, specifically using the congregation as hermeneutic of the gospel in doing so. This points to place as an essential component in Newbigin's description of neighborliness.

Newbigin's experiential evidence for neighborliness can be found in "Context and Conversion," where he identifies four characteristics of a growing church,[91] but it is the second of these characteristics that is important for this discussion. This second characteristic is that the members of the growing church are intimately engaged with the sorrows and conflicts of their neighbors and physically represent the church that is for others.[92] This is evidence of the local congregation being intimately involved in its neighborhood, with the results being that in the course of daily life the people of the neighborhood are brought into contact with the church through relationships. As well, in "Integration—Some Personal Reflection," Newbigin says, "I recognize that I can only share with others the life I have in Christ if I am willing to be part of their lives, to face their issues, to share their hurts."[93] This link moves from neighborliness to working towards the benefit of the neighborhood to preaching the gospel in word and deed.

Being a community of neighborliness speaks to the local congregation's reputation within their society, but it is only possible because they are the sign, instrument, and foretaste of the kingdom of God.[94] And they are only this because they have the original foretaste, the Holy Spirit, present within their community. Thus, being a community of neighborliness speaks to the presence of the Holy Spirit, leading the local congregation to be a community for others, living out its missionary nature within its society.

---

89. Porter, *Predicament of Place*, 320.
90. Porter, *Predicament of Place*, 320.
91. Newbigin, *Context and Conversion*, 6.
92. Newbigin, *Context and Conversion*, 6.
93. Newbigin, "Integration," 252.
94. This idea will be discussed more in chapter 4.

It Will Be a Community Where Men and Women Are Prepared for and Sustained in the Exercise of the Priesthood to the World

For Newbigin, the local congregation must be a community that prepares and sustains its members for the priesthood, so that it may function as the hermeneutic of the gospel in the world. Throughout all of Newbigin's writings on the subject, the concept of priesthood is often meant as the priesthood of every believer, what he refers to as the royal priesthood. "This priesthood of all believers is exercised in the working days of the week."[95] For Newbigin, every believer is meant to exercise their priesthood in all the days of the week and in all areas of life. Thus, the local congregation is a place where every member is enabled to live out their calling as a royal priesthood within everyday life outside of the church building. A topic that Newbigin discusses multiple times throughout his life, there are three major elements on which his discussion focuses on the most important points of the royal priesthood. First, Newbigin brings forth the necessary argument that *all* of God's people are called to this royal priesthood. Second, Newbigin discusses the need for a vast diversity of spiritual gifts to be exercised within this royal priesthood in order for it to be a priesthood that incorporates and ministers to all. Third, Newbigin highlights the importance of the local congregation to prepare, mobilize, and sustain its members to exercise the royal priesthood in the world.

Newbigin begins his discussion of the characteristic of preparing and sustaining members for the priesthood in the world by returning to the New Testament and pointing out that *all* Christians have been called to be a royal priesthood.[96] But what exactly does it mean to be God's royal priesthood? "The office of a priest is to stand before God on behalf of people and to stand before people on behalf of God."[97] Newbigin is saying that as God's royal priesthood, Christians are the intermediary between God and the rest of the world, representing God to the world and representing the world to God. Newbigin builds this concept of the royal priesthood of every believer upon the example of Jesus Christ as servant and priest.[98] To exercise this priesthood, Christians must enter the ordinary business of the secular world as Christ's representatives.[99]

---

95. Newbigin, "X-Ray to Make God Visible in the World," 7.

96. Newbigin, *Gospel in a Pluralist Society*, 229–30; Newbigin, "Christian Layman in the World and the Church," 185.

97. Newbigin, *the Gospel in a Pluralist Society*, 230.

98. Newbigin, "Lay Presidency at the Eucharist," 178–79.

99. Newbigin, *Gospel in a Pluralist Society*, 230.

Second, entering the world requires a diversity of gifts in order to reach all of the world, but also to represent the full range of spiritual giftings that exist within the church. Newbigin builds upon the letters of Paul to show in *The Holy Spirit and the Church* the necessity for a plurality of spiritual gifts within every congregation for the exercise of the royal priesthood to be fulfilled. Newbigin is saying that for the royal priesthood of every believer to be a full priesthood and reach the fullness of humanity, diversity must be lived out in the life and ministry of the church.[100] In contemporary society, especially in the West, there is a tendency for people to seek out uniform churches that look and act exactly like themselves. When this happens, churches become full of one or two gifts and devoid of all the others, which is not how God intends the church to be. Paul's letters stress the need for different gifts and different kinds of service with those gifts.[101] "Only when a congregation can accept and rejoice in the diversity of gifts, and when members can rejoice in gifts which others have been given, can the whole body function as Christ's royal priesthood in the world."[102] The local congregation must not only seek out those of different gifts, but it must be a place that rejoices and celebrates these different gifts. It is only in the differences that a fuller picture of the Triune God and a better enabling to represent that God in the world can happen.[103] One of Newbigin's best examples of this is the fullness of ministry that takes place when the church incorporates the handicapped in its activity and ministry.[104]

To prepare congregants for the royal priesthood, the church must be the place that rehearses the story of Christ and renews its membership for exercising the priesthood in the world for the coming week. "But the exercise of this priesthood is not within the walls of the Church but in the daily business of the world."[105] Newbigin is saying that Christians are to regularly worship together, and during worship they receive the renewing call to be God's royal priesthood, but then they must go into the world to represent God to the world. This makes one of the central jobs of pastors to be the preparation of their members for the exercise of the royal priesthood, and Newbigin shows that a major way that they do this is through preaching.[106] Thus, preaching is a cornerstone and uniquely explicit job of the ordained pastor. And in

---

100. Newbigin, *Holy Spirit and the Church*, 18–21.

101. Newbigin, *Gospel in a Pluralist Society*, 230.

102. Newbigin, *Gospel in a Pluralist Society*, 231.

103. Newbigin, "Mission of the Triune God," 1.

104. Newbigin, "Right to Fullness of Life," 345–46; Newbigin, "Not Whole without the Handicapped," 24.

105. Newbigin, *Gospel in a Pluralist Society*, 230.

106. Newbigin, *Good Shepherd*, 28–31, 74–82.

Preaching Christ Today, Newbigin reinforces the point that preaching is worthless without the activity of the congregation in the world, and that activity is given guidance and deeper meaning through gospel preaching.

In Newbigin's language, the church that prepares its members for the royal priesthood must also send and sustain them, thus the local congregation becomes like a mission station. "The congregation has to be a place where its members are trained, supported, and nourished in the exercise of their parts of the priestly ministry in the world."[107] For Newbigin, the local congregation must be the staging ground, the command center, the hospital, and the festival site for all of its members as they embark into the world as God's royal priesthood. Yet, this is not how pastors are trained. Too often pastors are trained for the pastoral care of their existing congregation and theologizing from a pulpit.[108] What is needed are pastors who prepare and send congregants to the front lines of missions in their communities. "There is a need for 'frontier-groups,' groups of Christians working in the same sector of public life, meeting to thrash out the controversial issues of their business or profession in the light of their faith."[109] Newbigin is saying that in order for the local congregation to fulfill its role in sustaining its members to be the royal priesthood, there must be groups established that connect members in the same industries, so that they may get together and theologize about the issues specific to their daily lives. These groups must be trained properly, but they must also be given regular support in order to support their members. This support comes primarily through two avenues. The first avenue is regular participation in congregational worship.[110] Every Sunday, Christians stand before God as the representative of the world. They are reminded of their sins, rehearse the redemption of the death and resurrection of Jesus Christ, and are sent out to be God's priests to the world. The second avenue, and attached to the first, is that the local congregation sustains its members for the priesthood through preaching Christ as both Saviour and Lord.[111] Such preaching provides spiritual renewal, but it also provides fodder for discussion and witness by the congregation.

The local congregation that prepares, sends, and sustains its members to be able to exercise their role as God's royal priesthood in the world does so only by the presence and leading of the Holy Spirit. Each and every member of

107. Newbigin, *Gospel in a Pluralist Society*, 230.

108. Newbigin, *Gospel in a Pluralist Society*, 231, 230; Newbigin, "Ministry and Laity," 479–81.

109. Newbigin, *Gospel in a Pluralist* Society, 230–31.

110. Newbigin, "Church as Witness," 8.

111. Newbigin, *Preaching Christ Today*, 5.

the church must be exercising their calling as God's royal priests in the world. This is only possible by the active presence of the Holy Spirit, guiding every member in how they should be royal priests and every congregation in how to prepare and sustain these members for this ministry.

It Will Be a Community of Mutual Responsibility

Mutual responsibility, for Newbigin, is the greatest example of the new social order that the church is supposed to model for the rest of society. Newbigin states that,

> We grow into true humanity only in relationships of faithfulness and responsibility toward one another. The local congregation is called to be, and by the grace of God often is, such a community of mutual responsibility. When it is such, it stands in the wider community of the neighborhood and the nation not primarily as the promoter of programs for social change (although it will be that) but primarily as itself the foretaste of a different social order.[112]

Here, Newbigin is saying that the local congregation is meant to be the model of a new social order, and that model is identified in society by the mutual responsibility of the local congregation. Mutual responsibility is an idea that Newbigin shows is important to the local congregation functioning as the hermeneutic of the gospel. For Newbigin, mutual responsibility has a very narrow definition—care for one another—but this definition has three very important ramifications.

The first ramification of Newbigin's mutual responsibility is binding together. This appears throughout many of his writings, but most notable within them is the connection to Christian unity, the pastoral care of each other by each member of a given congregation, and the connection between the church and the world. Newbigin notes that members of the Body of Christ are bound together in their imaging of Christ, their shared sense of debt to Christ, and in the presence of the Holy Spirit; the last of which creates in them a sense of responsibility to care for one another.[113] Within churches and across the Body of Christ, one way Newbigin envisions this caring for one another is "pluriformity."

> But these must always be held within a wider community of different kinds of groups, so that our smaller fellowships are not allowed to become self-sufficient. This suggests a great pluriformity in the

---

112. Newbigin, *Gospel in a Pluralist Society*, 231.
113. Newbigin, *Christ Our Eternal Contemporary*, 64, 74.

life of the Church—small intimate groups for spiritual growth, big public celebrations, tough and costly exercises in tackling situations where God's will is denied—all held together in loyalty to the whole family of the Church. We need that kind of pluriformity if our living together in Christ is to be the opportunity for receiving the gift of life and for giving it away in order to receive more abundant life.[114]

Newbigin is calling for the connection of small fellowships with the larger church, both within congregations and amongst congregations, as a form of living together that is necessary for the church. Responsibility for each other is doubly important within the congregation as Newbigin points to the reasonability of the laity to provide pastoral care for one another.[115] Newbigin shows that the role of pastoral responsibility to care for one another in the New Testament was not operated by ordained priests, but rather by the members of the congregation itself.[116] Nigel Peter Warner, in his MA Thesis from Anglia Polytechnic University in 2001, addresses this very issue. Warner uses the congregation as hermeneutic of the gospel as a framework for his chapter outlining Newbigin's ecclesiology, through which the kingdom can see the world and the world can see members of the kingdom.[117] Warner then uses this understanding to show the necessity for participatory mutual discipleship of every member of a congregation, thus placing pastoral care on the shoulders of the whole community rather than just the ordained pastors. Newbigin, while discussing mutual responsibility, points to the unity within a congregation and among congregations that happens when they bear responsibility for each other.[118] Newbigin also points to the covenant relationship of the church as the foundation for each congregation bearing witness to a new social order in the world.[119] Newbigin necessitates this new social order through his analysis of the current state of affairs, particularly in the West.

Newbigin begins his argument about the second ramification of mutual responsibility, bearing witness, by pointing out the fact that Western society has ventured deeply into the false premise of individualism. "The deepest root of the contemporary malaise of Western culture is an individualism which denies the fundamental reality of our human nature as given by God—namely that we grow into true humanity only in relationships of faithfulness and

---

114. Newbigin, "Living Together," 19.
115. Newbigin, "Church Union," 358–60.
116. Newbigin, "Church Union," 358–59.
117. Warner, "Missionary Ecclesiology of Leslie Newbigin," 4–12.
118. Newbigin, "Basis and the Forms of Unity," 10.
119. Newbigin, "Politics and the Covenant," 361.

responsibility toward one another."[120] As Newbigin points out here, Western society has sacrificed everything else at the altar of individualism, but this individualism runs in opposition to God's design of humanity. Humans are made to be in deep, intimate, faithful relationships with one another and are called to account for their brothers and sisters in these relationships. They are to bear each other's burdens, celebrate each other's accomplishments, and weep in each other's sadness. In this deep relationship, Newbigin affirms the unity of being children of God. "Being children of God must mean being—in some recognizable sense—members of one family.... That is why this wonderful prayer (*John 17:22-22*) is so filled with longing for the unity of Christ's people—'I in them and thou in me that they may become perfectly one.'"[121] The unity of being children of God is seen within the interdependence Newbigin calls for in the church.

Newbigin's characteristic of mutual responsibility also strikes at the heart of individualism to call the local congregation back to their original design of interdependence—an interdependence of deep and intimate relationships. In this interdependence, the local congregation becomes a new social order that calls all of society to return to its intended relational reality. "If the Church is to be effective in advocating and achieving a new social order in the nation, it must itself be a new social order.... When it is such, it stands in the wider community of the neighborhood and the nation not primarily as a promoter of programs for social change (although it will be that) but primarily as itself the foretaste of a different social order."[122] Newbigin is saying that the church is meant to provide a different social order for society, but for this to happen it must first model this new social order within itself. When it models this new social order, the church becomes the foretaste of the kingdom; then, it is the hermeneutic of the gospel to their society.

Newbigin's third ramification of mutual responsibility is that it provides the foundation for the church to be advocates of peace, justice, and liberation in society. Only when the members of the local congregation operate in the interdependence of mutual responsibility do they themselves experience the liberation of life fully lived in Christ. From this liberation, members of the local congregation can be advocates for the liberation of others. They already live in the true liberation of Christ, which they can only share once they inhabit that liberation themselves.[123] As well, the local congregation of mutual responsibility is meant to model justice for society. "In its (*the local*

---

120. Newbigin, *Gospel in a Pluralist Society*, 231.
121. Newbigin, *Is Christ Divided?*, 20; italics added.
122. Newbigin, *Gospel in a Pluralist Society*, 231
123. Newbigin, *Is Christ Divided?*, 18-25.

congregation's) corporate life and mutual care and discipline of its members it embodies (even if very imperfectly) the justice of God which both unmasks the sin and restores relation with the sinner."[124] Newbigin argues that it is mutual responsibility that enables the local congregation to begin to model justice in an unjust world. The church of mutual responsibility working for peace and justice, then, does so out of an abundance of life in Christ. "Its actions for justice and peace will be, and will be seen to be, the overflow of a life in Christ, where God's justice and God's peace are already an experienced treasure."[125] Thus, Newbigin sees that the church that lives in mutual responsibility experiences the fullness of God's peace and justice, and from that experience can begin to work for peace and justice in society. It is through experiencing peace, justice, and liberation in mutual responsibility that the local congregation becomes an agent of peace, justice, and liberation in society.

Thus, being a community of mutual responsibility is about caring for each other in a way that models the new social order for society. This is only possible by the presence of the Holy Spirit, leading and enabling the local congregation to care for and serve each other in this way. It is the presence of the Holy Spirit that spurs the local congregation to this loving care and builds toward the congregation functioning as the hermeneutic of the gospel in their society.

It Will Be a Community of Hope

Hope, as Newbigin discusses it, is always in the context of the gospel, as a future hope based on the resurrection and promised return of Jesus Christ. This hope is an exclusive hope found only in Christians and the Christian community that is formed around the gospel. But it is also an inclusive hope, where all are invited to join. The hope of the gospel is meant to be shared with others; it is the responsibility of Christians to bear witness to the hope that they have (1 Pet 3:15). Thus, gospel hope is the only true hope that exists in the world, for it is the only hope that comes from the Creator Father, is fulfilled in the Son Jesus Christ, is being fulfilled through the presence of the Holy Spirit, and will be fulfilled in the future new creation. Gospel hope draws the local congregation into the world as witnesses to and images of the hope of Jesus Christ. Newbigin discusses hope primarily in three ways.

First, the hope that Newbigin discusses is a patient-yet-eager hope, one that is based on the evidence of God's present kingdom, but longing for the fulfillment of God's future kingdom. This hope is part of what makes up the

---

124. Newbigin, "Whose Justice?," 311; italics added.
125. Newbigin, *Gospel in a Pluralist Society*, 231–32.

very identity of the church, as hope in the present/future kingdom of God is the grounds for understanding why the church serves the world as Christ served the world.[126] Newbigin developed this understanding and perspective on Christian hope through scripture, specifically the works of Paul and Peter on the subject.[127] In particular, Newbigin notes in Paul the role of Romans 8:18–25 for his understanding of Christian hope. Noting first that Paul has discussed suffering, Newbigin launches into a discussion on hope, "he goes on to say that our troubles are not worth mentioning in comparison with the greatness of what we hope for."[128] Newbigin is showing that the hope that Christians have is a hope in the future, one which makes all earthly troubles and struggles seem insignificant in comparison. And from Peter, Newbigin stresses the present reality of that hope.

> In that beautiful pastoral letter, the first letter of Peter, we have this little word: "Always be ready to give an answer to everyone who asks you to give the reason for the hope that you have, but do this with gentleness and respect" (I Peter 3:15). Notice two things about this. Firstly, it is the other person, the unbeliever, who asks the question. The authentic opportunity for evangelism is when the unbeliever asks the question because there is something about the Christian fellowship that prompts people to ask for the secret. Indeed, if you look through the record of Christian evangelism in the Acts of the Apostles you will find that the great majority, beginning with St. Peter's sermon on the day of Pentecost, are prompted by a question asked by the unbeliever: What is going on? What is your secret? And secondly, we note that the question is about 'the hope that you have'. A believing Christian congregation will be a community of hope in a world which is often without hope.[129]

Newbigin is stressing from Peter that Christians should live their hope in the world in such a way that others notice and ask about it. Hope, then, is part of the lived reality of the local congregation. Newbigin even connects this with future hope. "Christians are people who look forward to a glorious future—God's future. When that is so, people will notice it, and they will ask the question: 'What is your secret?' If that is not happening, a Christian congregation

---

126. Newbigin, *Household of God*; Newbigin, "Nature of the Christian Hope."

127. See Newbigin, *Mission and Unity of the Church*, 15–16; Newbigin, "Bible Study on Romans 8"; Newbigin, *Come Holy Spirit-Renew the Whole Creation*, 5–6; Newbigin, "Gospel as Public Truth," 7; Newbigin, *Christ Our Eternal Contemporary*, 31, 62; Newbigin, "Pastoral Ministry in a Pluralist Society," 151–52; Newbigin, "Evangelism and the Whole Mission of the Church," 5.

128. Newbigin, "Bible Study on Romans 8," 6.

129. Newbigin, "Pastoral Ministry in a Pluralist Society," 151–52.

must ask why."[130] Newbigin calls on congregations to be living the reality of hope in the world, and if they are not being asked about this hope, then they are not truly living the hope of Christ. He grounds the identifying marker of the church, the hope that it has in Jesus Christ, within the New Testament. This grounding directly distinguishes the difference between Christian hope and all other claims to hope in the world.

Second, Newbigin often discusses hope in the context of the distinguishing markers of Christian hope versus other claims of hope in the world. As early as the 1950s, Newbigin can clearly see that the world is wounded by hopelessness and in need, a need that can only be healed through the hopefulness of Jesus Christ,[131] as he differentiates between Christian hope and the meaningless hope that is found in the world in "The Present Crisis and the Coming Christ." This element of hope is expanded upon later in Newbigin's work as he calls out the false hope that exists in other religions and ideologies of the world, showing how dull and lifeless this false hope is when exposed to the light of the true hope of the gospel.[132] The biblical hope that Newbigin has established is one that looks to the future, yet it is also being manifested in the present age.[133] It is this hope that the church is called to bear witness to in the world, a world devoid of hope.

Third, at multiple points in Newbigin's discussion of hope, he establishes a firm link between hope and witness, because the message of hope is part of the gospel witness of the church in the world. Newbigin establishes hope as a key part of preaching, which is meant for both the church and the world.[134] This evangelistic preaching of hope, particularly in the West, is part of what is meant to define the witness of the local congregation as a community of Christ followers who function as the hermeneutic of the gospel for their society.[135] In sharing this hope with society, the local congregation is living in and witnessing to a new plausibility structure by which society can operate. The hope found in the plausibility structure of the gospel is so different from that of the world that it is unbelievable—to the world, hope found in a crucified rabbi is beyond comprehendible.[136] This is why it is the responsibility of the

---

130. Newbigin, "Pastoral Ministry in a Pluralist Society," 152.

131. Newbigin, "Present Crisis and the Coming Christ," 118–23.

132. Newbigin, "Mission of the Triune God," 8.

133. Newbigin, *Journey into Joy*, 81–99.

134. Newbigin, *Preaching Christ Today*, 4; Newbigin, "Pastor's Opportunities," 356; Newbigin, "Gospel And Culture," 2, 7.

135. Newbigin, "Can the West be Converted?," 7; Newbigin, "Evangelism and the Whole Mission of the Church," 5.

136. Newbigin, "Evangelism and the Whole Mission of the Church," 5.

local congregation to be immersed in the gospel and be a living example of gospel hope within the world.[137] The local congregation cannot simply do this in worship or in activities of missions and outreach, it must be a requisite part of the life of the congregation and all of its members. The local congregation must live out this hope in every area of public life that each of its members' ventures into on a daily basis.[138] Newbigin says,

> If the gospel is to challenge the public life of our society, if Christians are to occupy the "high ground" which they vacated in the noontime of "modernity," it will not be by forming a Christian political party, or by aggressive propaganda campaigns. Once again it has to be said that there can be no going back to the "Constantinian" era. It will only be by movements that begin with the local congregation in which the reality of the new creation is present, known, and experienced, and from which men and women will go into every sector of public life to claim it for Christ, to unmask the illusions which have remained hidden and to expose all areas of public life to the illumination of the gospel.[139]

Newbigin is stating that it is the responsibility of the local congregation to bring the light of the gospel hope into every aspect of public life through active engagement and public witness.

The hope which Newbigin builds the community of hope characteristic upon is biblical hope, which comes to the church through scripture and the Holy Spirit. But it is the presence of the Spirit leading the local congregation in living out this biblical hope in the world that makes them a community of hope, functioning as the hermeneutic of the gospel and testifying to the credibility of Jesus Christ as the last word in human affairs.

THE CONGREGATIONAL FRUIT OF THE SPIRIT

Newbigin has established that the constituting active presence of the Holy Spirit is essential for understanding the missionary nature of the church. When he discusses this nature throughout his ecclesiology, he uses lists to help depict key points. When Newbigin frames his missionary ecclesiology in the expression of the congregation as hermeneutic of the gospel, his list in this expression is a list of characteristics. These characteristics are actively being developed within local congregations as the Holy Spirit establishes and leads the church in each situation and generation it encounters. Thus, Newbigin's

---

137. Newbigin, "Evangelism and the Whole Mission of the Church," 5.
138. Newbigin, "Evangelism and the Whole Mission of the Church," 5.
139. Newbigin, *Gospel in a Pluralist Society*, 232–33.

characteristics of the congregation as hermeneutic of the gospel can be viewed as kind of congregational fruit of the Spirit, in the same mode as Paul's Fruit of the Spirit in Gal 5. Within this section I will first address the Fruit of the Spirit in Gal 5 (and particularly Newbigin's discussion of it), then I will show how Newbigin's characteristics should be viewed as congregational fruit of the Spirit.

The Fruit of the Spirit

In Galatians 5:13–26, Paul provides an overview of what it means to live with and by the Spirit for the individual Christian believer, supplying the Galatian church and subsequent readers with lists of both acts of the flesh and the Fruit of the Spirit. Many sermons have been preached and numerous books have been written trying to understand and apply the Fruit of the Spirit to the daily lives of Christians, but the most basic interpretation is that the fruit Paul outlines in versus 22–26 is evidence of the active presence of the Spirit in the life of individual Christians. They point to a growing relationship of obedience and discipleship between the Holy Spirit and individual Christians, where the Spirit is growing these fruit within the Christian and the evidence of that growth is seeing these fruit come to bear within their lives.

Investigating the Fruit of the Spirit must begin with a review of the pericope of Galatians 5:13–26. Paul's prayer and desire for all of the congregations he interacted with was "that out of his glorious riches he may strengthen you with power through his Spirit in your inner being, so that Christ may dwell in your hearts through faith" (Eph 3:16–17a). Thus, Paul's heart for the church, and every member in it, is that they would be filled with the power and presence of the Holy Spirit through their faith in Jesus Christ. This prayer for the Ephesian church can similarly be seen in all of Paul's letters, but when he comes to the Galatian church, Paul specifically addresses what it means for the power of the Spirit to be in Christians and their community, developing their hearts of faith in Christlikeness. New Testament scholar Bonnie Thurston notes that in this section of Galatians 5, "Paul employs a rhetorical device, a 'teaching tool' if you will, which he probably learned from Stoic philosophers, the vice and virtue list."[140] What Thurston is saying is that in Galatians 5:16–26, Paul is using a known philosophical device of comparing between vices and virtues. This section of scripture begins in verses 13–15, where Paul calls on the church to live according to love rather than the flesh, even though they are free to live however they choose. In verses 16–18, Paul shows that the flesh and the Spirit are in conflict with each other. Then, in verses 19–21, Paul explores the

---

140. Thurston, *Fruit of the Spirit*, 4.

vice list—sexual immorality, impurity and debauchery, idolatry and witchcraft, hatred, discord, jealousy, fits of rage, selfish ambition, dissensions, factions and envy, drunkenness, and orgies. This list, while detailed, should be understood broadly, including any activities that have any connection to those that Paul has listed. The end of this chapter, (Gal 5:26—"Let us not become conceited, provoking and envying each other") could be included in this vice list as well. Paul concludes, "I warn you, as I did before, that those who live like this will not inherit the kingdom of God" (Gal 5:21b) After this, Paul enters the virtue list, what is traditionally referred to as the Fruit of the Spirit. This list includes love, joy, peace, patience, kindness, goodness, faithfulness, gentleness, and self-control (Gal 5:22–23). Paul says this is because Christians have crucified the flesh and live by the Spirit, then they will show the evidence of the Spirit in their lives through the fruit he lists.

Versus 22–23, have received many different interpretations since the time of Paul. The interpretations of the Fruit of the Spirit cover a wide swath of teachings and traditions, but a few stand out. There are those who view the Fruit of the Spirit as gifts of the Holy Spirit, given to Christians for the purpose of spiritual maturity.[141] There are others who see the Fruit of the Spirit as virtues that are to be cultivated and worked on, and can be of particular use for things like leadership, discipleship, or mission.[142] And there are still others who see the Fruit of the Spirit as proof of redemption.[143] While all of these provide valuable perspective of the Fruit of the Spirit, there is a better interpretation which influences the Christian community as well as the individual.

Newbigin's discussions of Galatians 5 connect the new life of the Spirit with the visible evidence of the Fruit of the Spirit. "This new life of the Spirit in us is that which brings forth all manner of good fruit (Galatians 5:22–23) and the tree is known by its fruit (Matthew 7:16–20)."[144] Here, Newbigin is specifically talking about the individual Christian, living in the Spirit as evidenced by the Fruit of the Spirit in their lives—this points to the Christian being firmly planted in the tree that bears good fruit from Matthew 7. But Newbigin also provided a full study of Galatians during his time as Bishop of Madras. In *Set Free to Be a Servant*, Newbigin summarizes the epistle by saying, "The heart of the matter is this: the Cross of Jesus. That is the only thing that can provide us with our unshakable standing ground."[145] With this in mind, Newbigin talks about the role of the Fruit of the Spirit in this letter. He begins by showing that

---

141. Thurston, *Fruit of the Spirit*, 2–4; Wright, *Cultivating the Fruit of the Spirit*, 13–22.
142. Smith, *Inside Job*, 57–68.
143. Sanderson, *Fruit of the Spirit*, 14; Kenneson, *Life on the Vine*, 10.
144. Newbigin, *Household of God*, 90–91.
145. Newbigin, *Set Free to Be a Servant*, 71.

humans are free now to surrender to the Holy Spirit, but when they surrender their hearts to the Holy Spirit they will come into conflict between their old flesh and their new heart.[146] "But when he is describing the work off [sic] the Spirit he makes it clear that the essential work is this: to reproduce the life of Jesus in the life of men. Where we see this happening, we know that the Spirit is at work."[147] The Fruit of the Spirit is the evidence of the Spirit's work in the life of the Christian to craft them into Christlikeness. The Spirit is exercising an active presence in the life of the believer. The markers of this work are part of what binds us together with other Christians. "We are marked with the Cross in baptism in token of the fact that we have given up the other road absolutely, and are now committed to walk the way of the Cross together with all our fellow-believers."[148] The mark of the Cross binds Christians together, and its presence is made known through the evidence of the Holy Spirit working to form them in Christlikeness.

While Newbigin would agree with Arnold Prater that the Fruit of the Spirit is evidence of the presence of the Holy Spirit in the life of the Christian,[149] he argues that the Fruit of the Spirit is more than just evidence. Newbigin points to the Holy Spirit actively developing the traits within individual Christians that are seen outwardly as the Fruit of the Spirit. In this activity of the Spirit, the Fruit of the Spirit becomes both the nature of the Christian and the evidence that the Holy Spirit resides within them creating this nature. It is an active presence. It is this active presence that enables new ways of relating to each other, in love, which A. Sue Russell builds upon to share a vision of living anti-structurally within the structure of society.[150] Likewise, the Spirit is working in the local congregation to form them, corporately, in Christlikeness.

Newbigin's Characteristics as Congregational Fruit of the Spirit

Newbigin's characteristics of the congregation as hermeneutic of the gospel point to the evidence of the Spirit's work, they are congregational fruit of the Spirit. While there is not a direct one-for-one correlation between Paul's Fruit of the Spirit and Newbigin's community characteristics, following his line of thinking that the Holy Spirit is actively producing the nature of the Fruit and the evidence of the Spirit's work is seen by the Fruit in someone's life, then I

---

146. Newbigin, *Set Free to Be a Servant*, 64–66.
147. Newbigin, *Set Free to Be a Servant*, 66.
148. Newbigin, *Set Free to Be a Servant*, 67.
149. Prater, *Presence*, 140–47.
150. Russell, "Mimesis, Alterity, and Liminality," 14 (unpublished manuscript used with permission from the author).

am arguing that Newbigin's characteristics of the congregation as hermeneutic can be seen as congregational fruit of the Spirit. This comes about through the active presence of the Holy Spirit in the local congregation, constituting and growing them in the missionary nature of the church. This nature has the characteristics, Newbigin states, of praise, truth, neighborliness, exercising the royal priesthood of every believer, mutual responsibility, and hope. The evidence of the Holy Spirit actively developing these in the local congregation is to see these characteristics lived out by the congregation. These characteristics are not traits or activities that the congregation can develop, but rather they are expressions of the active presence of the Holy Spirit within the community, much like the Fruit of the Spirit serves as evidence of the active presence of the Holy Spirit in the lives of individual believers. Following Paul as a model for reviewing Newbigin's characteristics of the congregation as hermeneutic of the gospel, there are two key portions of it that are necessary to unpack in order to view his characteristic list as congregational fruit of the Spirit.

The first portion of the congregation as hermeneutic of the gospel, which needs further unpacking in the model of Paul's Fruit of the Spirit is the issue of the acts of the flesh (Gal 5:19–21). While Paul provides an extensive list of actions (from which subsequent readers can assume any activity that connects to this list is an act of the flesh as well), Newbigin notes, "The Spirit does not immediately obliterate all the old appetites and ambitions."[151] This leads to the struggle of the flesh and the Spirit which Christians continually battle throughout their lives. The closest comparison in Newbigin to the acts of the flesh from Gal. 5 would be his admonition to avoid neglecting either God or the world.

> A Christian congregation is defined by this twofold relationship: it is God's embassy in a specific place. Either of these vital relationships may be neglected. The congregation may be so identified with the place that it ceases to be the vehicle of God's judgment and mercy for the place and becomes simply the focus of the self-image of the people of that place. Or it may be so concerned about the relation of its members to God that it turns its back on the neighborhood and is perceived as irrelevant to its concerns.... The local congregation is the place where the proper relation is most easily and naturally kept.[152]

Being God's embassy for a specific place means that the local congregation must be the place that stays in proper relation to both God and the world.

---

151. Newbigin, *Set Free to Be a Servant*, 65.
152. Newbigin, *Gospel in a Pluralist Society*, 229.

Constituted by the Holy Spirit

Newbigin's reaction to Paul's acts of the flesh is simply to say, "There is a kind of life which you know very well, from your own experiences and from the world around you (verses 19–21). There is no need to talk much about this. All that is necessary is to say that this sort of life is simply excluded from God's kingdom."[153]

But what gets more attention in Newbigin is the second portion, the characteristics that can be associated with the Fruit of the Spirit. Each of the characteristics of the congregation as hermeneutic of the gospel builds upon the active presence and leading of the Holy Spirit because they are the evidence of the Spirit being present and active within the congregation. But they also testify to the congregation's corporate discipleship to the Spirit. As Paul says, the congregations which are identified by these characteristics have, "crucified the flesh with is passions and desires" (Gal 5:24), and they now "live by the Spirit" and must "keep in step with the Spirit" (Gal 5:25). These characteristics—praise, truth, neighborliness, royal priesthood, mutual responsibility, and hope—are identifying markers, both for the congregation and for the community they inhabit, that the Spirit is present and active, the kingdom of God is near, and that the gospel is credible as public truth.

Newbigin begins each characteristic by stating that the congregation that is the hermeneutic of the gospel will be a community either of, which, or that. These three terms point to the development of these characteristics within the congregation, but it is a development that is dependent upon the active work of the Holy Spirit within the congregation. It is this active presence of the Spirit, shaping the congregations in their intended missionary nature as modeled by Christ, which then produces the outward evidences (or fruit) of these characteristics being witnessed both by the congregation and by the surrounding community. Based on Newbigin's view (seen above) of the Fruit of the Spirit in Gal 5 as the Holy Spirit's active presence in Christians to create in them the nature of Christ which is then evidenced as the Fruit, these characteristics Newbigin uses within the congregation as hermeneutic concept can be seen as the same active presence leading to evidence of the Holy Spirit within congregations. There are glimpses of this which can be seen within the characteristics themselves.

In be a community of praise, which is "perhaps its most distinctive character,"[154] the congregation is visibly aligning itself with God. "Praise is an activity which is almost totally absent from 'modern' society."[155] Thus, to give reverence and thanksgiving to God is an act of the Spirit to change the 'modern'

---

153. Newbigin, *Set Free to Be a Servant*, 65.
154. Newbigin, *Gospel in a Pluralist Society*, 227.
155. Newbigin, *Gospel in a Pluralist Society*, 227.

heart of the congregation away from suspicion and towards adoration. Being a community of truth changes the plausibility structure of the congregation, an activity that can only be completed by the Holy Spirit in the revelation of both scripture and relationship (with individuals and the congregation). Being a community that focuses on the neighborhood requires maintaining the delicate balance of proper relation between God and the world, which can only happen in the power of the Holy Spirit keeping the congregation in that balance. Being the community of the royal priesthood is a calling to guide Christians in their dual role of representing God (to the world) and the world (to God). This too is only accomplished with the power, presence, and active leading of the Holy Spirit. Being a community of mutual responsibility is a calling God places on the Body of Christ to care for one another, which is only achievable through the power and leading of the Holy Spirit to be faithful and responsible toward one another.[156] And being a community of hope is to live the hope of the gospel in society, a hope that is only found in the presence of the Holy Spirit.

These characteristics describe who the congregation is, not what they do. And who the congregation is comes directly out of their establishing and sustaining relationship with the Holy Spirit. These characteristics are direct evidence of the credibility of the gospel in society because they point to the active presence of the Holy Spirit within the Christian community, and that community's indwelling belief and living out of the gospel. Ultimately, these characteristics are following the model of Paul, while also embracing the teaching of Jesus—from the heart comes either good or evil (Matt 15:16–20; Luke 6:44–46). Thus, Newbigin's concern in these characteristics is with the heart of the congregation, a heart that he sees as being derived dually from the gospel and the active presence of the Holy Spirit; and, Newbigin sees these characteristics as being expressed in different ways.

> I am, of course, not denying the importance of the many activities by which we seek to challenge public life with the gospel—evangelistic campaigns, distribution of Bibles and Christian literature, conferences, and even books such as this one. But I am saying that these are all secondary, and that they have power to accomplish their purpose only as they are rooted in and lead back to a believing community.[157]

Thus, it is not the activity (in this case of witness) that matters for Newbigin, it is the heart of the community which does these activities that matters. That

---

156. Newbigin, *Gospel in a Pluralist Society*, 231.
157. Newbigin, *Word in Season*, 67.

heart is one of knowing, believing, and living the gospel by the Christian community. This heart is evident through the characteristics Newbigin lists. These characteristics are the fruit of the active presence of the Holy Spirit in that community, establishing and leading their belief in and living by the gospel in the world.

Any deficiency in the congregational fruit of the Spirit points to a deficiency in the relationship of the congregation with the Holy Spirit. Conversely, any overdevelopment of a characteristic also points to a deficiency in the congregational relationship with the Holy Spirit. Discovering this deficiency requires deep investigation with the Spirit to diagnose the root cause and work on resolving that cause for the discipleship of the whole congregation. This means that the congregation must focus on listening to and discerning the voice of the Holy Spirit, seeking guidance to uncover why one of these characteristics is lacking or overdeveloped, and then embarking on a path to remedying this deficiency, under the guidance of the Spirit. There is no set program or guidelines for this process, except that it will always start with scripture and prayer, and may also involve other spiritual disciplines as well. This is a process that requires commitment and faith by the congregation, leaning on the Holy Spirit to lead them.

SUMMARY

The congregation as hermeneutic of the gospel builds upon the constituting and active presence of the Holy Spirit within the local congregation. It speaks to the relationship between God and the church, which is foundational for all the other elements of Newbigin's missionary ecclesiology. The active presence of the Spirit first establishes the congregation, then it builds it up to be God's embassy for a specific place (and time), then it leads it through that place (and time) for the glory of God. Thus, the active presence of the Holy Spirit is the starting ground for understanding Newbigin's missionary ecclesiology, and in particular the congregation as hermeneutic of the gospel concept. Within this concept, Newbigin's characteristics provide a kind of congregational fruit of the Spirit, in the mode of Paul's Fruit of the Spirit in Gal 5. Looking at the characteristics and the congregation as hermeneutic concept in this way very clearly shows the importance of the constituting active presence of the Holy Spirit for the local congregation. In understanding the congregation as hermeneutic of the gospel concept, being constituted by the Holy Spirit focuses on the God relationship of the church—keeping its eye focused on God.

4

Representing the Kingdom of God

INTRODUCTION

THE NEXT ELEMENT OF Newbigin's missionary ecclesiology is representing the kingdom of God. This element focuses on the relationship between the church and the world, which comes directly out of the active presence of the Holy Spirit leading the church into the world in fulfilling God's mission on earth. Newbigin's most common imagery for discussing this element is the church as the sign, instrument, and foretaste of the kingdom of God. Understanding Newbigin's imagery of the church as the sign, instrument, and foretaste of the kingdom of God is essential for fully understanding his vision of the congregation as the hermeneutic of the gospel. In being the sign, instrument, and foretaste of the kingdom, the local congregation attests to the credibility of Jesus Christ as the last word in human affairs. When talking about the kingdom in connection to the life and mission of the church, Newbigin highlights God's calling on the church to represent the kingdom (or reign or kingship)[1] of God both as a present and a future reality for all of humanity. The reign of God serves as the foundation for Newbigin's understanding of the missionary nature of the church and thus understanding it is essential for understanding the congregation as hermeneutic of the gospel. And Newbigin's most vibrant imagery of the relationship between the local congregation and the kingdom of God is the church as the sign, instrument, and foretaste[2] of the kingdom.

---

1. Throughout his life, Newbigin used these terms interchangeably, though Kingdom and reign became more common than kingship later in his writings.

2. In some earlier works, Newbigin also used the term first fruits along with foretaste, but as he utilizes this imagery in his retirement years, foretaste became the more common expression.

Representing the Kingdom of God

In this chapter, I will unpack Newbigin's imagery of the church as the sign, instrument, and foretaste of the kingdom, investigate what it means for the local congregation to represent the kingdom of God, and address the role of the local congregation in representing the kingdom of God.

SIGN, INSTRUMENT, AND FORETASTE

Newbigin's most poignant description of the connection between the kingdom and the church is his phrase the sign, instrument, and foretaste of the kingdom of God. This phrase is used multiple times throughout Newbigin's writings, in some combination of one, two, or all three of these images. Moreover, he connects it to his discussions of first fruits and the new reality, or the New Creation. Understanding Newbigin's imagery of the church as the sign, instrument, and foretaste of the kingdom of God is essential for fully understanding his vision of the local congregation as the hermeneutic of the gospel for their society. Ultimately, being the sign, instrument, and foretaste of the kingdom in the world is related to what makes the congregation as hermeneutic of the gospel the credible witness to the gospel's claim that Jesus Christ is the final word in human affairs. Specifically, Newbigin distinguishes the church as something unique because it is the sign, instrument, and foretaste of the kingdom of God on earth.

> What distinguishes the Church from other human corporations is that it is that body which has been sent into the world by God for the specific purpose of being the sign, instrument and foretaste of His kingdom. God's kingly rule is at work of course in all spheres of human life. His providence upholds all spheres of human life. His mercy surrounds all spheres of human life. The Church is not simply one of these spheres. It is the place, the only place, to exist solely for the purpose of bearing witness to the one who is the word made flesh.[3]

Newbigin makes a direct link between the church and the kingdom by showing that the church is the only place where the combination of sign, instrument, and foretaste of God's kingdom exists. And this exclusive position for the church requires witnessing to the gospel in the world, in all that the church is, does, and says. Being the sign, instrument, and foretaste is first about who the church is, and from that the church now acts as these things within society. But both being and acting as the sign, instrument, and foretaste is always in pointing back to the kingdom of God. Thus, Newbigin's imagery of sign, instrument, and foretaste speaks to the church representing the kingdom

3. Newbigin, "On the Gospel as Public Truth," 3.

in the world based out of the constituting of the Holy Spirit in the missionary nature of Christ's mission.

Hunsberger, in *Bearing the Witness of the Spirit*, takes up (in part) the issue of the local congregation as the sign, instrument, and foretaste of the kingdom of God within Newbigin. In this book, Hunsberger combines his doctoral research on Newbigin's doctrine of election with some of the theological discussions of the Gospel and Our Culture Network (GOCN) (specifically the developing missional theology discussion at that time) to look at Newbigin's theology of cultural plurality. Within this book, Hunsberger crafts a sense of "an implicit 'theology of cultural plurality,'" which "rests on the 'missionary character' of the biblical doctrine of election" within Newbigin.[4] Hunsberger goes on to show that Newbigin's doctrine of election is about being elected for witness.[5] In this discussion, Hunsberger notes the role of the congregation as hermeneutic of the gospel in understanding the witness of the church.[6] Hunsberger notes that it is

> the interpretive lens through which people will see and read what the gospel has to do with them and the world in which they live. It has the power to open up dynamic ways for churches to be living, speaking, acting signs of the reign of God ... to sustain the church as a community that gives living demonstration that God is known and God's purposes are achieved in the life, death, and resurrection of Jesus Christ, and that it is both thinkable and feasible to live as though that is true![7]

For Hunsberger, the congregation as hermeneutic is a vitally important component for understanding Newbigin's theology of cultural plurality, and specifically his affirmation of the local congregation to be the sign, instrument, and foretaste of the kingdom of God. To fully understand this phrase and its connection with the hermeneutic of the gospel, it is necessary to take a deeper look at Newbigin's most significant uses and explanations of it throughout his life. Within this section, I will take a deeper look at Newbigin's use of sign, instrument, and foretaste of the kingdom, connecting it back to how the local congregation represents the kingdom of God, and ultimately to the congregation as hermeneutic of the gospel concept.

---

4. Hunsberger, *Bearing the Witness of the Spirit*, 235.

5. See Hunsberger, *Bearing the Witness of the Spirit*, chap. 3.

6. The reference to *GPS*, 222–23, on 101, was added to the citation in his original 1987 dissertation when it was edited for this 1998 publication. George R. Hunsberger, personal conversation with author via Zoom, August 9, 2021.

7. Hunsberger, *Bearing the Witness of the Spirit*, 279. Acknowledged as an edition to this specific publication. George R. Hunsberger, personal conversation with author via Zoom, August 9, 2021.

Representing the Kingdom of God

Throughout Newbigin's life, the imagery of the church as the sign, instrument, and foretaste (or first fruit) of the kingdom is used often. He regularly used one, two, or all three of these words in various combinations to describe the relationship between the kingdom of God and the church. Beginning in the 1950s with *The Household of God*, Newbigin used this image of that relationship hundreds of times throughout his lifetime of writings. But in all of those uses, there is a commonality in his meaning of this image: (1) it is derived from the presence of the Holy Spirit in the church, as the original foretaste/first fruit of the kingdom; and (2) it describes how the church represents the kingdom of God in the world.

While not the first time that Newbigin used the terms, *Sign of the Kingdom* is the most significant usage of sign, instrument, and foretaste of the kingdom as it relates to the congregation as hermeneutic of the gospel concept. As shown earlier, this book addresses the renewal of the theme of kingdom-centric mission within the conversations of mission conferences that were presently underway at the time of its writing. Newbigin shows that this understanding of mission is derived directly from the ministry of Jesus, who claims the presence of God's kingdom within Himself.[8] While reviewing the Johannine literature, Newbigin specifically states that the Holy Spirit alone is the foretaste and first fruit of the kingdom of God presently on earth and that the church becomes the sign, instrument, and foretaste of the kingdom only by the presence of the Holy Spirit within it.[9] This ultimately leads to Newbigin's description of what the church, as sign, instrument, and foretaste of the kingdom, will be.[10] Within this book, Newbigin states that he sees the church as the sign, instrument, and foretaste of the kingdom because of the active presence of the Holy Spirit within it.[11] This is Newbigin's definition of the relationship between the church and the kingdom.

In *The Open Secret*, Newbigin frequently references the church as the sign, instrument, and foretaste of God's reign on earth. Deriving from the trinitarian foundations of missions that Newbigin builds in this book, he points to the church as the sign, instrument, and foretaste of the present and future reign of God through actively engaging the issues and problems of their society, representing the gospel in deeds and words.[12] In *Foolishness to the Greeks*, Newbigin shows that the church, as the sign, instrument, and foretaste of the kingdom, is to be an active participant in all areas of society, witnessing

---

8. Newbigin, *Sign of the Kingdom*, 29–31.
9. Newbigin, *Sign of the Kingdom*, 40–43.
10. Newbigin, *Sign of the Kingdom*, chap. 3, "Ecclesial Characteristics."
11. Newbigin, *Sign of the Kingdom*, 40.
12. Newbigin, *Open Secret*, 54.

to and being the evidence of God's kingdom within every area of society.[13] Within *The Gospel in a Pluralist Society* (*GPS*), Newbigin uses the sign, instrument, and foretaste imagery in arguing for the necessity of mission and the place the church has within global mission—a place which is always pointing back to the kingdom of God.[14] In *A Word in Season*, Newbigin argues that because the church is the foretaste (due to it having the foretaste) it can then be an instrument of God's justice, peace, and freedom, and be a visible sign pointing people to the reality of the kingdom.[15] And while all of these uses show Newbigin's firm understanding of the church being the sign, instrument, and foretaste of the kingdom of God, it is also helpful to look at how Newbigin discusses each of these images separately.

Having discussed either in part or in total, the imagery of the church as sign, instrument, and foretaste of the kingdom of God throughout his life, Newbigin explained specifically what he means with each of these images in "On Being the Church for the World." Newbigin begins his description in reverse order from how he normally uses the combined, three-word phrase, first addressing *foretaste*. Newbigin begins with foretaste because he sees it as the starting point for understanding the rest of this imagery of the church-kingdom relationship.

> I was once making an elaborate explanation of this word *arrabōn* in a class in the Selly Oak colleges and explaining how scholars used to be puzzled by it because it is not a classical Greek word. And then they dug up a lot of parchments in the sands of Egypt and found that they were shopkeepers' accounts and that *arrabōn* was just the word that the shopkeepers all used for cash on deposit, a pledge for a bill that you would pay at the end. . . . And that's the word that St Paul uses over and over again for the Holy Spirit. . . . Now, the Holy Spirit is the *aperitif* for the messianic banquet. It is something which you enjoy now and that is the great thing in the charismatic moment. You enjoy it. There is something really to enjoy and celebrate now. It is not just an IOU, a promissory note. But the whole point of it is that it is a foretaste, that it assures you of a greater reality still to come. And in that sense the Church is a foretaste of the Kingdom.[16]

---

13. Newbigin, *Foolishness to the Greeks*, 124–25.
14. Newbigin, *Gospel in a Pluralist Society*, 118–19, 128–29, 136–37.
15. Newbigin, *Word in Season*, 60–63.
16. Newbigin, "On Being the Church for the World," 37–38. A similar, though not identical, version of this chapter was published as "Does Society Still Need a Parish Church?" in *A Word in Season*, referenced in n15 above.

Newbigin has laid out here his basic understanding of foretaste. He is saying that Paul uses the term *arrabōn* to describe the Holy Spirit, meaning the Holy Spirit is a deposit of the kingdom to come. But Newbigin furthers this idea, saying that the Holy Spirit is more than a deposit, but a first taste of the coming kingdom meant to be enjoyed and shared. He then makes note that the church, established and inhabited by the Holy Spirit, becomes the foretaste of the kingdom in the World. Newbigin goes on to say,

> The Orthodox have always stressed the point that the Church is first of all a communion in the Holy Spirit in the life of the triune God, so that you must define the Church in ontological terms and not just in functional terms. The Church is defined by what it is. It is already a sharing in the life of God. . . . The first thing therefore, is that the Church is a foretaste, and that means it will be different from the world. If it isn't, it's no good.[17]

Here, Newbigin shows that Christians everywhere can learn from the Orthodox tradition the understanding of the church as a participation in the Trinity, and therefore a different community from the world. He even goes so far as to say that a congregation that is not different from the world is no good. And while this understanding of foretaste is outlined in 1988, it is implicit in Newbigin's uses of the term throughout his life, most notably in the texts already mentioned, as well as *The Household of God* and *One Body, One Gospel, One World*. In *The Household of God*, Newbigin uses foretaste as his primary way of describing the connection between the church and the kingdom of God. Newbigin particularly uses foretaste in describing the church receiving the gift of the Holy Spirit, and from that gift engaging the world in missions.[18] In this discussion, Newbigin concludes that the church, as the community witnessing to the gospel, lives out the foretaste of the kingdom of God for all the nations to experience.[19] Later, in *One Body, One Gospel, One World*, Newbigin uses foretaste to describe the church as it relates to Christ's mission in the world, noting that it is the foretaste of forgiveness, peace, and eternal life that is to come in the fulfillment of God's kingdom.[20] "The characteristic fruit of the Holy Spirit is always a foretaste, something that points beyond itself to the fullness of redemption in Christ."[21] Newbigin is using foretaste here to describe the church that is constituted by the Holy Spirit, pointing beyond itself

---

17. Newbigin, "On Being the Church for the World," 38–39.
18. Newbigin, *Household of God*, 138.
19. Newbigin, *Household of God*, 138.
20. Newbigin, *One Body, One Gospel, One World*, 19–21.
21. Newbigin, *One Body, One Gospel, One World*, 20.

in the present world to the fulfillment of Christ's redemption in the kingdom, both now and in the future.

Newbigin expressed his understanding of *instrument* in many different ways throughout his life. In particular, Newbigin discusses instrument in a variety of ways throughout *The Household of God*. He ultimately concludes, "Precisely because the Church is here and now a real foretaste of heaven, she can be the witness and instrument of the kingdom of heaven."[22] Thus, Newbigin sees one of the ways the church represents the kingdom of God is by being its instrument on the earth. Returning to his more detailed description in "On Being the Church for the World," Newbigin says that the church "in so far as it is a foretaste, it can also be an instrument."[23] Thus, being the foretaste of the kingdom also means the church is the instrument of God in the world. "It can be an instrument through which God's will for justice and peace and freedom is done in the world. That takes the church out into the secular world with whatever is relevant to the real needs of that secular world. If that is not happening, how is the world going to know that the reality we talk about is true?"[24] Here, Newbigin is explicitly challenging the church to enter the world and to be an instrument of God's peace, justice, and freedom throughout the world. If the church fails to do this, then if fails to faithfully represent the kingdom of God. Newbigin then ventures into a discussion of Matthew 10, showing that Jesus gave his followers authority to go cast out evil spirits and heal, and only after they have done these deeds are they to preach the message of the kingdom of God at hand.[25] "The preaching explains the happenings. . . . In other words, that the words without the deeds lack authority! The deeds without the words are dumb, they lack meaning. The two go together."[26] Newbigin is claiming that there is a necessary link between deeds and words in representing the reign of God in the world. This is similar to the way Newbigin uses instrument in other writings.

In *The Relevance of Trinitarian Doctrine for Today's Mission*, Newbigin notes the role of the evangelist as an instrument in the Holy Spirit's work of conversion.[27] Newbigin points out that the Holy Spirit is always at work in society, and that the evangelist has a role to play; their words are instruments of the Holy Spirit to bring about the explanation of the Holy Spirit's work in that society. As well, in *A Word in Season*, Newbigin makes a similar

---

22. Newbigin, *Household of God*, 147–48.
23. Newbigin, "On Being the Church in the World," 39.
24. Newbigin, "On Being the Church in the World," 39.
25. Newbigin, "On Being the Church in the World," 39.
26. Newbigin, "On Being the Church in the World," 39–40.
27. Newbigin, *Relevance of Trinitarian Doctrine for Today's Mission*, 31–34.

connection, noting that the personal witness of Christians is one of the instruments the Holy Spirit uses to reach out to the world.[28] Newbigin also mentions in *A Word in Season* the role of the church as an instrument of the Holy Spirit within a city. He notes that the church should be "an *instrument* (not the only one) that God can use for his work of healing, liberating, and blessing."[29] Thus, the church must show that it cares for the city before it can preach to the city.[30] Here, Newbigin notes that the church can be the instrument of God's kingdom by being engaged with the world, but he also notes that it is not the only instrument. "And the Church, in so far as it is a foretaste of the reign of God, can also be an instrument of the reign of God.... Not the only instrument of course.... I think we have too much neglected this, that God has other instruments for the doing of His will in the world. But it is only the Church which can be the foretaste, the *arrabon* of the Kingdom."[31] Newbigin is careful to warn the church that it is not the only instrument of God, but it is the only instrument that is also the foretaste of the kingdom.

"The point of a sign is that it points to something that is not yet visible.... The point of a sign is that it points to something which is real but not yet visible—which is not visible, not because it does not exist, but because it is over the horizon."[32] This is Newbigin's most basic understanding of what it means for the church to be a *sign* of the kingdom—pointing to a reality that is not quite visible (or not yet fully visible). And like being an instrument, Newbigin links being a sign back to being the foretaste of the kingdom.

> Now, the Church is a sign of the Kingdom, in so far as it is a foretaste. The Church is a sign of the Kingdom, pointing people to a reality which is beyond what we can see. And the necessary "other-worldliness" of the Church seems to me to be something that has to be absolutely held on to. We do not compete with all the other agencies in the world that are offering solutions to human problems here and now. We are not offering utopian illusions. We are pointing people to a reality which lies beyond history, beyond death. But we are erecting in this world, here and now, signs—credible signs—that make it possible for people to believe that that is the great reality and, therefore, to join us in going that way.[33]

---

28. Newbigin, *Word in Season*, 21–32.
29. Newbigin, *Word in Season*, 33.
30. Newbigin, *Word in Season*, 33–39.
31. Newbigin, "On Being the Church for the World," 40.
32. Newbigin, "On Being the Church for the World," 40.
33. Newbigin, "On Being the Church for the World," 40.

Newbigin's view of the church as the sign of the kingdom is that it points to the reality of the kingdom to come, which marks it as different from the rest of the world and all the other instruments God is using to bring about His will in the world. It is thus that, by being a foretaste and an instrument of God's kingdom in the world, the church is a sign of the future reality of the kingdom, coming to its fulfillment in New Creation. Newbigin is careful to make sure that this connection to the church as the sign of the kingdom is firmly grounded in the presence of the Holy Spirit in the church in his book *A Faith for This One World?* Here, Newbigin points to the Holy Spirit being the foretaste of the kingdom in the church, and from that the church is the sign and foretaste of the kingdom in the world.[34] Thus, being a sign of the kingdom is a result of being the foretaste of the kingdom through the presence of the foretaste, the Holy Spirit. One of the elements of being the sign of the kingdom that Newbigin envisions is dialogical evangelism through the laity. The church, being the sign of the kingdom, is the place of training, sending, and supporting of its members for gospel witness in the world, which Newbigin believes includes dialogical presentations of the gospel story.[35] Thus, the church as the place where the Holy Spirit dwells as the first fruit and foretaste of the kingdom of God, is also the place through which signs of God's reign are made throughout the world.

Newbigin's usage of the imagery of sign, instrument, and foretaste of the kingdom is a description of his understanding of the relationship between the church and the kingdom of God.

> The Church does not exist for the sake of its members; it exists to continue the mission of Jesus. But this does not make the Church a mere programme agency. The Church continues the mission of Jesus first by being itself a foretaste of the kingdom, a community in which the freedom and joy of the kingdom are already tasted and celebrated in praising and adoring God. It can thus also be a sign of the kingdom, pointing beyond itself to God's love and holiness. And it may also be an instrument which God can use (among other instruments) for doing his will in the world. So the Church is neither to be identified with the kingdom nor separated from it. Jesus did not manifest the kingly rule of God by taking over the government of the world. That remains in the Father's hand. Jesus manifested it by his perfect obedience of the Father's will. The Church is called to do the same. But the kingdom is not to be set against the Church, as though we could seek the kingdom of God by looking elsewhere than to Jesus. The Church, in the

---

34. Newbigin, *Faith for This One World?*, 92–94.
35. Newbigin, *Word in Season*, 155–57.

power of the Spirit, is called to be sign, foretaste and instrument of the kingdom.[36]

Newbigin shows the deep connection between his imagery of the sign, instrument, and foretaste of the kingdom, and the church. Thus, understanding Newbigin's use of sign, instrument, and foretaste provides the necessary context for understanding the congregation as hermeneutic of the gospel. Within this investigation of Newbigin's imagery, foretaste provides the starting ground for the other two images. It should be noted that Newbigin also used the term first fruits in connection to foretaste in his earlier writings. And at times he changes the order of sign, instrument, and foretaste, or he discusses one or two of them without the other. Yet, the foretaste is the Holy Spirit, and because the church is constituted by the Holy Spirit, it becomes the foretaste, and from having and being the foretaste, it is also the sign and the instrument of the kingdom. This is because Newbigin saw the Holy Spirit as the foretaste of the kingdom, and the church, being constituted by the Holy Spirit, becomes the foretaste of the kingdom in the world. To differentiate, it may be helpful to envision the Holy Spirit as the invisible foretaste[37] and the church as the visible foretaste, noting that the church can only be the visible foretaste of the kingdom by the presence of the invisible foretaste of the Holy Spirit. In being the visible foretaste, the church will also be an instrument of God's activity in the world, and the sign of the present and future kingdom. Being an instrument of God's activity in the world is the present focus of being the visible foretaste of the kingdom, participating in the world to seek God's justice, peace, freedom, liberation, and mercy. While being the sign of God's reign is the future focus of the visible foretaste of the kingdom, the church points to the fulfillment of the reality of God's kingdom, both now and in the future. The church is all these things simultaneously, following the lead of the Holy Spirit in being the foretaste, instrument, and sign of God's kingdom. Yet, Newbigin notes that the Holy Spirit also has other instruments, and I would argue erects signs of the kingdom outside of the church. But it is only the church that is also the foretaste of the kingdom because it is established and sustained by the invisible foretaste of the kingdom—the Holy Spirit. Thus, to represent the reign of God, Newbigin believes that the church must be the sign, instrument, and foretaste of the kingdom in the world, both for now and for the future. So, being the sign, instrument, and foretaste of the kingdom is the beginning of representing God's reign in society, giving credible witness to Jesus Christ as the final word in all human affairs.

36. Newbigin, "Church," 6.

37. This idea aligns with Flett's Barthian argument of the visible and invisible in connection with the congregation as hermeneutic of the gospel. See chapter 1.

The Congregation as Hermeneutic of the Gospel

Newbigin, in explaining his views of representing the reign of God explicitly addresses the important role of the local congregation, provides a foundation for understanding the authority of the church to preach the gospel, and finally provides an image of the church-kingdom relationship. And Newbigin makes sure to associate all of this with individual congregations in a specific place and time. "The Church is sign, instrument and foretaste of God's reign for that 'place', that segment of the total fabric of humanity, for which it is responsible—a sign, instrument and foretaste for *that* place with its particular character."[38] Here, Newbigin is calling on each congregation to be the sign, instrument, and foretaste for the specific place God has sent it to in the world (both geographically and historically). Newbigin also envisions the proclamation of the kingdom as an intimate engagement with the world for a church that bears the presence of the Holy Spirit in its very being.

> Concretely I think this means that the congregation must be so deeply and intimately involved in the secular concerns of the neighbourhood that it becomes clear to everyone that no one and nothing is outside the range of God's love in Jesus. Christ's message, the original gospel, was about the coming of the kingdom of God, that is to say God's kingly rule over the whole of his creation and the whole of human kind. That is the only authentic gospel. And that means that every part of human life is within the range of the gospel message; in respect of everything the gospel brings the necessity for choice between the rule of God and the negation of his rule. If the good news is to be authentically communicated, it must be clear that the church is concerned about the rule of God and not about itself. It must be clear, that is, that the local congregation cares for the well-being of the whole community and not just for itself.[39]

Here, Newbigin is sharing that the congregation which represents the reign of God must live and act in such a way that their care for the community above and beyond themselves is explicitly noticeable. This is the continuation of Jesus' mission of representing the kingdom come. This way of living speaks to the authority of Jesus Christ over all areas of life. Or, as Abraham Kuyper puts it, "There is not a square inch in the whole domain of our human existence over which Christ, who is Sovereign over *all*, does not cry, 'Mine!'"[40] This often-quoted statement from Kuyper agrees with Newbigin, that all aspects of human life are under the sovereignty of God. This is signified by the

---

38. Newbigin, "On Being the Church in the World," 37.
39. Newbigin, "Pastor's Opportunities," 357.
40. Kuyper, "Sphere Sovereignty," 26.

congregation living out their obedience and discipleship to the Holy Spirit in each context that the Spirit leads and directs them into. The expression of the church representing the reign of God will be different for each congregation, there is no universal model or method for it. This requires that each congregation live a contextualized life, as the hermeneutic of the gospel for a specific place and time.

While sign, instrument, and foretaste points back to the kingdom, within this imagery each point has a deep connection to what it means to represent the kingdom of God. For sign, the focus is upon pointing to the not-yet fully visible reality of the kingdom of God, both present and to come. Thus, the church is pointing back to the reality of the kingdom which is both present and to come fully at a later time. For instrument, the church is one of God's tool for bringing about justice, peace, and freedom in the world. As this tool, the church is grounded in the justice, peace, and freedom of God's kingdom and working to bring those about in the world. For foretaste, the link is back to the Holy Spirit. The Spirit is the foretaste of the kingdom, and since the Spirit is in the church, the church is the foretaste as well. Having the foretaste of the kingdom, the church can now become that foretaste in the world. In all three cases, the church is always connecting back to the kingdom of God, pointing to both its present and future reality for all of the world to see.

REPRESENTING THE KINGDOM OF GOD

Having seen Newbigin's usage and meaning of the imagery of the church as the sign, instrument, and foretaste of the kingdom, this now leads to the question, "What exactly does it mean to represent the kingdom of God?" For Newbigin, it means that all the church says, does, and is points back to the present and future reality of the kingdom, which enters the world with Jesus Christ. And while this should be the central message of the church, Newbigin notes the waxing and waning focus the kingdom has received in recent times.

> The Kingdom of God was the central theme of the preaching of Jesus as we find it in the New Testament.... And yet it cannot be said that it has been a central theme in the great classical traditions of Christendom.... The message of the Kingdom has often been seen as something wider, more inclusive, less sectarian than the message of salvation through Jesus Christ. The recent conference of the World Council of Churches in Australia, on the theme 'Your Kingdom Come', has brought the theme back again into the center of missionary thinking.[41]

---

41. Newbigin, *Sign of the Kingdom*, vii–viii.

The Congregation as Hermeneutic of the Gospel

Newbigin asserts that the kingdom of God is central to the message of Christ, but it has not been central to the church in modern history, even though recently it has re-emerged in missiological discussions. In this section, I will unpack what it means for the local congregation to represent the kingdom of God, and the relevance of this for the hermeneutic of the gospel concept.

While representing the kingdom is one of the elements of Newbigin's missionary ecclesiology and its expression as the congregation as hermeneutic of the gospel, there are only a few times where Newbigin explicitly states this. The most explicit place Newbigin makes this argument is in *The Open Secret*.

> The church represents the presence of the reign of God in the life of the world, not in the triumphalist sense (as the "successful" cause) and not in the moralistic sense (as the "righteous" cause), but in the sense that it is the place where the mystery of the kingdom present in the dying and rising of Jesus is made present here and now so that all people, righteous and unrighteous, are enabled to taste and share the love of God before whom all are unrighteous and all are accepted as righteous. It is the place where the glory of God ("glory as of an only son") actually abides among us so that the love of God is available to sin-burdened men and women (John 17:22–23). It is the place where the power of God is manifested in a community of sinners. It is the place where the promise of Jesus is fulfilled: "I, when I am lifted up from the earth, will draw all men to myself" (John 12:32). It is the place where the reign of God is present as love shared among the unloved.[42]

Newbigin is identifying the church as the place through which God's reign is present in the world; the place where the love of God and the glory of God shine into the brokenness of the world. Newbigin later says, "The Church exists for the world as Christ exists for the world, in judgement and in promise. It shares in the mission of Christ: 'as the Father sent me, so I send you.' . . . [T]he Church is to be seen, and will rightly be judged, as a foretaste and instrument of God's Kingdom, offering an experience of the life of the Kingdom, while pointing beyond itself to a consummation beyond history."[43] Here, Newbigin again affirms the place of the church in representing the kingdom of God to the world, in the same manner as Jesus Christ. In representing the presence of the reign of God, the church is to continually point back to Jesus Christ who initiated the presence of the kingdom in his life, ministry, death, and resurrection. Thus, the church represents the kingdom of God in the world.

---

42. Newbigin, *Open Secret*, 54.
43. Newbigin, "On Being the Church of the World," 25.

Newbigin also argues that the only way the church can represent the kingdom is in the same manner as Jesus Christ. "The church can only represent the righteousness of God in history in the way that Jesus did."[44] Here Newbigin establishes that representing the kingdom of God is based upon Jesus Christ and how he represented the kingdom in the world. Later, he would say, "The Church is not authorized to represent the reign of God, his justice and his peace, in any other way than that in which Jesus represented it, namely by being partners with him in challenging the powers of evil and bearing in its own life the cost of the challenge."[45] Newbigin is arguing that the church must follow Christ in representing the kingdom by challenging the powers and principalities that attempt to supplant God as the center of creation. Thus, seeking God's justice and peace in the world does not take the form of political power or legal might, but that of a servant, like Jesus Christ, the Lamb of God. This leads Newbigin to later ask the question, "What does this say about the way in which the Church is authorized to represent the kingdom of God in the life of society?"[46] This is the beginning of Newbigin's questions about holding in balance the two key relationships of the church, with God and the world. Newbigin goes on to say that representing the kingdom excludes the use of power which is seen in the world, or that the church simply "responds to the aspirations of the people," or uses modern techniques only to attract members.[47] Newbigin's fundamental question here, "How can the Church be fully open to the needs of the world and yet have its eyes fixed always on God?," is also behind the question of the credibility of the gospel in society.[48] And his answer is, "a congregation of men and women who believe it and live by it."[49] Thus, representing the kingdom is at the heart of Newbigin's expressing the missionary nature of the church in the congregation as hermeneutic of the gospel concept. And this representing begins with Jesus Christ.

Jesus began his earthly ministry by saying "Repent, for the kingdom of heaven is at hand" (Matt 4:17), making this statement in full knowledge and meaning of the Hebraic understanding of kingship.[50] In this statement, Jesus is announcing a new event in history, which is public news of God's sovereignty as the present reality for creation, thus all are called to repent and turn towards the King, which is a response of faith, and is both an immediate event and a

---

44. Newbigin, *Open Secret*, 111.
45. Newbigin, *Gospel in a Pluralist Society*, 134.
46. Newbigin, *Gospel in a Pluralist Society*, 226.
47. Newbigin, *Gospel in a Pluralist Society*, 226.
48. Newbigin, *Gospel in a Pluralist Society*, 226.
49. Newbigin, *Gospel in a Pluralist Society*, 227.
50. Newbigin, *Sign of the Kingdom*, 21–24.

The Congregation as Hermeneutic of the Gospel

calling on all of humanity.[51] Both the present and the future reality of God's reign are part of the kingdom message which Jesus lived and preached. During the time between Christ's resurrection and ascension, He commissions His followers to continue preaching this message in deeds and words, continuing God's mission on earth by making the present kingdom reality known.[52] But, "Faithfulness to the mission and message of Jesus absolutely required that the early Church should have Jesus as the centre of their gospel."[53] What Newbigin is saying is that though the mission is about representing the kingdom of God in deeds and words, the central component of that message is Jesus Christ. Emulating His way of living and His preaching of the kingdom is how congregations continue His mission. And Jesus, after His ascension, fulfills His promise to send a helper for the church to be able to do this (Acts 2). The Holy Spirit, as the foretaste of the kingdom, dwells within the church and turns the church into the foretaste of the kingdom for the world. "Positively, the only hermeneutic of the message of the Kingdom is the presence of a community in which the foretaste of the kingdom, the Spirit, is already present.... The *hermeneutic* can only be the living reality of a community in which the first fruits of the Kingdom are already being enjoyed and shared."[54] Newbigin is saying that the congregation is the hermeneutic of the gospel through the presence of the Holy Spirit making it the hermeneutic. This presence is expressed through the local congregation enjoying and sharing it both within the congregation and with the society in which the congregation dwells. Newbigin presents all of this within a framework of the triangular relationship between church, gospel, and culture. "Newbigin's model helps us become more discriminating in our concern to avoid both syncretism and irrelevance, more focused upon inhabiting the biblical vision as part of a multi-cultural Christian community, and more open to the ongoing dialogue with our own culture which is as much an inner dialogue as an outer one."[55] Hunsberger claims that Newbigin's triangulation provides help for avoiding syncretism and irrelevancy, while also opening the local congregation to more authentic and intimate dialogue with its culture.

Newbigin's understanding of the kingdom of God comes directly out of his reading of the New Testament, and specifically the life and ministry of Jesus.[56] Newbigin saw that the reality of the kingdom was entrusted to Je-

---

51. Newbigin, *Sign of the Kingdom*, 24–26.
52. Newbigin, *Sign of the Kingdom*, 33–34.
53. Newbigin, *Sign of the Kingdom*, 32.
54. Newbigin, *Sign of the Kingdom*, 42, 43.
55. Hunsberger, "Newbigin Gauntlet," 10.
56. See Newbigin, *Christ Our Eternal Contemporary*; Newbigin, *Holy Spirit and the Church*; Newbigin, "Holy Spirit."

Representing the Kingdom of God

sus' followers, which they accepted on faith, and were commissioned to bear witness to it throughout their lives. "It means that God does indeed reign, that his reign is the final reality, but that it is a reality known by faith and not by common sight."[57] Thus, Christians are to accept the reign of God on faith and to share that reign with the world as public fact which has been entrusted to them. This fact is then lived out in the actions of Christians in the world. "They are not the *means* by which God established His Kingdom. They are the witnesses to the present reality of His Kingdom."[58] Here, Newbigin is saying that Christians are the witness of the kingdom come. "The kingdom is the kingdom of God—God's active putting forth of his kingly power. So also, *ecclesia* is shorthand for *ecclesia tou Theou*, the assembly of God—God in action to draw all persons to himself in the crucified and risen Christ."[59] Here, Newbigin is clarifying the definition of the church as the gathered body of Christ, through which God draws people to follow Christ in the power of the Holy Spirit. "We are indeed stewards entrusted with the precious treasure of the secret of God's kingdom, and we have to be faithful stewards. But faithfulness does not consist simply in holding fast to the tradition we have received. It has been entrusted to us for a purpose, namely that it should be put into the commerce of the world so that it may grow."[60] Newbigin is calling on the church to actively witness to the kingdom in the world. This active witness is the central calling of the church.

When Newbigin calls on the church to represent the reign of God he beckons every congregation and every Christian to continue Christ's ministry, the mission of God on earth, making the present reality of the kingdom of God known and experienced throughout the world. "The gospel is news of a fact—the presence of the kingdom of God in Jesus. . . . The kingdom of God is, quite simply, God's reign; it is not our programme."[61] This very simple understanding of the gospel as the message of the presence of the kingdom (the reign of God) in Jesus Christ is the foundation for understanding Newbigin's view of the kingdom or reign of God. While this understanding may appear to be simple, there is a lot that must be unpacked to fully comprehend what Newbigin is saying about representing the kingdom of God. For instance, to represent the message that Jesus proclaimed, it is necessary to explain who Jesus is. Newbigin's explanation of Jesus is that, "He is the Son, sent by the Father and anointed by the Spirit to be the bearer of God's Kingdom to the

57. Newbigin, *Gospel and Culture*, 2.
58. Newbigin, "Mission of the Triune God," 18.
59. Newbigin, "Basis and the Forms of Unity," 7.
60. Newbigin, *Christian Witness in a Plural Society*, 24.
61. Newbigin, *Mission in Christ's Way*, 16.

nations."[62] Newbigin's explanation of Jesus points to Him as a member of the Trinity, who's life and ministry was about the message of God's kingdom. But Newbigin also highlights that Jesus explicitly claims the presence of the kingdom within himself.[63] Thus, the kingdom of God has come into the present reality. Newbigin also notes that the mission of the church, derived from and a continuation of Jesus' mission, is about pointing back to Jesus and His message. "The mission of the church is in fact the church's obedient participation in that action of the Spirit by which the confession of Jesus as Lord becomes the authentic confession of every new people, each in its own tongue."[64] Here, Newbigin makes a connection between the mission of the church to point back to Jesus and His message of the kingdom; the goal, following the Spirit's leading, is to make the confession Jesus is Lord authentic amongst all peoples and in every nation. This mission requires the life of the church to continually point to the message and person of Jesus Christ, and in this the kingdom is experienced in the presence of the Holy Spirit through each local congregation.

In its most basic form, Newbigin uses the term evangelism to mean communicating the good news of Jesus Christ.[65] But, giving a priority to the verbal form of this communication—as Newbigin sees often happening in Western Evangelicalism—is a misunderstanding of the term.[66] Instead, Newbigin focuses on the issue of witness as a broader understanding of the calling to proclaim the kingdom of God in the world,[67] which includes both deeds and words. "The authentic opportunity for evangelism is when the unbeliever asks the question because there is something about the Christian fellowship that prompts people to ask for the secret."[68] Newbigin believes, and he also argues from Acts,[69] that the church should live in such a way (modeling a new social order) that those outside of the church will ask questions; only then are words used to explain the actions of the church. So, it is in living the gospel that the church is invited to vocally communicate the gospel. Both, living the gospel and preaching the gospel, come together to form the local congregation in representing the kingdom of God in their society. And Newbigin also notes the necessity of the whole church in this proclamation. "The Church's

62. Newbigin, *Open Secret*, 24.
63. Newbigin, *Sign of the Kingdom*, 38–40.
64. Newbigin, *Open Secret*, 20.
65. Newbigin, "Evangelism and the Whole Mission of the Church," 7.
66. Newbigin, "Evangelism and the Whole Mission of the Church," 7.
67. Newbigin, "Integration," 251–52.
68. Newbigin, "Pastoral Ministry in a Pluralist Society," 151.
69. Newbigin, *Sign of the Kingdom*, 38–43; Newbigin, *Gospel in a Pluralist Society*, 128–40.

evangelistic force is—or ought to be—its entire membership, nothing less."[70] Here, Newbigin is insisting that evangelism, in its vocal and visual sense, only happens through the full membership of every congregation living and preaching the gospel wherever they go in life. "Evangelism is, therefore, part of the normal life of every Christian congregation . . . from the moment of its birth."[71] Newbigin's point is that no one is born a Christian, all come to faith through hearing the message of Jesus Christ, therefore every church and every Christian arises from evangelism of some form. Thus, evangelism should be part of the life of every Christian and congregation. As well, Newbigin points out that evangelism and witness require every Christian since it takes the fullness of the community living and preaching the gospel to reach the fullness of society.[72] David Lowes Watson, in his contribution to *The Church between Gospel and Culture* ("Christ All in All") specifically discusses evangelism within the work of Newbigin. Connecting evangelism with the congregation as hermeneutic of the gospel, Watson argues for the church's Christocentric understanding of itself as the hermeneutical locus of evangelism. "As an integral feature of the *missio Dei*, evangelism cannot be undertaken apart from such communities."[73] Thus, Watson is arguing that evangelism takes place through communities who are the hermeneutic of the gospel for their society. These communities, Watson says, must remain focused on the world rather than internal congregational concerns. "The gospel of Jesus Christ is for the world, not the church, and congregations must regard themselves solely as Christ's messengers, with all the discretion and self-effacement that such a role implies."[74] Thus, Watson reminds the church that it is other-focused, and can only bear witness to the gospel by remaining other-focused. But there is another issue that must be addressed when discussing the local congregation representing the kingdom of God in the world.

The Tension of Representing the Kingdom of God

One portion of Newbigin's discussion of the kingdom of God is the already/not-yet tension of the present and future realities of the kingdom of God; or the already/not-yet tension of the kingdom. Newbigin clearly saw God's reign as the present reality of human history through Jesus Christ, but he also saw the future hope of the fulfilled kingdom of God in New Creation. "For the

---

70. Newbigin, "Christian Layman in the World and in the Church," 185.
71. Newbigin, "Pattern of Ministry in a Missionary Church," 8.
72. Newbigin, "Pattern of Ministry in a Missionary Church," 8.
73. Watson, "Christ All in All," 185–86.
74. Watson, "Christ All in All," 186.

future it has Christ's promise: it is your Father's good pleasure to give you the Kingdom. And for the present it has His assurance: Be of good cheer; I have overcome the world."[75] Here, Newbigin makes clear that the kingdom has both a present reality and a future promise—the promise of the fullness of the coming kingdom, present in the confidence of Christ's victory over sin and death. Having explicitly voiced his call for the church to bear gospel witness to all nations in *Foolishness to the Greeks*, Newbigin's first point about this witness is that it requires a recovery of proper eschatology. "The first must be the recovery and firm grasp of a true doctrine of the last things, of eschatology. The gospel is good news of the kingdom, and the kingdom is an eschatological concept. A true understanding of the last things is the first essential."[76] Thus, representing the reign of God requires a firm understanding and careful attention to eschatology. In Western theology, Newbigin saw two major false eschatologies—one being the private salvation of Christians apart from society,[77] and the other being that the future hope as distant, rather than imminent.[78] Newbigin saw the imminent completion of God's reign in New Creation, which pushes the church to active engagement in the world.[79] Thus, the promise of the kingdom is both present and future. This future promise is the hope for New Creation, the promised fulfillment of God's reign, where all of creation will bow and worship the King.[80] Thus, Newbigin calls for a renewal of true eschatology, which sees Jesus Christ as the last word in human affairs, and the return of Jesus as the end of human history.[81]

There is a dual position of eschatology in relation to the kingdom of God in Newbigin, where both the present and the future reality of eschatology sit in tension with one another. Jürgen Schuster investigates this tension in his 2006 PhD dissertation from Trinity International University, and he assesses that central to that tension is the congregation as hermeneutic of the gospel concept. Schuster remarks that as the hermeneutic of the gospel, the local congregation is the first fruits of God's kingdom, and the living embodiment of the gospel for the world.[82] His analysis of Newbigin's concept of the congre-

75. Newbigin, "Mission of the Triune God," 32.
76. Newbigin, *Foolishness to the Greeks*, 134.
77. Newbigin, "Which Way for 'Faith and Order'?," 18–119.
78. Newbigin, "Evangelism and the Whole Mission of the Church," 5–6.
79. Newbigin, *Foolishness to the Greeks*, 136–37.
80. Newbigin, "Authority," 4.
81. See Newbigin, "Nature of Christian Hope," 282–84; Newbigin, *Finality of Christ*; Newbigin, *Household of God*, 136–39; Newbigin, *Word in Season*, 77–78; Newbigin, *Signs Amid the Rubble*, 19–30, 31–45.
82. Schuster, "Significance of the Kingdom of God," 269, 268.

gation as hermeneutic is that the glory of the Son should be seen within the community of Christ in the world.[83] He goes on to state what he believes are the implications of this. "The visible community of believers becomes the key for the world to see the meaning and relevance of the gospel, to understand God's goal for human life and to enter into the truth. . . . Thus the community of believers is the hermeneutic of the gospel which translates God's story of salvation into the life of people and invites them to become part of this story."[84] Schuster's view of the congregation as hermeneutic of the gospel is that it is the foundation for the local congregation understanding its role and place, its identity, in the world as the interpretive key for the gospel to confront the world and the world to confront the gospel. Thus, through the local congregation being the hermeneutic of the gospel for their society, the eschatological reality of the kingdom is made known in the world.

The present/future reality of the kingdom of God is part of what representing the kingdom means for every local congregation. They are the visible community of the kingdom which is already present in part, but in the future will come into fullness. By representing the kingdom, the church testifies to the credibility of Jesus Christ as the final word in human affairs. As well, within an understanding and proclamation of the kingdom of God, the church and all of its members are reminded of the proper position of itself in God's story of redemption. "The Kingdom is the kingdom of God i.e., God assuming his sovereign power. The Church is the assembly of God, God drawing people by the power of the Spirit into the allegiance of Christ."[85] Thus, Newbigin is basing all of conversion squarely on the shoulders of God, reminding the church that its place is as the community of Christ followers, pointing back to Jesus Christ and living out their experience of the reign of God as the Spirit leads. It is the church's duty to witness; it is the Spirit's duty to transform hearts through the witness of the church. But this witness is not something that can be tasked to professional evangelists and missionaries, it is the responsibility of every Christian to live the witness of the gospel.

THE ROLE OF THE LOCAL CONGREGATION

The individual Christian community, the local congregation of the Body of Christ, has a role in training, sending, supporting, and celebrating gospel witness in each one of its members. The local congregation, then, is a place where the Holy Spirit is present (see chapter 3), and through which the Spirit

83. Schuster, "Significance of the Kingdom of God," 156.
84. Schuster, "Significance of the Kingdom of God," 157.
85. Newbigin, "Basis and the Forms of Unity," 7.

makes the kingdom of God known in the world. Thus, the local congregation serves as the instrument of the Holy Spirit for representing the reign of God for a specific place and time. Newbigin addresses the local congregation as the place where "a certain kind of shared life"[86] is lived through which the reign of God is made known in society. But what exactly is this 'certain kind of shared life'? In this section, I will address the role of the Holy Spirit in the shared life of the local congregation, the actions of the local congregation to train, send, support, and celebrate its members in gospel witness, how this is lived out in the deeds and words of the congregation, and finally the role of the ordained pastor in the shared life of the local congregation.

In chapter 3 the issue of the presence of the Holy Spirit establishing, sustaining, and leading the church was addressed. When it comes to the individual local congregation, the presence of the Holy Spirit operates in the same way, guiding the local congregation into experiencing and living the kingdom of God within its given context. Newbigin's description of this relationship between the Holy Spirit and the local congregation comes through his use of the term *arrabōn*. "The presence of the kingdom in the Church is the presence of its foretaste, its first fruit, its pledge (*arrabōn*) in the Spirit."[87] The kingdom comes to the local congregation through the presence of the Holy Spirit, which serves as the foretaste of the reality of the kingdom for that community. Newbigin continues on to show that this *arrabōn* binds the congregation together in a shared life.[88] This idea of the Holy Spirit as the first fruit of the kingdom is something Newbigin picks up from Luke and John,[89] and its binding together of the local congregation into a shared life of the Spirit in the kingdom reality he derives from Paul.[90]

But Newbigin sees that these two ideas are linked, and he expresses that link through discussing the presence of the Holy Spirit as a foretaste of the kingdom for the church, binding it together and leading it to share that foretaste with the world. Newbigin sees this all happening in the local congregation, which is the hermeneutic of the gospel for their society. George Vandervelde, in a 1996 conference presentation that was published in a 2010 edition of *Trinity Journal for Theology and Ministry*, also acknowledges the importance of the local congregation in Newbigin's discussions of his missionary ecclesiology. Vandervelde specifically identifies the local congregation as the locus of salvation and the presence of God in the world within Newbigin's

---

86. Newbigin, *Word in Season*, 152.
87. Newbigin, *Gospel in a Pluralist Society*, 119–20.
88. Newbigin, *Gospel in a Pluralist Society*, 119–21.
89. Newbigin, *Sign of the Kingdom*, 37–38, 40–42.
90. Newbigin, "Bible Study on Romans 8."

Representing the Kingdom of God

thought—a view he associates with the congregation as hermeneutic of the gospel.[91] Vandervelde continues by discussing the role and importance of the six characteristics of the congregation as hermeneutic of the gospel for showing what a community who believes and lives the gospel can be in the world.[92] Thus, Vandervelde reinforces the importance of the local congregation for the congregation as hermeneutic of the gospel, specifically for making the presence of the kingdom known in the world.

One way for the local congregation to live and express the presence of the kingdom is through training of its members. This training must entail preparing members for engaging the public sectors with which they intersect with daily, and Newbigin envisions this as happening through groups that meet and theologize about the issues of their lives within the public sector. "There is a need for 'frontier-groups,' groups of Christians working in the same sector of public life, meeting to thrash out the controversial issues of their business or profession in the light of their faith."[93] Newbigin is saying that for the local congregation to fulfill its role in training its members, they must establish groups that connect members in the same industries, so that they may get together and theologize about the issues specific to their daily lives. This will also require teaching those members how to study the bible and theologize about the important issues that arise. This training will never be fully completed because there will always be new issues and new public sectors that need addressing.

Next, the local congregation must send its members into the world to represent the reign of God in deeds and words (more on this below). Within the modern Western Church, sending has too often been associated with the sending of missionaries to foreign lands, so a better term may be *releasing*. In this, Newbigin would argue for the local congregation to release its members for full and active ministry of gospel living and representing the kingdom in their society. "We forget that the Church is the laity, the People of God, and that the Christian layman in his office, field or factory is precisely the Church's frontline soldier in her engagement with the world."[94] Newbigin calls on the local congregation to remember that representing the kingdom happens through every member living and sharing the gospel story in every sphere of their lives. This sharing is not about giving a personal testimony, though that certainly may be included, but about living in a way that represents the kingdom in everything that a Christian says, does, and thinks as they go about

91. Vandervelde, "Church as Missionary Community," 120.
92. Vandervelde, "Church as Missionary Community," 123.
93. Newbigin, *Gospel in a Pluralist Society*, 230–31.
94. Newbigin, "Christian Layman in the Word and in the Church," 185.

their life. Thus, there is a need to remind and release members to live out and preach the gospel wherever they go.

The local congregation must also remember to support its members in representing the kingdom of God in the world. "The congregation has to be a place where its members are trained, supported, and nourished in the exercise of their parts of the priestly ministry in the world."[95] Supporting and nourishing members for their role as God's royal priesthood in the world is essential for representing the reign of God. This royal priesthood "is to stand before God on behalf of people and to stand before people on behalf of God."[96] Living this royal priesthood requires support, and Newbigin calls on the local congregation to provide that support to its members. Every Sunday, Christians stand before God as the representative of the world; they are reminded of their sins, rehearse the redemption of the death and resurrection of Jesus Christ, and are sent out to be God's priests to the world.

Then, the local congregation must also be a place that celebrates the way the Holy Spirit is leading them to represent the kingdom of God in their society. In giving thanksgiving to God in the act of worship, the local congregation celebrates with its members all that God has done, is doing, and will do in society. "The Christian congregation meets as a community that acknowledges that it lives by the amazing grace of a boundless kindness."[97] In acknowledging this grace, the local congregation celebrates the way God's grace and mercy have worked in and through them, touching the world with the reality of the kingdom.

Deed and Word

The connection between deeds and words is a tenuous one, receiving attention in New Testament epistles from Paul (Romans and Colossians), Peter (1 Peter), John (1 John), and James (James). The fundamentalist/progressive split of the Western Church in the twentieth century saw deeds and words again as one of its central topics, taking on the terms social action (deeds) and evangelism (words). But Newbigin saw deeds and words as inextricably linked, one cannot exist without the other. His understanding of deeds and words makes three very important points. The first is that Newbigin sees the congregation as living by the gospel through deeds and words in the world. Thus, the gospel forms the basis for how the congregation acts in the world, and for the explanation the congregation gives for those actions. Second, both deeds and words arise from the shared life of the Christian community. They

---

95. Newbigin, *Gospel in a Pluralist Society*, 230.
96. Newbigin, *Gospel in a Pluralist Society*, 230.
97. Newbigin, *Gospel in a Pluralist Society*, 228.

are the outpouring of the community's love for God and gospel formation. Third, Newbigin notes that most often the deeds precede words. While deeds and words are linked, Newbigin believes that the congregation must act before it can preach. To fully understand what Newbigin means by calling on the congregation to represent the kingdom, it is necessary to investigate his understanding of deeds and words.

Newbigin's understanding of deeds and words is that they are linked together with an unbreakable bond. "They mutually reinforce and interpret one another. The words explain the deeds, and the deeds validate the words."[98] Thus, Newbigin sees that it is insufficient to have deeds without words to explain them and that using words without deeds that reinforce them makes the words meaningless. Newbigin goes on to provide a biblical foundation for this view, showing how Jesus and the disciples always witnessed to the gospel in deeds and words, usually with the deeds preceding the words.[99] This is because neither deeds nor words, by themselves, explicitly represent the gospel and challenge society with the new reality of the present kingdom. "Healings, even the most wonderful, do not call this present world radically into question; the gospel does, and this has to be made explicit. On the other hand, the preaching is meaningless without the healings. They are the true explanation of what is happening, but if nothing is happening no explanation is called for and the words are empty words."[100] Newbigin's point is that for the gospel to be shared, it must come in both deeds and words, together, as they define and support each other. Newbigin also connects deeds and words with the shared life of the church in the gospel.

> By its witness—in word and deed and common life—to the centrality of the work of Jesus in his ministry, death, and resurrection it offers to all people the possibility of understanding that the meaning and goal of history are not to be found in any of the projects, programs, ideologies, and utopias which offer themselves in competition with one another . . . but that it is to be found in a person and a history which breaks decisively through this endless succession by breaching the final barrier of death and opening a new horizon for human affairs, a hope which on the one hand affirms and energizes all those human hopes which correspond to God's purpose as revealed in Christ, but yet on the other hand transcends them all.[101]

---

98. Newbigin, *Gospel in a Pluralist Society*, 137.
99. Newbigin, *Gospel in a Pluralist Society*, 131–34.
100. Newbigin, *Gospel in a Pluralist Society*, 132.
101. Newbigin, *Gospel in a Pluralist Society*, 129.

Here, Newbigin links deeds, words, and the shared life of the community as the witness that points to the new reality of Jesus Christ as the final word in all human affairs. But Newbigin also stresses that all of this is an action of God, and the church is following God's lead in its witness to the gospel.[102] Newbigin continues this idea by affirming the place of mission in deeds and words within the leading of the Holy Spirit. "The mission is an expression of the authority Jesus has on earth and in heaven as he sits at God's right hand. It is manifest in the powers which the presence of the Spirit confers on the Church so that it becomes—both in its words and in its deeds—a witness to the reign of Jesus."[103] Newbigin is placing mission underneath the Lordship of Jesus Christ, calling all congregations to witness in deeds and words as part of its obedience and discipleship to Christ, and its representing of the kingdom. Newbigin concludes that "it is clear that to set word and deed, preaching and action, against each other is absurd. The central reality is neither word nor act, but the total life of a community enabled by the Spirit to live in Christ, sharing his passion and the power of his resurrection."[104] Thus, Newbigin is affirming the bond between deeds and words within the congregation as a living out of the gospel. But Newbigin also has something to say explicitly about the relationship between deeds and words.

Ultimately, Newbigin draws deeds and words together because they are part of the same witness to the truth and reliability of the gospel. "Words and deeds both point to the same reality, the active presence of the reign of God."[105] Newbigin believes that both deeds and words are pointing to the reality of the present and future kingdom of God. Thus, Newbigin goes on to say "The mission of the church, following that of Jesus, has to be both word and deed and the life of a community which already embodies a foretaste of God's kingdom."[106] Newbigin is saying that deed and word go together in the local congregation, living the gospel because it embodies the foretaste of the kingdom. This foretaste is made possible in the local congregation because the foretaste of Jesus' initiation of the kingdom, the Holy Spirit, resides within the church. This foretaste is what makes the church different from all other evidence of the kingdom on earth. And this foretaste must be lived out in the local congregation who knows and believes the gospel and through their witness to the gospel in deeds and words within society.

---

102. Newbigin, *Gospel in a Pluralist Society*, 134–37.
103. Newbigin, *Gospel in a Pluralist Society*, 108.
104. Newbigin, *Gospel in a Pluralist Society*, 137.
105. Newbigin, "Evangelism and the Whole Mission of the Church," 8.
106. Newbigin, "Missionary's Dream," 6.

The Role of the Ordained Pastor

Another important portion of Newbigin's discussion about the role of the local congregation in representing the kingdom of God in society is specifically about the role of the pastor. Pastors, especially in the Western Church, have often developed into the professional Christian, the one who is supposed to do all of the ministry and lead all of the spirituality for the Christian community. For Newbigin, the role of an ordained pastor is meant not to exercise the ministry of the church, but to equip every member to exercise the church's ministry. In Newbigin's expression of the missionary nature of the church as the congregation as hermeneutic of the gospel, the role of the ordained pastor must change. Having discussed the congregation as hermeneutic of the gospel in chapter 18 of *GPS*, Newbigin's next chapter deals with ministerial leadership. He asks, "If the gospel is the good news of the reign of God over the whole of life, public no less than private; if the Church is therefore called to address the whole public life of the community as well as the personal lives of men and women in the private and domestic affairs, what kind of ministerial leadership is needed?"[107] Newbigin, assuming that all he has said about the church up to this point is true, asks about the type of ministerial leadership the church needs to live out its missionary nature. Newbigin's answer to this question is that the pastors of the local congregation must be servants of their congregations, engaging with the communities that they inhabit, and modeling the type of life that represents the kingdom in all they do and say before the watching world. "The minister's leadership of the congregation in its mission to the world will be first and foremost in the area of his or her own discipleship, in that life of prayer and daily consecration which remains hidden from the world but which is the place where the essential battles are either won or lost."[108] Newbigin is calling on pastors to be models of discipleship to Jesus Christ and representing the kingdom of God to the world, which the congregation can learn from and emulate as they too go about their lives publicly and privately.

Likewise, in "Pastoral Ministry in a Pluralist Society," Newbigin asserts that Christians do not, nor should they, live in a Christian bubble, but rather are involved all the time with non-Christians.[109] Newbigin then places the role of the pastor as that of training members to bear witness to the gospel among the non-Christians with which they are regularly involved.[110] Thus, because Christians are naturally engaged with peoples of other faiths or no faith in

---

107. Newbigin, *Gospel in a Pluralist Society*, 236.
108. Newbigin, *Gospel in a Pluralist Society*, 240–41.
109. Newbigin, "Pastoral Ministry in a Pluralist Society," 151.
110. Newbigin, "Pastoral Ministry in a Pluralist Society," 151.

their daily operation of business, social life, and family, then they must be prepared for bearing witness to the gospel among those people. This preparation should come through the local congregation and from the pastors of that congregation. Newbigin points out that the responsibility for each other within the local congregation is vitally important.[111] The church is too large for ordained pastors alone, thus Newbigin lays this responsibility for pastoral care on the laity. But they learn about pastoral care from the pastors who must train them in how to care for one another.

While Newbigin develops this need for a new type of leader, he also critiques the traditional pastor and pastoral training in the West. Newbigin does not want to diminish the role of the ordained pastor within the church, instead, he shifts the focus of this role from ministering to the congregation and the world to one of preparing and sustaining the members of the congregation for their exercise of the role of the royal priesthood within the world. As well, Newbigin gives the ordained pastor the responsibility to help maintain order and tradition within the church.[112] In the Polanyian view of Christianity as a sense of knowing within a tradition (see chapter 2), ordained pastors have the responsibility of training and regulating the tradition of Christianity. Thus, a new type of pastoral leader is needed for the local congregation being the hermeneutic of the gospel for their society. Too often pastors are trained for the pastoral care of the existing congregation and theologizing from a pulpit, which orients them away from their and the church's missionary calling.[113] What is needed is pastors who prepare and send congregants to the front lines of mission in their communities.

This call for a new type of pastor in Newbigin is also addressed in the book *Missional Church*. Calling on the North American Church to understand itself as God's sent community, *Missional Church* addresses several important topics within its discussion of recovering the missionary nature of the church. One of those issues is the need for "Missional Leadership" which focuses on equipping congregations for God's mission in their context.[114] The new type of leadership that the authors are calling for in this chapter is an implication of local congregations that are full of men and women who believe the gospel and live by it, engaging their highly plural societies as the hermeneutic of the gospel.[115] In particular, *Missional Church* calls for leaders who follow the leading of the Holy Spirit in reshaping their congregations into covenant

---

111. Newbigin, "Church Union," 358–60.
112. Newbigin, "Ministry and Laity," 482.
113. Newbigin, *Gospel in a Pluralist Society*, 231, 230.
114. Guder, *Missional Church*, 183–93.
115. Guder, *Missional Church*, 219.

communities formed in the character of the kingdom.[116] Understanding the missionary nature of the church in the way Newbigin expresses it in the congregation as hermeneutic of the gospel concept reinforces the necessity for this type of leader for the local congregation.

Though constituted by the Holy Spirit, the foundation of the local congregation is Jesus Christ, who formed, discipled, and sent a community of believers to continue His mission in the world. After all, the Holy Spirit is also referred to as the Spirit of Christ. This is the community that Jesus left behind; a community of disciples that are grounded in His message of the kingdom and that preach that message everywhere they go, in everything they do. "This community has at its heart the remembering and rehearsing of his words and deeds, and the sacraments given by him through which it is enabled both to engraft new members into its life and to renew this life again and again through sharing in his risen life through the body broken and the lifeblood poured out."[117] Thus, such a community is shaped around Christ and draws its life from Christ—living out this internal shaping in the same way that Christ did, in service to the world. This community will then become "the place where men and women and children find that the gospel gives them the framework of understanding, the 'lenses' through which they are able to understand and cope with the world."[118] This local congregation becomes the place where worldview is shaped and public truth is lived. From this re-shaped world view, Christians are to enter the world, representing in deeds and words, the message of the present and the future kingdom of God.

While all of this may seem like a large task for one local congregation to complete, Newbigin would note the importance of ecumenical unity throughout a city. Congregations from different theological traditions must work together in a city for the full proclamation of the gospel to happen in that city. Therefore, Newbigin promotes diversity within the local congregation,[119] a diversity that extends to all congregations within a given locale. And this is why Newbigin became an advocate for the inclusion of handicapped Christians in gospel ministry,[120] because without all members of the Body of Christ working together, the fullness of the gospel story will not be made known to the world. As well, Newbigin notes the issues that current pastoral training has when confronted with an understanding of the local congregation as the

---

116. Guder, *Missional Church*, 199–200.
117. Newbigin, *Gospel in a Pluralist Society*, 227.
118. Newbigin, *Gospel in a Pluralist Society*, 227.
119. Newbigin, *Gospel in a Pluralist Society*, 231.
120. See Newbigin, "Right to Fullness of Life"; Newbigin, "Not Whole without the Handicapped."

staging ground, the command center, the hospital, and festival site for all its members engaging in representing the reign of God to their society.

SUMMARY

Throughout his life, Newbigin saw representing the kingdom of God as an essential element of the missionary nature of the church. This element focuses upon the relationship between the church and the world, an essential relationship for the community which has the foretaste of the kingdom of God (in the presence of the Holy Spirit) and is called to live out God's mission by bringing that foretaste into the world. His imagery of the church as sign, instrument, and foretaste points back to the kingdom of God. As well, representing the kingdom is part of what makes the church unique within the world, because it focuses on those outside of the church while pointing to something larger than the church. This places the church in a tension of the already/not-yet reality of the kingdom, keeping one eye focused on the present world and the other eye focused on the fulfillment of the kingdom to come. In this, the role of the local congregation is bear witness to the kingdom in deeds and words, enabling each and every Christian to daily live out their calling as God's royal priests. Requiring a new type of pastoral leader who trains and sends members to this lifestyle ministry. All of which comes in the active, leading presence of the Holy Spirit within the local congregation. Thus, in understanding the congregation as hermeneutic of the gospel concept, representing the kingdom focuses on the outward relationship of this concept, which keeps the local congregation open to the needs of the world.

5

Living by the Gospel

INTRODUCTION

THE FINAL ELEMENT WITHIN Newbigin's missionary ecclesiology is living by the gospel. This element focuses on the internal relationship of the church, being the Body of Christ formed by the presence of the Holy Spirit, and both individually and collectively representing the kingdom of God in the world. Living by the gospel, which includes believing it within the congregation as hermeneutic of the gospel concept, is specifically the answer Newbigin provides to the question of the credibility of the gospel in a plural society. Thus, for Newbigin, living by the gospel is a part of the missionary nature of the church, but he adds it to this expression of the missionary nature as part of Newbigin's call on the Western Church to regain its missionary nature. Because it focuses on the internal relationship of the church, the element of living by the gospel engages life both within individual congregations and between different congregations. Living by the gospel is expressed in the shared life of the local congregation that is formed around the gospel and models the new reality of the kingdom of God as a testament to the gospel as public truth. Being formed by and living by the gospel story marks the local congregation as something different within society, a new social order which indwells the gospel in all that they are, say, and do. This element is broken into two primary pieces, 'living by' and 'the gospel'. Within living by, the focus is the binding together of the local congregation in a shared life, which is modeled by Jesus Christ. This makes the shared life of the community one that is shaped by the Cross. The gospel piece speaks to the gospel as public truth and how that nature is internalized and lived by the local congregation. In this chapter, I will discuss what it means for the local congregation to live by the gospel, including its shared life, cruciformity, and its role in society as a new social order. Then, I will discuss understanding the gospel as public truth, which will include the issues of the gospel as universal human history and the authority of the local congregation to present the gospel as public truth in a plural society.

LIVING BY

Newbigin's answer to the question of the credibility of the gospel message in a pluralist society to claim Jesus Christ as the final word in human affairs specifically calls for congregations to believe and live by the gospel. Believing and living by the gospel is following in the model of life which Christ modeled for the church.

> Jesus, as I said earlier, did not write a book but formed a community. This community has at its heart the remembering and rehearsing of his words and deed, and the sacraments given by him through which it is enabled both to engraft new members into its life and to renew this life again and again through sharing in his risen life through the body broken and the lifeblood poured out. It exists in him for him. He is the center of its life. Its character is given to it, when it is true to its nature, not by the characters of its members but by his character. Insofar as it is true to its calling, it becomes the place where men and women and children find that the gospel gives them the framework of understanding, the "lenses" through which they are to understand and cope with the world.[1]

Newbigin is saying the local congregation which is true to its character, the character given to it by Jesus Christ, will live a life that is centered on Christ. This life is modeled for the congregation in the gospel, and it is a life which is Cross-shaped and public. This living by the gospel requires that every member of the congregation first knows the gospel, then believes the gospel, and finally that they live their beliefs in every facet of their lives. In this, the local congregation, formed by the gospel around the Cross, will maintain a certain kind of shared life. This understanding of living by the gospel in the shared life of the congregation is something that Newbigin addresses at different times and from different perspectives throughout his life. In reviewing all these different discussions of living by the gospel, it is clear that Newbigin has a distinct view of what it means to live by the gospel, that this view requires a certain kind of life, this life is a shared life, and in this shared life

---

1. Newbigin, *Gospel in a Pluralist Society*, 227.

the congregation is also participating in the Trinity; thus, it is a shared life that is formed around the Cross. In this section, I will discuss the shared life of the local congregation, its relation to cruciformity, and finally how all of this comes together to point to living by the gospel as the foundation for the congregation being a new social order in society.

Shared Life

For Newbigin, living by the gospel is inhabiting the story of the gospel and then living that story as the new reality within the public square. He claims that the new reality is made known in society through three things, the first of which is a specifically different type of shared life within the congregation.

> The first and foremost one is a certain kind of shared life. At the heart of that will be praise.... A community of people that, in the midst of all the pain and sorrow and wickedness of the world, is continually praising God is the first obvious result of living by another story than the one the world lives by.... And where there is a praising community, there also will be a caring community with love to spare for others. Such a community is the primary hermeneutic of the gospel.... But a congregation that has at its heart a joyful worship of the living God and a constantly renewed sense of the sheer grace and kindness of God will be a congregation from which true love flows out to the neighbors, a love that seeks their good whether or not they come to church.[2]

In Newbigin's description of the certain kind of shared life of the local congregation, he notes the centrality of praise, the binding together of the community, and the reaching out of that community into their society. These things mark the congregation as a new society that is grounded in the new reality of the present/future kingdom. It is the community that lives by the gospel, which is the hermeneutic of that gospel to society. They represent and interpret the gospel for their society to witness. Their character is formed by the presence of the Holy Spirit, around the gospel, and witnessed in the characteristics discussed above (see chapter 3). But Newbigin also provides a warning within this description, first that praise can become stale (to which his solution is prayer for the Holy Spirit's renewal), and second that the love of the congregation can become insular (which is a false love).[3] Both of these are issues that the local congregation must be aware of and watching out for, within itself. In this description of the "certain kind of shared life," Newbigin

---

2. Newbigin, *Word in Season*, 152–53.
3. Newbigin, *Word in Season*, 153.

depicts the local congregation as a place through which the gospel is known, believed, and lived both publicly and privately. The shared life of the congregation is one that is shaped by the gospel and nurtured by the Holy Spirit.

Cruciformity

The centrality of the Cross as the forming principle of the life of the congregation, what is referred to as cruciformity (cruci—meaning the Cross, and formity—meaning formation), is essential to understanding living by the gospel. For the local congregation to live by the gospel is to live a Cross-shaped life. While Newbigin regularly discusses the Cross of Jesus Christ throughout his writings, one of the particularly important discussions of the Cross is in relation to the local congregation living by the gospel. The initial question Newbigin asks that warrants his answer of the congregation as hermeneutic of the gospel specifically asks how a man hanging on a cross could be seen as the last word in human affairs.[4] This makes the Cross central to understanding what it means to be a community of men and women who believe and live by the gospel. The Cross is the place where all of the world is called together to witness God's salvific action. For those that believe in Christ's atoning sacrifice, the Cross binds them together in a shared life of discipleship to Jesus Christ.

In particular, Newbigin's discussions of the Cross point to it as the rallying point—the starting point, returning point, and point of reference—for the shared life of the local congregation, ultimately drawing the congregation into the life of the Triune God. The true mark of the church's life in the flesh is the mark of the Cross, of life through death, of "'bearing about in the body the dying of Jesus, that the life also of Jesus may be manifested in our body' (II Cor. 4:10)."[5] Thus, the Cross is essential for understanding the reality of Jesus Christ as Son,[6] that His message of the presence of the kingdom is validated, and that the sins which separate humans from God are eliminated. The Cross (in relation to the Resurrection) becomes the visible sign of the redemption God offers to His creation, drawing fallen humanity back into relationship with Himself. "The cross was a public execution visible to all—believers and unbelievers alike. The resurrection was as much a fact of history as the crucifixion, but it was made known only to the chosen few who were called to be

---

4. Newbigin, *Gospel in a Pluralist Society*, 227.

5. Newbigin, *Household of God*, 82.

6. The incarnation, ministry, resurrection, and ascension of Jesus also speak to the reality of Jesus Christ as the Son of God, but the Cross is what I am focused on here. Because of this focus and a limitation of space, I will not be engaging these other pieces, though they all hold equal weight in validating the presence of the kingdom and the redemption of creation.

the witnesses of the hidden kingdom."[7] The Cross also forms the type of life which the congregation is to be in living by the gospel in the world. In speaking of the church as the sign of God's reign, Newbigin remarks that "Its only sign is and must be the sign of the cross, placed not merely on its altars and its buildings, but on its corporate life."[8] Thus, the Cross must mark the life of the local congregation.

Michael J. Gorman, in his book *Becoming the Gospel*, picks up the topic of cruciformity for the third time,[9] though in this version of his discussion of cruciformity, Gorman addresses cruciformity in relation to the church. The foundation of Gorman's argument in this book is that the understanding that theosis in the cruciform life of Christ is the ground from which mission emerges. Gorman states, "theosis—Spirit-enabled transformative participation in the life and character of God revealed in the crucified and resurrection Messiah Jesus—is the starting point of mission and is, in fact, its proper theological framework."[10] Gorman continues on to show that as God's community, the church lives in anticipatory participation in the world, embodying the gospel for all to see.[11] The local congregation, as Gorman sees it, is anticipating the age to come while it participates in the current age.[12] For Gorman, this is a participation in God, which necessitates a missional stance toward the world because God is missionary by nature. Gorman's understanding of the church is primarily a missionary one, as he shows in his opening quotes, one of which is Newbigin's concept of the congregation as hermeneutic of the gospel.[13]

This issue of cruciformity is also discussed by John G. Flett when he specifically addresses the congregation as hermeneutic of the gospel. Flett, having established his understanding of the church as the visible community of God as it is seen in Murray Rae,[14] goes on to show how this view of the visible community can be combined with Barth's discussion of the church living in cruciformity.[15] Flett argues from Barth that the resurrection is a revelation of God, and thus invisible, while the Cross is part of visible history—all of which is made known in the church by the presence of the Holy Spirit.[16] So,

---

7. Newbigin, *Gospel in a Pluralist Society*, 108.

8. Newbigin, *Open Secret*, 113.

9. See Gorman, *Cruciformity*; Gorman, *Inhabiting the Cruciform God*.

10. Gorman, *Becoming the Gospel*, 4.

11. Gorman, *Becoming the Gospel*, 15–20.

12. Gorman, *Becoming the Gospel*, 15–20.

13. Gorman, *Becoming the Gospel*, 1–2.

14. Flett, "What Does It Mean for a Congregation to Be a Hermeneutic?," 198–203.

15. Flett, "What Does It Mean for a Congregation to Be a Hermeneutic?," 203–6.

16. Flett, "What Does It Mean for a Congregation to Be a Hermeneutic?," 203–6.

the local congregation lives as the hermeneutic of the gospel when it is filled with the Holy Spirit in order to live out the visible Cross and the invisible resurrection as it is revealed by God. "This dialectic of cross and resurrection, of the church's special visibility, is central to Newbigin's understanding of the congregation as hermeneutic of the gospel."[17] Flett places the congregation as hermeneutic of the gospel within the conversation of the Cross and resurrection, connecting the notion of visible and invisible revelation from Barth, with Newbigin's understanding of the missionary nature of the church. Flett, in combining Barth and Newbigin says,

> Or, Jesus Christ's resurrection from the dead, though a historical fact—indeed, the center of history—is not visible to everyone. The visibility of the resurrection, the visibility of Jesus Christ as the Lord of all creation, is and remains an act of God. The cross, by comparison, is generally visible. For the church to live in the resurrection, to be visible as participant in the new reality inaugurated by Jesus Christ in the power of the Spirit, is to be seen in history as the people of the cross. It is only because of the resurrection that the church can have this cruciform visibility—the cross is not the end. For this reason, even while stressing the invisible, Barth describes the truth of the Christian community's earthly historical existence as "not a matter of general but a very special visibility." The church is visible for what it is only as an act of God. Barth's position is interesting here because in *The Gospel in a Pluralist Society* Newbigin articulates an identical position. In his discussion "Christ, the Clue to History," Newbigin conceives the church in terms of Jesus Christ's own earthly ministry. The church lives now after the cross but before the final revelation of Jesus Christ in his glory. This time, Newbigin argues, is "marked by suffering, and by the presence of the signs of the kingdom." This "double character," which forms the "substance of the mission to the nations," is related "in the same way as cross and resurrection were related to each other in the ministry of Jesus (cf. 2 Cor. 4:10). The cross was a public execution visible to all—believers and unbelievers alike. The resurrection was as much a fact of history as the crucifixion, but it was made known only to the chosen few who were called to be the witnesses of the hidden kingdom."[18]

Flett's overlapping of Barth and Newbigin shows that the Cross is the visible gathering ground for the church, while the resurrection is equally its invisible gathering point. For Flett, the cruciformity of the congregation as

17. Flett, "What Does It Mean for a Congregation to Be a Hermeneutic?," 205.
18. Flett, "What Does It Mean for a Congregation to Be a Hermeneutic?," 204–5.

hermeneutic of the gospel concept is that it continues the visible revelation of God in the world. This concept connects to the Cross in forming the Christian community through the life, death, and resurrection of Jesus Christ.[19]

There is also Charles J. Fensham's article about missiological method published in *Missiology* in 2019. In this article, Fensham argues for a learning posture in engagement with other cultures as a christomorphic[20] response to scripture, and that this learning posture will influence the methodology for presenting the gospel to cultures.[21] "By christomorphic I mean the shape and Spirit of Christ as a posture in the world."[22] One of the keys of this christomorphic response is Newbigin's congregation as hermeneutic concept. "The way that those outside the Christian movement know and see the gospel and make sense of the teaching of Scripture is through encountering the lives, witness, and preaching of faithful loving Christians in the world."[23] Fensham is stating that the congregation as hermeneutic of the gospel provides the foundation for this christomorphic response, and in doing so he approaches Newbigin's concept from the perspective of presenting the gospel to a new culture. So like Gorman and Flett, Fensham is arguing for the centrality of the Cross in shaping the Christian community; a community which, as Fensham also points out, lives this christomorphic (or cruciform) in being the hermeneutic of the gospel.

The shared life of the congregation is derived from the Cross-shaped understanding of itself. "It has been so from the beginning and it is always so, that the presence of the Spirit creates this deep sense of responsibility for one another, of caring for one another, because we are together acknowledging our infinite debt to Christ."[24] The debt to Christ, which Newbigin portrays, is a debt that is formed by the Cross, which then shapes how the church sees history, the world, and their place within society.[25] Because of the Cross, the whole world has been turned upside down, and in the shadow of the Cross, the congregation is shaped to live by the model of Jesus Christ. Thus, the Cross forms the shape of the community, which must bear the marks of the Cross within itself in order to live by the gospel in the world. "Here, however, the Church is recognizable as the bearer of the Kingdom, the presence of the Kingdom, in so far as it is marked by the scars of the Passion. And the

---

19. Newbigin, *Gospel in a Pluralist Society*, 107–8.
20. Fensham, "Methodology of Missiology," 303.
21. Fensham, "Methodology of Missiology," 301–3.
22. Fensham, "Methodology of Missiology," 303.
23. Cronshaw and Taylor, "Congregation in a Pluralist Society," 303.
24. Newbigin, *Christ Our Eternal Contemporary*, 64.
25. Newbigin, *Gospel in a Pluralist Society*, 86, 151–52, 159, 181, 194–95.

Passion of Jesus is not passive submission to evil, but the price paid for an active challenge to evil. The Passion is what the theologians call the Messianic tribulation, that which occurs at the frontier, where the reign of God challenges the rulers of this world."[26] Here, Newbigin highlights that the church must bear the marks of the Cross, marks which come from Jesus' challenge to the principalities and powers of the world.[27] Thus, Newbigin notes that the church only bears these marks when it too challenges these principalities and powers. "And that frontier runs right through the whole of human life and it is when the Church is at the frontier that it bears in its body both the marks of the Passion and the power of the risen life, of the Lord."[28] Newbigin is calling on every congregation to challenge the principalities and powers of the world, and in doing so embrace and live out the Cross-shaped life of the gospel. This challenge comes in the model of Christ, who suffered and died as a result to his own challenge, and the congregation must be willing to suffer and die as Christ did. In living this cruciform life, the local congregation is incorporated into the life of the Triune God.

All of this comes to mean that the congregation, living a shared life which is shaped by the Cross, will be different from every other community in society. Living a shared life that is shaped by the Cross means that the local congregation will be a place of humility, vulnerability, sacrifice, love, and grace. This shared cruciform life is the congregational equivalent of taking up the cross and following Christ, willingly giving up its life for the sake of Christ's mission (Mt. 16:24–26). This shared cruciform life also beckons the local congregation to live different from the world, they must be a new social order that reflects the new reality of the Cross.

Being a New Social Order

The congregation living by the gospel is also living into the new reality ushed in by the Cross, a reality which leads them to live a different way of life, which Newbigin refers to as a "new social order."[29] Newbigin often uses some form of this phrase throughout his writings to call on the church to be witnessing to the gospel through the shared life of the community which is Cross-shaped, Christocentric, and Holy Spirit led, providing a glimpse of the kingdom of God. This new social order is what Newbigin is calling the church to be today. And this new social order both challenges culture and functions within it,

26. Newbigin, "On Being the Church for the World," 34–35.
27. Newbigin, *Gospel in a Pluralist Society*, 198–210.
28. Newbigin, "On Being the Church for the World," 35.
29. Newbigin, *Gospel in a Pluralist Society*, 223.

changing it from inside. But it is a new social order that is defined by the shared life of the community of Christ.

Newbigin mentions in *The Gospel in a Pluralist Society* (*GPS*) that as Roman society crumbled, it turned to the church as the "integrating power for a new social order."[30] Living within the structure of Roman society, the early church was a martyr church, challenging the social order of the Roman Empire, and it was in the disintegration of that empire that the church was called upon.[31] Today, as the West is going through cultural shifts again, Newbigin is "cultivating 'ways of Christ' for people living in the midst of the cultural transition from modern worldviews to postmodern."[32] But Newbigin also notes that, "If the Church is to be effective in advocating and achieving a new social order in the nation, it must itself be a new social order."[33] This new social order is modeled in the shared life of the congregation living by the gospel, as an expression of their cruciformity.

Newbigin's idea of the new social order of the shared cruciform life of the congregation has similarities with other authors. "If the gospel of Jesus Christ is to be more than an intriguing idea, it must become visible in a people whose life together is the first fruit of the new social order intended by God for the whole of creation."[34] This quote from Inagrace Dietterich associates the new social order and the shared life of the congregation, noting that they are part of God's intention for creation. While not quoting directly from Newbigin here, Dietterich builds heavily upon the congregation as hermeneutic of the gospel in this article to form her idea of the missionary spirit of the church, and Newbigin's influence on the idea and language Dietterich uses here is noticeable. There is also Mary Jo Leddy's idea of parallel cultures. Building off of the writings of Doug Hall and Miroslav Václac Havel, Leddy develops the idea of parallel cultures that exist as sub-cultures within an already dominant culture, in which people can learn to become the people of God, and eventually begin to speak out against the dominant culture in hopes of changing it.[35] Leddy's idea of 'parallel cultures' aligns with Newbigin's call on the Church to be a new social order existing, challenging, and changing culture from within it.

As a new social order, Newbigin points to the publicness of the church. This publicness is based in the church's embrace and living by the gospel, which Newbigin argues is a public testament to public truth. Thus, the publicness of

---

30. Newbigin, *Gospel in a Pluralist Society*, 223.
31. Newbigin, *Gospel in a Pluralist Society*, 223.
32. Hunsberger, "Renewing Faith during the Postmodern Transition," 11.
33. Newbigin, *Gospel in a Pluralist Society*, 231.
34. Dietterich, "Vision for the Sending of the Church in North America," 35.
35. Leddy, "People of God as a Hermeneutic of the Gospel," 310–13.

the church grounded in the gospel as public truth is the second piece of the element of living by the gospel.

THE GOSPEL

Newbigin firmly believed that the gospel is universal and public, and as such it is truth. This understanding of the gospel is something that Newbigin always maintained, and it served as an assumption for much of his writings on topics of the church, missions, evangelism, witness, conversion, and a plethora of other topics. But the gospel as public truth received much more focused attention and discussion during Newbigin's retirement and his call for the missionary encounter between the gospel, the church, and Western culture. At the beginning of his discussion of the congregation as hermeneutic of the gospel, Newbigin states the need of the church to assert the gospel as public truth. "To be faithful to the message which concerns the kingdom of God, his rule over all things and all peoples, the Church has to claim the high ground of public truth."[36] Newbigin is saying that the gospel message, since it speaks to universal and public reality, must be reasserted as the public truth for society. As well, Newbigin's discussion of the gospel as public truth has been utilized by many contemporary authors as a foundation for the conversations about public theology and public missiology. In discussing the gospel as public truth, Newbigin provides another part of the definition of what it means for the congregation to live by the gospel as it functions as the hermeneutic of the gospel for its society. In this section, I will discuss Newbigin's understanding of the gospel as public truth in connection to the congregation as hermeneutic, and highlight two requisite components of this understanding: the gospel as universal human history, and the authority of the church to preach the gospel as public truth.

Newbigin states that "if our model of truth is embodied in a story, a story of which we ourselves are a part, then the only available form of knowledge is by faith in the One who is the author of the story."[37] In this, Newbigin is claiming that the gospel is a true story which necessitates faith in the author of that story, God. "The Gospel is the story of things which have happened. What has happened has happened and cannot be changed."[38] Thus, the gospel is unchanging because it is the story of what has happened in history. This story is made known only by a community that believes it and lives by it for others to see. "But when the Church affirms the gospel as public truth it is

---

36. Newbigin, *Gospel in a Pluralist Society*, 222.
37. Newbigin, *Truth and Authority in Modernity*, 80.
38. Newbigin, "Gospel as Public Truth," 1.

challenging the whole of society to wake out of the nightmare of subjectivism and relativism, to escape from the captivity of the self turned in upon itself, and to accept the calling which is addressed to every human being to seek, acknowledge, and proclaim the truth."[39] Newbigin is calling on the church to witness to the gospel as public truth, awake to the nightmare of relativism/subjectivism, and to accept the truth that gives life meaning and purpose. Thus, Newbigin's view is that if the gospel is true, then it is public truth, and if it is public truth, then it must be proclaimed. And that proclamation comes through the community that believes and lives the gospel, the congregation that functions as the hermeneutic of the gospel for society.

In Newbigin's first book, *Christian Freedom in the Modern World*, he discusses the public nature of the gospel. For Newbigin, real Christian morality stems from its foundation in the good news,[40] which focuses moral development on character over just doing good deeds (though certainly good deeds would flow from good character).[41] Later, Newbigin states, "Jesus' message was about the kingdom of God. The good news is that this kingdom, this sovereign rule of God, is at hand. That *is* the gospel."[42] Newbigin argues that the kingdom come is the truth that the church has received and the message to which it is to bear witness. By 1988, "Response to David M. Stowe" for *The International Bulletin of Missionary Research*, Newbigin is engaging in a conversation about what is public truth and how the gospel is public truth. In this discussion, he concludes, "The gospel is the announcement of those happenings that are the cure to the whole cosmic history, the clue to the story of which every human life is a part. It is good news, gloriously good news. It has to be announced as public truth."[43] Here, Newbigin is saying that because the gospel is the true story of cosmic and human history then it is public truth, and thus it must be proclaimed in the public square. In *GPS*, Newbigin shows that Europe was formed around the gospel as public truth, a truth which has been lost in that society and to which he is beckoning the church to return to in its witness in society.[44] Newbigin uses the foundation of the gospel as

---

39. Newbigin, *Truth to Tell*, 13; a more thorough examination of the gospel as public truth in Newbigin can be found in Weston, "Lesslie Newbigin," 7–9.

40. "The Christian Gospel is good news precisely because at this point it announces that God has done something which in the nature of the case man could never do for himself." Newbigin, *Christian Freedom in the Modern World*, 81–82.

41. Newbigin, *Christian Freedom in the Modern World*, 87–88.

42. Newbigin, *Mission in Christ's Way*, 6.

43. Newbigin, "Response to David M. Stone," 153.

44. Newbigin, *Gospel as Public Truth*, 222–24, 228. This call on the Church to proclaim the gospel as public truth is reiterated in "Christianity and Culture." The gospel as public truth is then the central focus of Newbigin's 1991 article, "Gospel as Public Truth" in

public truth for the vision of sufficient Christian influence upon society in his unpublished manuscript, "What Kind of Britain?," which can also be seen in fuller development within *Faith and Power*. "I believe that the Gospel is truth, and therefore that it is public truth, and therefore that it must determine the kind of society which we seek to nurture."[45] Here, Newbigin clearly states his view of the gospel as public truth and foundation for society. This issue of the gospel as public truth is again the focus of Newbigin's response to the colloquium of neo-Calvinists at the University of Leeds in 1996, where Newbigin regularly addresses the needed interaction between the gospel and the public square.[46] Throughout all of these perspectives, Newbigin's discussions of the gospel as public truth point to it as foundational for understanding what it means for the local congregation to live by the gospel as they function as the hermeneutic of the gospel within society.

During the 1990–91 academic year, Newbigin was invited to give the Osterhaven Lectures at Western Theological Seminary (MI), which were later published as *Truth to Tell*. Newbigin prefaces the published version of the lectures with two important assumptions that will undergird the rest of his remarks. "I believe that every human being has a responsibility to seek to grasp the truth about the reality which meets us and encompasses us and to state the results of that search, knowing that full comprehension is always beyond us. For the Christian this search is sustained by the promise that, while we know only in part, a day will come when we shall know as we are known."[47] For Newbigin, the truth which the Christian has found and must claim in the public square is Jesus Christ. Newbigin states,

> The great objective reality is God but he is also the supreme subject who wills to make himself known to us not by a power that would cancel out our subjectivity, but by a grace that calls forth and empowers our subjective faculties, our power to grow in knowledge through believing. We believe in order to understand, and our struggle to understand is a response to grace. Real understanding

---

preparation for the 1992, "Gospel and Our Culture" programme consultation, the opening statement of that consultation ("The Gospel as Public Truth: Swanwick Opening Statement"), then again in a supplement after that consultation ("The Gospel as Public Truth"), and as the introduction to a series of articles about the consultation in *The Church of England Newspaper* ("Introduction: The Gospel as Public Truth"). Each of these re-states Newbigin's argument for the gospel as universal human history, and thus it is truth that must be proclaimed in the public sphere, and they provide a different aspect of Newbigin's view in conversation with others who interacted with this consultation.

45. Newbigin, "What Kind of Britain?," 5.
46. Newbigin, "On the Gospel as Public Truth."
47. Newbigin, *Truth to Tell*, 5.

> becomes possible not by seeking a certitude apart from grace, but by accepting the calling to seek understanding while knowing that full understanding will be a gift of grace beyond the horizon of our own searching.[48]

Newbigin is claiming that God is both the ultimate object and subject of knowing, and by believing in Him humanity may know truth. This knowledge, Newbigin says, is a gift of grace that those who believe in God accept while understanding that they will not enter the fullness of knowing and understanding simply by searching.

Newbigin also very clearly associates the gospel and the Christian community. "The book *(the Bible)* is the book of the community, and the community is the community of the story that the book tells. Neither can be understood without the other."[49] This inter-relationship between the gospel and the church is essential, they make sense of each other. Newbigin also states that, "The Bible cannot function with any authority except through the lives of those whose story it is, those who 'indwell' the story."[50] It is not just that scripture and the church are related, the church must indwell the gospel story for that story to have any authority within society. Thus, the credibility of the gospel to be asserted as public truth in a pluralist society is predicated upon a community which believes, indwells, and lives the gospel story throughout their lives. In this, the gospel is asserted and testified to as public truth.

Several people have incorporated Newbigin's discussion of the gospel as public truth into their own arguments, most notably the public missiology group of the American Society of Missiology (ASM). In Hunsberger's 2006 *Missiology* article, "The Missional Voice and Posture of Public Theologizing" he addresses what he sees as a necessary connection for post-Christendom North America, between missional church and public theologizing. He argues that public theologizing is an essential activity of the church and will need to have the proper voice and posture for bearing witness, which includes a spirit of companionship,[51] humility in Truth-telling,[52] particularity in discourse,[53] courage in public action,[54] and an eye on the horizon.[55] Hunsberger asserts

---

48. Newbigin, *Truth to Tell*, 36–37.
49. Newbigin, *Truth and Authority in Modernity*, 49; italics added.
50. Newbigin, *Truth and Authority in Modernity*, 43.
51. Hunsberger, "Missional Voice and Posture of Public Theology," 20–22.
52. Hunsberger, "Missional Voice and Posture of Public Theology," 22–23.
53. Hunsberger, "Missional Voice and Posture of Public Theology," 23–24.
54. Hunsberger, "Missional Voice and Posture of Public Theology," 25–26.
55. Hunsberger, "Missional Voice and Posture of Public Theology," 26–27.

that the church sits on both sides of the gospel-culture encounter, which leads the church to a continuing conversion in the same manner as Darrell Guder argues.[56] It is in sitting on both sides of this encounter, Hunsberger argues, that the church functions as "the 'hermeneutic' of the gospel by which they (society) see it (the gospel) taking shape within their own culture."[57] It is in this function that the gospel is proclaimed as public truth for society.

Hunsberger's 2005 article for *Swedish Missiological Themes*, "The Mission of Public Theology: An Exploration" provides an overview of the mission of public theology, which is deeply grounded in Newbigin. Hunsberger first establishes the need for theologizing in the public square, but then turns the majority of his argument onto the topic of the church encountering culture with both acceptance and challenge.[58] Hunsberger believes this encounter will include a gracious comradeship, a humble epistemology, a courageous particularity, risk-taking proposals and actions, and a hope-filled horizon.[59] In his discussion of the public encounter between church and culture in which public theologizing happens, Hunsberger shows that the church expressly proclaims the gospel as public truth. It should be noted that these two articles are so similar because they draw upon each other—the 2006 article comes from Hunsberger's 2005 address at the ASM meetings and influenced the article for the *Swedish Missiological Themes*, which is why it appears first here.[60]

In 2017, Hendrick R. Pieterse's *Missiology* article, "A New Global Theology?," discusses intercultural theology as a means of public theologizing for the global church. Pieterse uses the congregation as hermeneutic of the gospel in his definition of the church as a public formed by the gospel for the sake of presenting the gospel to the public world for its healing and redemption.[61] Thus, Pieterse establishes that his view of public witness is derived from understanding the church as indwelling the gospel and the world seeing the gospel within the church—the church, then, is the lens by which the public square encounters the gospel. There is also Gregg Okesson's book, *A Public*

---

56. Hunsberger, "Missional Voice and Posture of Public Theology," 21. Guder's call for the continuing conversion of the church can best be summed up in one of his final statements. "We are to be, to do, and to say witness to the saviorhood and lordship of Jesus Christ as God's good news for the world. To do this, the church must be continually converted from her reductions of the gospel to its fullness." Guder, *Continuing Conversion of the Church*, 206.

57. Hunsberger, "Missional Voice and Posture of Public Theology," 21; italics added.

58. Hunsberger, "Mission of Public Theology," 317–19.

59. Hunsberger, "Mission of Public Theology," 322–24.

60. Recounting of this timeline was shared in an email from George R. Hunsberger, January 24, 2022.

61. Pieterse, "New Global Theology?," 139.

Missiology, which bases his argument on the claim that "Congregations are . . . the hermeneutic of the gospel and the basic unit of a new society."[62] Okesson provides a way for local congregations to critically engage and witness to the multitude of publics that it encounters every day. As such, Okesson argues that their witness to the publics that exist within the networks of peoples connected to local congregations must be thickened.

Thomas Andrew West's doctoral dissertation from Southeastern Baptist Theological Seminary, "A Genuinely Missionary Encounter," connects the congregation as hermeneutic of the gospel with discussions of public witness and local congregations indwelling the story of the gospel. West builds a theology of missionary encounter within Newbigin's works and uses that theological lens to review Newbigin's theological method and project, and doctrine of scripture. West poignantly remarked, "He (Newbigin) believed the Church was 'the hermeneutic of the Gospel' because the Church is that utterly unique people who are interpreting the message of the Bible in the midst of their life—both down through the centuries as well as today. . . . Newbigin believed it is the responsibility of the Church to communicate this message afresh in every generation and cultural situation."[63] This belief in the uniqueness of the people of God for interpreting scripture to the world is done through the presence of the Holy Spirit in the local congregation. Thus, local congregations bear the presence of the Spirit within the public square through public witness.

West and contributors to the ASM public missiology conversation all have understood and applied the gospel as public truth within the congregation as hermeneutic of the gospel concept, in conversations about public witness and public missiology. And all of them have made this application by seeing the connection between public witness to the truth of the gospel and the congregation as hermeneutic of the gospel. This public witness is based on Newbigin's view of the gospel as the message of Truth, and the path to knowledge about truth for those who believe it and live by it.

The Gospel as Universal Human History

In understanding the gospel as public truth, one of Newbigin's important points is to see the gospel as an interpretation of universal human history. This is because Newbigin believes that the gospel is public truth, speaking to all of humanity, and that includes all of human history. Newbigin's view is that the gospel is God's revelation of Himself and His interaction with human history. As the author of creation, God is the only one who can authoritatively

---

62. Okesson, *Public Missiology*, 157.
63. West, "Genuinely Missionary Encounter," 109.

The Congregation as Hermeneutic of the Gospel

speak meaning and purpose into human history, and into the lives of humans. Within the revelation that God gives of Himself in the gospel, God is also providing the purpose of all of creation. Newbigin argues that the gospel is universal human history because it is God's revelation about how to understand and interpret history within God's purpose. Thus, Newbigin sees the gospel as universal human history, with Jesus as the central figure of that history, and indeed he calls Jesus the clue to human history.[64]

Flett also picks up on the gospel as universal human history in Newbigin within his discussion of the visibility of the church.

> By contrast, when the church moves beyond itself, impelled by the Spirit to participate in Jesus Christ's own mission to the world, when it unmasks and challenges "the powers of darkness and bearing in its own life the cost of their onslaught, then there are given to the Church signs of the kingdom, powers of healing and blessing which, to eyes of faith, are recognizable as true signs that Jesus reigns." Such missionary movement defines the nature of the church's visibility, its being a hermeneutic of the gospel.[65]

What Newbigin has developed and Flett has highlighted, is a perspective of the gospel as universal history, which is a key piece of the congregation as hermeneutic of the gospel concept; particularly, how this concept speaks to the credibility of the gospel's witness that Jesus Christ is the final word in human affairs.

In "The Gathering Up of History into Christ," an article that Newbigin wrote during his time with the IMC, he notes the one commonality throughout the whole world is the drawing of all of humanity towards a linear history whose center is the Cross.[66] From this perspective, Newbigin highlights, through the lens of the New Testament, five different ways of interpreting the world: (1) while the world belongs to Christ, it is currently in the power of the devil; (2) while Christ came to save and not to judge, His coming pronounces judgment on the sinful world; (3) while Christ came to gather all of humanity to Himself, in this gathering the Antichrist emerges trying to draw humanity away from Christ; (4) while Christ leads people to be in the world but not of the world, God's chosen people are being judged by the world for their apostasy from it; and (5) while all of humanity is judged by their relationship

---

64. See Newbigin, *Gospel in a Pluralist Society*, chap. 9.

65. Flett, "What Does It Mean for a Congregation to Be a Hermeneutic?," 206, quoting *GPS*, 108.

66. Newbigin, "Gathering Up of History into Christ," 81–82.

to Christ, Christ is hidden in the world.[67] Within this discussion, Newbigin has expressed a view of history through the lens of the gospel, which he then comments on in order to nudge the church into reading and acting both the gospel and history in the same way.

Later, Newbigin would write *A Faith for this One World?*, which addresses a different perspective he has on the issue of the gospel as universal history. Newbigin, in building his argument for the authority of the revelation of Christ, acknowledges a presupposition, which is that the personal God is acting in human history through an elect people.[68] This activity, Newbigin shows, is the universal clue to understanding all of human history, and thus it is the responsibility of every Christian to participate in the apostolic witness of the revelation of Jesus Christ.[69] The church, then, is a community formed around the gospel with the express purpose and authority to pass on the message of the gospel to every other group of people on earth, and subsequent generations of those peoples. "Our thesis here is that the Church has the duty and authority to preach the gospel to the whole world, not only because in it the new reality of God's era is present, but also because in it the nature of the end to which human history looks is known, known on the basis of revelation."[70] Newbigin is arguing that the church has the authority and the duty to preach the gospel, not just because it is the story of God's activity in human history, but also because it is an expression of the end of human history. Gospel witness provides purpose and prophecy to human history, defining both the meaning of the past and the direction of the future.

Within *Christ Our Eternal Contemporary*, Newbigin argues for the fact of Jesus Christ. Here, Newbigin clearly voices his understanding of Jesus as the focus and turning point of human history.[71] Newbigin bases this understanding on his reading of history through the lens of the New Testament. In this reading, Newbigin sees that in Jesus Christ, God has changed all of human history, creating a whole new world.[72] In light of this fact, Newbigin says that all of humanity must make a choice whether or not to worship Jesus as God; a choice that confronts those of the first century as well as those today.[73] Here, Newbigin is showing his understanding of Jesus as the linchpin of history,

---

67. Newbigin, "Gathering Up of History into Christ," 84–86.
68. Newbigin, *Faith for this One World?*, 87–90.
69. Newbigin, *Faith for this One World?*, 87–90.
70. Newbigin, *Faith for this One World?*, 94–95.
71. Newbigin, *Christ Our Eternal Contemporary*, 23–24.
72. Newbigin, *Christ Our Eternal Contemporary*, 34–35.
73. Newbigin, *Christ Our Eternal Contemporary*, 2.

around which all purpose and meaning, all connection to the past and the future, is bound.

The Finality of Christ builds out Newbigin's philosophical and theological argument for seeing Jesus as the final word in all human affairs. Within this book, Newbigin again expresses his understanding of Jesus as the central clue to interpreting and understanding human history. "To claim finality of Christ is to claim that his is the true clue to history, the standpoint from which one truly interprets history and therefore has the possibility of being relevantly committed to the service of God in history now."[74] Christ is the clue to human history, and as such the congregation must seek to serve God in the place and time where they are situated. This service is a participation in God's continuation of human history in light of the turning point of Christ.

Later, in *Journey into Joy*, Newbigin is discussing the reorientation of life to focus upon Jesus, in which he ventures into a discussion of Christian hope. Newbigin associates this hope with the kingdom of God, but he does so by connecting the future kingdom with the present world. "There is a road which leads through world history to the Kingdom of God, but it is a road which goes down through the valley of death and there is no bridge. The powers of evil have to be overcome in this world through the voluntary suffering of Christ and his people."[75] Newbigin's point is that there is a hope for all of human history. This hope is found in Jesus Christ and is only witnessed in history by a community of Christ followers who live by the gospel, suffering the persecution and death that Christ suffered at the hands of evil in the world. Thus, in bearing witness to the gospel as universal human history, the church must endure suffering like Christ—a suffering that connects the church to its cruciform existence.

Now in retirement back in England, Newbigin contributed to a book called *Incarnation and Myth*, in which his "The Centrality of Jesus for History" directly addresses statements from an early book, *The Myth of God Incarnate*. Throughout this chapter, Newbigin is calling out false assumptions he sees within *The Myth of God Incarnate*, highlighting three major assumptions that he is explicitly rejecting. First, Newbigin refutes the idea that Jesus must be understood in the general historical experience of humanity by showing Jesus, as God's Word, is the active presence of God in the world and that the Cross stands out as the specific historical event that changes human history.[76] Second, Newbigin confronts the presumption that there is no more knowledge learned from specific history than from general history by affirming that

---

74. Newbigin, *Finality of Christ*, 86–87.
75. Newbigin, *Journey into Joy*, 90.
76. Newbigin, "Centrality of Jesus for History," 197–201.

salvation is about the whole person (not just their soul).[77] Lastly, Newbigin addresses the idea that facts about Jesus are not accessible because they do not fit the general definition of history with the recounting of the shift in the understanding of history since the eighteenth century. This shift has a false presupposition of development, removing the possibility of divine intervention in history, thus it cannot adequately assess Jesus' place in history.[78] In this chapter, Newbigin effectively refutes the assumptions, which underlie the argument of the incarnation as religious myth, and his refutations start with reading and understanding the gospel as universal human history.

By *GPS*, Newbigin uses this understanding of the gospel as universal human history as the foundation for his discussions about mission, and ultimately for his understanding of the missionary nature of the church, which he expresses as the congregation as hermeneutic of the gospel. Within chapters 6–9 of *GPS*, Newbigin has a section of chapters that deal with issues of history. He starts his argument with a discussion of the role of revelation in history as the mode by which God interacts and forms personal relationships with humanity.[79] This relationship is the basis of election, whereby the community of the followers of Christ is called into a personal relationship with God so that it may be the witnesses to the offer of salvation to all of creation.[80] The Bible serves as God's revelation of His story in human history, given to the community of believers in order that they may pass it on to others—scripture is the universal history of humanity.[81] As universal history, Christ serves as the clue both to understanding the past and the hope for the future.[82] The present role of Christians is bearing witness to Christ as they patiently and excitedly await His return, and the church then is the body of that witnessing and waiting. Thus, each congregation must be the lens of interpretation of the gospel for the segment of society in which God has called and placed them. They will be the hermeneutic of the gospel for their society.

In *A Word in Season*, Newbigin touches on the gospel as universal human history a few different times, but two chapters have significant interaction with this idea. Chapter 9, "Our Missionary Responsibility in the Crisis of Western Culture" focuses on seeing culture through the lens of the gospel, rather than the gospel through the lens of culture.[83] Newbigin notes that often

77. Newbigin, "Centrality of Jesus for History," 201–7.
78. Newbigin, "Centrality of Jesus for History," 207–10.
79. Newbigin, *Gospel in a Pluralist Society*, chap. 6.
80. Newbigin, *Gospel in a Pluralist Society*, chap. 7.
81. Newbigin, *Gospel in a Pluralist Society*, chap. 8.
82. Newbigin, *Gospel in a Pluralist Society*, chap. 9.
83. Newbigin, *Word in Season*, 98–99.

in Western culture, the gospel is viewed through the lens of culture. He then states that the first step for reversing this view upon the world and scripture is to read and interpret scripture as universal history and then relate it to the historical story told by individual cultures.[84] In chapter 11, "Mission in the World Today," Newbigin takes a broader perspective by viewing the current state of global missions through his understanding of the cosmic and universal history of the Cross. Newbigin's conclusion is that the biblical story is the story of God's chosen people for God's chosen purpose, thus it is not about salvation but about relationship. "If we believe that the Christian revelation gives us an interpretation of the human story that is true, then we will not be embarrassed about missions."[85] Newbigin is saying that faith in the gospel as true universal human history necessitates witnessing to the gospel in the public square.

The Authority of the Church

One of the questions Newbigin addresses whenever he talks about the gospel as public truth is the question of the authority of the church to preach the gospel as truth in the public square. In *GPS*, and especially in the 1990s, the question of authority was a major component of Newbigin's discussions about the encounter between gospel and Western culture. Hunsberger highlights the congregation as hermeneutic of the gospel as vital for understanding the rationale and authority for the church both to exist and to witness. "The presence of the Christian community functions as a hermeneutical key, an interpretive lens through which onlookers gain a view of the gospel in the living colors of common life."[86] Thus, the church is the lens through which society witnesses the gospel as public truth. But to fully understand this perspective within Newbigin, it is necessary to survey his discussions of the authority of the church throughout his writings.

As early as 1948 in "The Duty and Authority of the Church to Preach the Gospel," Newbigin is seeking to answer the question of authority. Newbigin begins his discussion by relaying the foundational truth that he bases everything else upon, "The duty and authority of the Church to preach the Gospel derives from Christ, and from no other source."[87] Thus, Newbigin sees the church's authority to preach the gospel coming directly from Jesus Christ's own authority to preach the gospel. Newbigin then spends the majority of this paper exegeting a biblical foundation for this authority around the doctrines of

---

84. Newbigin, *Word in Season*, 109–12.
85. Newbigin, *Word in Season*, 130.
86. Hunsberger, "Renewing Faith during the Postmodern Transition," 13.
87. Newbigin, "Duty and Authority of the Church to Preach the Gospel," 20.

creation,[88] the fall,[89] election,[90] redemption,[91] and consummation.[92] Throughout, Newbigin connects this discussion of the biblical authority to preach the gospel with the Christian community, or more specifically local congregations within society. "The preaching of the Gospel is indissolubly linked with the existence of a people called and set apart by God to be its bearers."[93] Thus, the preaching of the gospel is derived from Christ, but it is exercised through the local congregation.

While leading the CWME of the WCC, Newbigin's book *A Faith for This One World?*, expands upon his biblical understanding of the authority of the church to preach the gospel by enlarging his exploration of the doctrines he addressed in "The Duty and Authority of the Church to Preach the Gospel." In his discussion of redemption and consummation, Newbigin makes a firm link between the church and the kingdom of God. "The Church is the instrument of the kingdom because it is the first fruit of the kingdom, it is therefore from the beginning a sent body. It not merely has a mission; it *is* a mission, the continuation of God's mission."[94] Here, Newbigin sees a link between the mission of God, the kingdom of God, and the church; one which necessitates the preaching of the gospel—a preaching which derives its authority from Christ through the participation in the kingdom and continuation of the mission of God. Newbigin acknowledges the eschatological tension of the church, living with one foot in the new reality of the kingdom and with the other foot still in the fallen world. "Thus, the real resolution, so to say, of this tension between having and hoping is the world-wide mission of the Church."[95] His solution is for the church to continue witnessing to and preaching the gospel around the world. Thus, missions are the duty of the church, derived from its authority and responsibility to continue Christ's mission.

In *Christ our Eternal Contemporary*, Newbigin's presentations to the Christian Medical College of Vellore in 1966, he approaches the question of authority from a different perspective, this time seeking to understand "What gives us the authority to say about anything, 'I know'?"[96] Newbigin then outlines three major responses to the question. First, he shows that all knowledge

---

88. Newbigin, "Duty and Authority of the Church to Preach the Gospel," 24–26.
89. Newbigin, "Duty and Authority of the Church to Preach the Gospel," 26–28.
90. Newbigin, "Duty and Authority of the Church to Preach the Gospel," 28–31.
91. Newbigin, "Duty and Authority of the Church to Preach the Gospel," 31–33.
92. Newbigin, "Duty and Authority of the Church to Preach the Gospel," 33–35.
93. Newbigin, "Duty and Authority of the Church to Preach the Gospel," 29.
94. Newbigin, *Faith for This One World?*, 93.
95. Newbigin, *Faith for This One World?*, 94.
96. Newbigin, *Christ Our Eternal Contemporary*, 7.

comes from the process of learning, which can only take place within a community that both teaches and regulates knowledge based on a set of principles and assumptions that they accept by faith.[97] Second, Newbigin shows how this faith forms the foundation for knowing, and that all new knowledge comes from accepting a new set of assumptions, on faith, which challenge and critique the old assumptions.[98] Third, Newbigin asserts that religion is on the search for coherence, in which most religions depict a cyclical understanding of human history and a veiled world of the metaphysical.[99] Newbigin does add a caveat to the discussion here, noting that in the Hebrew bible, knowledge is based upon relationships, and in that context the revelation of God is part of the divine-human relationship.[100] From this perspective, Newbigin makes the point that the Christian understanding of the divine-human relationship is a different sort of knowledge of coherence, which makes time, human history, and the physical world relevant as the place where God interacts with humanity.[101] Thus, Christianity's claim to knowledge comes through its relationships with Jesus Christ.

In *The Open Secret*, Newbigin acknowledges that missionaries, through the course of their missionary activities in society, will be questioned by what authority they go and preach the message of the gospel. Here, Newbigin returns to his original answer, saying that the authority to preach the gospel comes directly from Jesus Christ. But he adds to this answer by saying that this authority is a personal commitment distinguished from others because it provides meaning to everything,[102] this commitment points to Jesus as the clue for the community to understand all of life (public included),[103] and that this commitment is led by God (who has "laid hold of" and commissioned Christians to this commitment).[104] Thus, the missionaries, throughout their whole lives, proclaim their faith in Jesus Christ. "The Christian mission is thus to act out in the whole life of the whole world the confession that Jesus is Lord of all."[105] Newbigin is saying that this confession is the continuation of the foundation and authority of the Holy Spirit for the missionary to preach the gospel, and it is verified in the way the missionary lives. This already shows his

---

97. Newbigin, *Christ Our Eternal Contemporary*, 7–12.
98. Newbigin, *Christ Our Eternal Contemporary*, 12–16.
99. Newbigin, *Christ Our Eternal Contemporary*, 16–22.
100. Newbigin, *Christ Our Eternal Contemporary*, 18–20.
101. Newbigin, *Christ Our Eternal Contemporary*, 20–22.
102. Newbigin, *Open Secret*, 15–16.
103. Newbigin, *Open Secret*, 16–17.
104. Newbigin, *Open Secret*, 17.
105. Newbigin, *Open Secret*, 17.

understanding of how the missionary nature of the church is lived out in the local congregation, which is an important component of the congregation as hermeneutic of the gospel.

Within *GPS*, Newbigin takes a different approach to the question of authority, but he maintains his biblical understanding of the authority of the church to preach the gospel deriving directly from its relationships with Jesus Christ. Here, Newbigin begins with the Polanyian understanding of the tradition of science—regulating itself, apprenticing new members, debating new knowledge[106]—noting that the Christian tradition of knowing operates similarly. "Like the scientist, the Christian believer has to learn to indwell the tradition."[107] Newbigin calls for Christians to indwell the gospel, forming their beliefs and patterns of behavior around the story of God's redemption of creation through the sacrifice of Jesus Christ.

In *A Word in Season*, Newbigin uses different angles of reflection on the question of authority. In chapter 8, "By What Authority?," Newbigin addresses the way this question has been answered in the church through scripture,[108] tradition,[109] reason,[110] and experience.[111] Newbigin concludes that authority comes from Jesus Christ, passed to Christians by the Holy Spirit present in the gathered community of Christ followers, who are directed to believe and live out the Christ story in the world.[112] Newbigin notes that this presence only comes through those who "abide" in Jesus, again asserting the need to deeply indwell the gospel and from that God's authority is passed on.[113] In chapter 9, "Our Missionary Responsibility in the Crisis of Western Culture," Newbigin asks the question, "Do you try to understand the gospel through the spectacles provided by your culture, or do you try to understand your culture through the spectacles provided by the gospel?"[114] Once he has responded to this question, Newbigin shows that in order to embark on mission to the West, the church must see the Bible as the authoritative interpretation of universal history, which connects to the historical story of the culture—both challenging the cultural story of history, and reinterpreting the purpose of

---

106. See chapter 2.
107. Newbigin, *Gospel in a Pluralist Society*, 49.
108. Newbigin, *Word in Season*, 81–86.
109. Newbigin, *Word in Season*, 86–89.
110. Newbigin, *Word in Season*, 90–93.
111. Newbigin, *Word in Season*, 93–95.
112. Newbigin, *Word in Season*, 95–97.
113. Newbigin, *Word in Season*, 96–97.
114. Newbigin, *Word in Season*, 99.

that history.[115] In each of these discussions, Newbigin shows the authority of the church is derived, at least in part, from the authority of the gospel—all of which originates in the authority of Jesus Christ. In both of these examples, Newbigin provides a thickening context to his understanding of the authority the church has to preach the gospel in the world.

Newbigin's investigation into the issues of faith and doubt in Western society, *Proper Confidence*, addresses the authority of the church, without using that term. Within Newbigin's discussion of "Holy Scripture," he builds a case for the biblical authority of the gospel as public truth. Here, Newbigin raises the issue of revelation as a different form of knowledge, and as such, the Bible functions as an authoritative source of truth to be tested in the public sphere.[116] This will require a different critical approach to studying scripture, apart from the historical-critical method, which also sees this study as an act of discipleship.[117] This places the Christian in a unique position within society, that of a pilgrim. "A pilgrim is one who turns his back on some familiar things and sets his face in the direction of the desired goal. The Christian is called to be a pilgrim, a learner to the end of her days. But she knows the Way."[118] Thus, Newbigin is calling on all Christians to be pilgrims in society, living by the gospel as they follow the leading of the Holy Spirit.

In Newbigin's discussion of authority in the book *Truth and Authority in Modernity*, he begins his argument by showing that God, the Creator, is the ultimate authority of life, but also that modern Western society has tried to replace God with science and reason.[119] Newbigin then goes on to argue for the re-emergence of revelation as the foundation for authority, by grace[120] and by faith.[121] The source of this revelation, Jesus Christ, passes His authority to Christians through the community of disciples he left behind, and which the Holy Spirit leads.[122] This community has expressed this authority of the truth of the gospel through the Wesleyan Quadrilateral.[123] "All the four elements

---

115. Newbigin, *Word in Season*, 105–12.
116. Newbigin, *Proper Confidence*, 85–92.
117. Newbigin, *Proper Confidence*, 85–92.
118. Newbigin, *Proper Confidence*, 92.
119. Newbigin, *Truth and Authority in Modernity*, 7–10.
120. Newbigin, *Truth and Authority in Modernity*, 13–17.
121. Newbigin, *Truth and Authority in Modernity*, 17–24.
122. Newbigin, *Truth and Authority in Modernity*, 25–32.

123. Newbigin does not actually refer to these as the Wesleyan Quadrilateral, though that is their origin. Instead, Newbigin refers to these as the primary words to describe how Christians have attempted to answer the question of authority. Having spent decades as a bishop within the CSI, which incorporated Methodist (from whom he most certainly learned about this idea), Anglicans, Reformed, and Congregationalists, Newbigin was

we have considered have their place in our recognition of and submission to the authority of God, but only as they are inseparably combined."[124] Newbigin sees a relationship between these four elements—balanced and properly combined—and the authority of God in the world, exercised through the church. Thus, Newbigin calls on the church to share the gospel, pointing the world to Jesus Christ, who is the truth and authority for all of human history (which covers the entirety of the last chapter of this book).[125] Newbigin specifically addresses this call to the church in the West, a culture that has a biblical foundation but increasingly is divorcing itself from that foundation.[126] Throughout this book, Newbigin has rehearsed many of his previous arguments about the authority of the church to preach the gospel, placing them specifically in the context of contemporary Western culture.

Faith in a Changing World is a collection of presentations that Newbigin gave at Holy Trinity Brompton's School of Theology in the early 1990s. Compiled and edited by Newbigin scholar Paul Weston, this book covers the topics of trinitarian faith, the church and unity, epistemology, the current crisis of Western culture, the cultural separation of facts and values, knowing and believing, and reason and revelation.[127] Within these topics, Newbigin addresses the issue of the authority of the church multiple times, and this book provides an overview of Newbigin's arguments for the authority of the gospel as public truth and the authority of the church to preach the gospel in society. This overview makes up Part Two of the book, with each chapter taking up a different topic concerning the authority of the church to preach the gospel as public truth. These chapters include discussions of authority: in how Christians know truth,[128] in scripture, tradition, reason, and experience,[129] in the doctrine of creation,[130] in the doctrine of salvation,[131] in the role of the church in continuing Christ's mission (in Christ's authority),[132] and in the doctrine

---

adept at integrating theological ideas from multiple denominations/traditions. For more about the Wesleyan Quadrilateral, see Thorsen, *Wesleyan Quadrilateral*; see Newbigin, *Truth and Authority in Modernity*, 32–63.

124. Newbigin, *Truth and Authority in Modernity*, 62.
125. See Newbigin, *Truth and Authority in Modernity*, chap. 3.
126. Newbigin, *Truth and Authority in Modernity*, 64–69.
127. Newbigin, *Faith in a Changing World*, 17–23 (introductory outline of the central themes of the book).
128. Newbigin, *Faith in a Changing World*, chap. 4.
129. Newbigin, *Faith in a Changing World*, chap. 5.
130. Newbigin, *Faith in a Changing World*, chap. 6.
131. Newbigin, *Faith in a Changing World*, chap. 7.
132. Newbigin, *Faith in a Changing World*, chap. 8.

of eschatology.[133] Weston's organization of these presentations show the importance and role of authority in Newbigin's thought throughout his theological discussions and provides a good overview of Newbigin's arguments on the questions of authority.

Throughout Newbigin's life, the questions of authority persisted, though he approached them from diverse perspectives, providing a thick understanding of the authority of the church to preach the gospel. Thus, talking about Newbigin's answer to the questions of authority requires a robust response. For Newbigin, the authority of the church comes directly from Jesus Christ, given to those whom He discipled, and passed on to the community of Christ through the presence of the Holy Spirit. Newbigin sees this discussed within the church through the avenues of scripture, tradition, reason, and experience. This gives Newbigin the foundation for an argument for divine revelation as the source of knowledge. This divine revelation then, as it is provided in the gospel, is the authoritative interpretation of human history because it comes directly from the Creator. Thus, Newbigin sees the gospel as public truth. And as public truth, Newbigin calls on local congregations to share the gospel in the public square, envisioning Christianity acting with a Polanyian sense of knowing within a tradition, verifying the authority of the gospel as public truth.

SUMMARY

The element of living by the gospel is focused upon the internal relationship of the church, both within individual congregations and between different congregations. Calling on the Western Church to recover its missionary identity, Newbigin uses living by the gospel as a key piece to his expression of this missionary nature of the church as the congregation as hermeneutic of the gospel concept. This piece is about the internal life of the congregation being formed by the gospel, around the Cross, and living that formation in every aspect of everyday life. The community that lives by the gospel testifies to the gospel as public truth, but it does so by focusing on the shared life which is formed by the gospel. The community is living out a different story, a new social order, shaped by the Cross, and which grows out of the history-changing Jesus event and always points back to the kingdom of God. This element focuses on the internal relationship of the congregation, speaking to the inner self and its formation by the gospel. It is a key element to Newbigin's ecclesiology and understanding of the congregation as hermeneutic of the gospel because it is an implication of the congregation which is constituted by the Holy Spirit and

---

133. Newbigin, *Faith in a Changing World*, chap. 9.

also represents the kingdom. Thus, it is the final element to gaining the fullness of understanding of Newbigin's congregation as hermeneutic concept as it answers the question of the credibility of the gospel within a pluralist society. This element speaks to the pattern of life for the local congregation that is the hermeneutic of the gospel for their society. It is the mode of life of the community which is nourished in its nature of being a missionary congregation.

6

So What?

INTRODUCTION

THIS STUDY HAS ARGUED that Newbigin's concept of the congregation as hermeneutic of the gospel voices a vision for local congregations that are constituted by the Holy Spirit, represent the kingdom of God, and live by the gospel, making credible "that the power which has the last word in human affairs is represented by a man hanging on a cross."[1] These elements provide the theological context for the congregation as hermeneutic of the gospel, and thus the fullest understanding of this concept will incorporate all three of these elements. As well, each element describes a different aspect of Newbigin's understanding of the missionary nature of the church. They build upon each other and support each other so that it is impossible to have one without the others. They are bound together as one whole, supporting and nurturing each other. Thus, having one of these elements means that the local congregation will necessarily have all three of them. These elements are part of what make up the missionary nature of the church, as Newbigin understood it, and they are essential for understanding this concept. Stated in chapter 1, my focus on the congregation as hermeneutic of the gospel has been to better understand Newbigin's intended meaning, this concept's place within his ecclesiology, and its relevance for the twenty-first century North American Church. Throughout, I have fleshed out what I believe is Newbigin's intended meaning by calling local congregations the hermeneutic of the gospel and have located it within his ecclesiology. This now leaves one last question, "So what does all

---

1. Newbigin, *Gospel in a Pluralist Society*, 227.

of this mean for the North American Church today?" This chapter will draw together all of the research of this study to show the relevance of the congregation as hermeneutic of the gospel for the North American Church, and also address some avenues of further research.

SO WHAT DOES ALL OF THIS MEAN FOR THE NORTH AMERICAN CHURCH?

Newbigin's concept of the congregation as hermeneutic of the gospel is an expression for depicting his view of the missionary nature of the church, particularly as a response to the questions about the credibility of the gospel as public truth within the plural Western context. In this understanding, I have discussed three elements to Newbigin's concept of the congregation as hermeneutic of the gospel, and in investigating these three elements I have expressed a fuller understanding of this concept. Within this section, I will review the key arguments for this thesis, and discuss what all of this means for the North American Church.

What Has Already Been Said?

To argue for my interpretation of the congregation as hermeneutic of the gospel, I began by showing that it is a specific expression Newbigin uses to describe his understanding of the missionary nature of the local congregation—connecting this concept to Newbigin's life, work, and view of the missionary nature of the church. This expression aligns and overlaps with Newbigin's other expressions of the missionary nature of the church. I also defined Newbigin's use of hermeneutic in this concept to mean that he sees the local congregation as the interpretive body of the gospel in their society. As well, I showed that this expression has a specific place within Newbigin's retirement writings, where he discusses the need for a missionary encounter between the gospel and Western culture.

The first element of the congregation as hermeneutic of the gospel concept is that the local congregation is constituted by the Holy Spirit. Being constituted by the Holy Spirit means that each local congregation is established, shaped, led, and sustained by the active presence of the Holy Spirit within its body. This presence of the Holy Spirit is evidenced by the six characteristics Newbigin lists within *The Gospel in a Pluralist Society* (GPS).[2] These characteristics are evidence of the presence of the Holy Spirit, like Paul's Fruit of the Spirit (Gal 5:22–26), thus they form, what I am calling "a congregational fruit of the Spirit," showing the presence and leading by the Holy Spirit of each

2. Newbigin, *Gospel in a Pluralist Society*, 227–33.

local congregation. This congregational fruit of the Spirit points not to activity, but to the character of the local congregation, as evidence of its corporate relationship with the Spirit. If one of these characteristics is lacking within a congregation, it points to a deficiency in the relationship between that congregation and the Holy Spirit. Identifying, diagnosing, and fixing such a deficiency requires a deep and thorough investigation of the congregation and its members through asking self-reflective questions and prayer, with the leading of the Holy Spirit. This will require cultivating the congregational relationship with the Spirit, including discipleship and immersion in the gospel to discern the voice of God and follow the leading of the Spirit.

The next major element for understanding the congregation as hermeneutic of the gospel is the local congregation representing the kingdom of God. The local congregation which represents the kingdom of God attests to the credibility of Jesus Christ by being the sign, instrument, and foretaste of the kingdom in the world. They are only these things because they have received the foretaste, the Holy Spirit, and then they live out that foretaste in all their deeds and words in the world. The local congregation, formed in the character of the presence of the Holy Spirit, is always pointing to the kingdom of God, sharing its present and future reality with their society. This means that the local congregation must always be asking itself whether they represent the kingdom or distort the kingdom in their deeds and words in society.

Darren Cronshaw and Steve Taylor, researching how Newbigin's concept is experienced in the lived reality of missional churches, show what type of lived hermeneutic these congregations are within their society.[3] They conclude with four key themes they uncovered: these churches are local in mission,[4] they are holistic in mission,[5] they affirm the whole people of God in mission,[6] and they engage in dialogue for mission.[7] These themes all point back to how the local congregation represents the kingdom of God in their society.

The last element for the congregation as hermeneutic of the gospel concept is living by the gospel. For the local congregation, living by the gospel binds them to a shared life which models the reality of the kingdom of God, testifying to the gospel as public truth. This living by the gospel requires a certain type of shared life, one that is different and distinct from the rest of society. This makes the local congregation an alternative society, living out the new reality of the kingdom of God through the presence of the Holy Spirit

---

3. Cronshaw and Taylor, "Congregation in a Pluralist Society," 207–8.
4. Cronshaw and Taylor, "Congregation in a Pluralist Society," 215–18.
5. Cronshaw and Taylor, "Congregation in a Pluralist Society," 218–20.
6. Cronshaw and Taylor, "Congregation in a Pluralist Society," 220–22.
7. Cronshaw and Taylor, "Congregation in a Pluralist Society," 222–25.

within its shared life. Living by the gospel is also the way that the local congregation attests to the gospel as public truth and the foundation for society. Living by the gospel means that the local congregation must be firmly immersed in the gospel through biblical preaching, study, and discipleship within their shared life together. This necessitates deep and intimate relationships where brothers and sisters in Christ care for one another, supporting and exhorting each other to deeper engagement with and living by the gospel throughout their lives.

Some, like Fyfe Blair, see this element of living by the gospel as an essential inroad to the local congregation living as the hermeneutic of the gospel. Blair, using the agricultural cultivation definition of culture, says it "suggests to me that our role is not so much the creating of culture, as it is learning to cultivate the habits and disciplines of Biblical faith that mark the church as a particular people with a distinctive identity in communion with the trinitarian God. This is our starting point for regarding the congregation as hermeneutic of the gospel."[8] Blair is saying here that being the congregation as hermeneutic starts in the community of Christ which cultivates a lifestyle of faith through spiritual habits and disciplines. Thus, living by the gospel is the beginning of Blair's usage of the hermeneutic of the gospel concept. Trevor Hutton's dissertation on the trinitarian foundations for church planting also addresses the congregation as hermeneutic of the gospel from the element of living by the gospel. Hutton draws from *The Open Secret* and Newbigin's uses of John 20:21 in other writings to understand Newbigin's trinitarian missiology. In this understanding, he shows how Newbigin specifically applied his gospel foundation of mission to the contextual issue of the Western Church. "In response to these contextual challenges, Newbigin declares that the church must become the hermeneutic of the gospel embodying and interpreting the gospel to the world."[9] Thus, Hutton sees the congregation as hermeneutic concept as Newbigin's solution to the contextual issues confronting the church in the West, a solution that comes out of a community which is grounded in the gospel. Finally, there is Thomas F. Foust's dissertation, which combines the work of Newbigin and Dean E. Walker in developing a missiology for Western culture. "Newbigin contended that the local congregation that stays faithful to its charge from Christ is the best hermeneutic of the gospel."[10] For Foust's interpretation of Newbigin, indwelling the gospel and staying faithful to it is part of what makes the local congregation the hermeneutic of the gospel for

---

8. Blair, "Making Our Culture Attractive," 15.
9. Hutton, "Rooting the Practice of Evangelical Protestant Church Planting," 223.
10. Foust, "Christology, Restoration, Unity," 158.

The Congregation as Hermeneutic of the Gospel

their society. Thus, living by the gospel stands out most in Foust's usage of 'the congregation as hermeneutic' concept.

The fullest understanding and usage of the congregation as hermeneutic of the gospel comes through combining all three of these element. In combining all three elements, the local congregation will attend to the presence of the Holy Spirit, point back to the present and the future kingdom of God in all that they say and do, and live by the gospel in a shared life. For the twenty-first century North American Church, understanding these elements is essential for recovering its identity as a missionary church in a plural context. It means that the local congregation must focus on developing its corporate relationship with the Holy Spirit (as well as the individual relationship of each member), pass every decision through the question of how this will represent the kingdom of God in their society, and build a shared life that is grounded in and shaped by the gospel. None of these things has a program or activity that dictates a 'how to' or a correct way of doing them, instead, they point to the nature of the local congregation in their character being formed by the Holy Spirit and lived in deeds and words within society. It forces every congregation to walk the line between abandoning society and over-identifying with society, by focusing on God and focusing on the world.

Throughout all these elements of the congregation as hermeneutic of the gospel, there is a measure of interdependency. The Holy Spirit constitutes and leads the local congregation in representing the kingdom of God and living by the gospel in society. Thus, it is impossible to have the presence of the Holy Spirit without representing the kingdom of God or living by the gospel; or to represent the kingdom of God without the presence of the Holy Spirit or living by the gospel, or to live by the gospel without the presence of the Holy Spirit or representing the kingdom of God. These elements are not about activities, but rather about the nature of the local congregation, a missionary nature that Newbigin expresses as the congregation as hermeneutic of the gospel. Within the context of a necessary missionary encounter between the gospel and Western culture—a culture that is calling into question the credibility of the gospel which claims Jesus Christ as the final word in human affairs—the hermeneutic of the gospel concept provides a vision for the church to recover and live its missionary nature. Thus, in calling the local congregation the hermeneutic of the gospel, Newbigin is incorporating all these elements to affirm the credibility of the gospel's claim through the life, character, and visible presence of every local congregation.

So What?

What Does This Mean for the North American Church?

Newbigin's vision of the missionary nature of the church as expressed in the congregation as hermeneutic of the gospel provides both a challenge and a hopeful image for the North American Church. It is a challenge for this church to regain its missionary nature, living its calling to continue Christ's mission in their society, and speak the truth of the gospel into the changing situation of North American culture. It is a hopeful image in that it provides a clear depiction of who and what the North American Church is, and the impact it can have within its society. Thus, understanding this vision helps in providing a revitalization of the North American Church for the twenty-first century.

Newbigin often critiqued the current state of Western culture and in particular, the place which the church has taken within that context. He laments the passive position that the church has taken within this context and wonders, "Can we accept God's forgiveness for the arrogance and greed and cruelty of which we have been guilty as people of this nation, and can we recover confidence in the Gospel which will enable us to come out of the private sector and proclaim the Gospel as truth for all?"[11] This is a challenge from Newbigin, in this case specifically to Britain, but one which can be expanded to all of Western Society. It is a challenge to recover the missionary nature of the church and venture into the public sphere proclaiming the gospel as public truth in all that it does and says. This is a return to the religiously plural context in which Christianity was born,[12] and a call on the church to return to that which caused it to grow in that early stage—living the gospel in deeds and words throughout society. And, as Newbigin would argue, this is especially needed in the current context of Western culture. "We are witnessing the collapse of the whole glorious human enterprise of seeking to know the truth, to make contact with reality, to know God as God truly is."[13] What Newbigin is saying is that the human seeking of truth, as a way to understand reality, is quickly disintegrating in society. But Newbigin also argues that truth is not something that is owned by any culture or person.[14] This is what makes Christians witnessing to gospel truth such an important task as it counters the cultural captivity of truth-claims, with the universal person of Jesus Christ.[15] Newbigin also states, "The Church exists to embody and to tell the story which

---

11. Newbigin, "Witness to the World," 7–8.
12. Newbigin, "Religious Pluralism: A Missiological Approach," 227.
13. Newbigin, "Religious Pluralism and the Uniqueness of Jesus Christ," 52.
14. Newbigin, "Religious Pluralism and the Uniqueness of Jesus Christ," 53–54.
15. Newbigin, "Religious Pluralism and the Uniqueness of Jesus Christ," 53–54.

is the true story, the story which truly renders the character of God."[16] Which begs the question, "Can we recover the faith that our true story is the one we share with all human beings and that it is the story which the Bible tells?"[17] All of these point to the challenge of the congregation as hermeneutic of the gospel for the North American Church today.

The challenge that Newbigin gives is also answered with the congregation as hermeneutic of the gospel. "It is when there are congregations of men and women and children who are living the story now, here, that the Bible will become good news for secularized people."[18] Thus, the hope of the church in North America is living the gospel, being the hermeneutic of the gospel, for their society. This only happens in the combination of the three elements discussed throughout this study. And in the current state of change from modern to post-modern within Western Culture, the church stands in a position to speak gospel truth into that change. Newbigin highlights that for this to happen, the church must recover its confidence in the gospel, establish a firm foundation for biblical authority, and focus on creating unity across denominational/traditional lines.[19] Only then will it be able to bear witness to the living hope for the redemption of all of creation. Thus, in being the hermeneutic of the gospel for society through the presence of the Holy Spirit, representing the kingdom of God, and living by the gospel, the local congregation in Twenty-first Century North America presents the New Testament truth of Jesus Christ for its society.

> The New Testament repeatedly asserts, in one way or another, that the whole fact of Christ (his incarnation, ministry, death and resurrection) is either a stone of stumbling, to be discarded, or else the corner stone on which the whole building is itself constructed. It is not something which can be fitted into another kind of edifice, a structure of belief, built on another foundation. It is either something to be rejected, or something which becomes the new starting point for all thought and all action. If the Jesus whom we know through the apostolic witness is truly the word through whom and for whom all things have their being, then there cannot exist any more comprehensive frame of thought into which he could be fitted.[20]

---

16. Newbigin, "Gospel and Modern Western Culture," 7.
17. Newbigin, "Witness to the World," 8.
18. Newbigin, "Bible," 6.
19. Newbigin, "New Birth into a Living World," 6–9.
20. Newbigin, "Gospel in Today's Global City," 7.

So What?

Newbigin is showing that Jesus Christ is either a stumbling block for society or the foundation on which society is built. For the local congregation, which is the hermeneutic of the gospel, it is the foundation that they are to proclaim for their society, the hope for a new social order which they are to model for society. "But we should insist that the Christian doctrine, with its prime model in the doctrine of the Trinity, ought to be playing an explicit and vigorous part in the public debate that makes up the life of the public square."[21] This new social order should be grounded in the Trinity, and the hermeneutic of the gospel is a pathway to participating in the Trinity while continuing the mission of Jesus Christ in North America today.

Michael W. Goheen, in discussing the impact of Newbigin's ecclesiology, notes the challenge and hopefulness of the congregation as hermeneutic of the gospel and mentions that it will lead the local congregation to live a different life. "A community that lives like this will be a 'foretaste of a different social order.' They will be congregations that renounce an introverted concern for their own lives and recognize that they exist for the sake of those who are not members. The self-giving and outward oriented life will be a 'sign, instrument, and foretaste of God's redeeming grace for the whole life of society.'"[22] This different life of the local congregation is exactly what the North American Church can be when it embraces Newbigin's vision of its missionary nature. Jürgen Schuster also addresses the church as the hermeneutic of the gospel as being a different community based upon its relationship with Jesus Christ. "The church takes its bearings for its being in the world from the fact that Christ is inaugurated as Lord of all. . . . It is the provisional incorporation of humankind into Christ which will find its consummation in the eschatological establishment of the new humankind in the new creation."[23] Schuster is calling out that the church is a different kind of community due to its relationship with Jesus Christ. "The eschatological tension between the inauguration of Christ's reign in the past and the manifestation of his reign in the future characterizes the life of the church."[24] Thus, the church is a body with one foot in the present and one in the future. The foot in the present must work towards the fulfillment of the future by witnessing to the gospel in the public sphere. And this witness will carry the church into contention with the powers and principalities currently striving to supplant Christ at the center of society. Gregg Okesson points out that living as this new social order, there will also be witnessing to the principalities and powers that work in the structures of

---

21. Newbigin, "Trinity as Public Truth," 1.
22. Goheen, *Church and Its Vocation*, 81.
23. Schuster, "Clue to History," 44.
24. Schuster, "Clue to History," 45.

The Congregation as Hermeneutic of the Gospel

society. He highlights from Newbigin that, "Gospel witness must take both aspects seriously: the structures, along with the spiritual realities—'behind, within, and above human beings.'"[25] Thus, the congregation as hermeneutic of the gospel also leads the local congregation to conflict with the principalities and powers which currently attempt to take Christ's place in the center of society. This life of the local congregation is both present and eschatological and confronts the principalities and powers in the world, is the exact type of life that the congregation as hermeneutic of the gospel fosters in the local congregations of North America today.

Newbigin's vision of the missionary nature of the church as the congregation as hermeneutic of the gospel, is a compelling vision for the North American Church. Therefore, it has so often been utilized by scholars and pastors all over North America in the Twenty-first Century. Yet, part of what makes it compelling is that it also aligns with the New Testament, and if the North American Church is to embrace this image it must also firmly plant its embrace within scripture. This alignment starts with one of Newbigin's favorite verses in scripture, John 20:21 (Again Jesus said, "Peace be with you! As the Father has sent me, I am sending you.").

> Forty times in this Gospel Jesus is described as the one sent by the Father, now he sends them to continue and to complete his mission. This mission wholly defines the nature of the church as a body of men and women sent into the public life of the world to be the bearer of that peace which Christ has wrought "by the blood of the cross." They will participate in his mission as they participate in his passion.[26]

Newbigin's foundation for understanding the church as missionary by nature comes from this verse, and he explains here that it is such by participating in and bearing witness to the Cross of Christ. This marks the way of life for the church, the way of Christ. "This is how we know what love is: Jesus Christ laid down his life for us. And we ought to lay down our lives for our brothers and sisters" (1 John. 3:16). In this, the North American church can heed Paul's call to "live a life worthy of the calling you have received" (Eph 4:1). This calling requires that each congregation lives "so that in every way they will make the teaching about God our Savior attractive" (Titus 2:10), and in living this way they must "Always be prepared to give an answer to everyone who asks you to give the reason for the hope that you have" (1 Pet 3:15b). This brings the congregation back to living their faith in deeds and words (Jas 2:14–26),

---

25. Okesson, "Christian Witness to Institutions," 145.
26. Newbigin, *Light Has Come*, 268.

as James says, "Show me your faith without deeds, and I will show you my faith by my deeds" (Jas 2:18b). The congregation as hermeneutic of the gospel aligns behind all of these pieces of scripture, affirming the way of life of the local congregation in society.

If a local congregation begins to catch Newbigin's vision of the missionary nature of the church, it must remember to stay faithful to all three elements. It may be tempting to focus on one and develop specific programs or activities to fulfill that component, but doing this forgets two important points: (1) all three are necessary for a full expression of the congregation as hermeneutic of the gospel, and (2) these elements are about the nature of the local congregation, not about what they do. Thus, in staying faithful to all three elements, the local congregation can begin to re-develop its missionary nature, becoming the hermeneutic of the gospel through the leading of the Holy Spirit, pointing to the kingdom of God, and with a foundation in the gospel. With that being said, there are a few useful things the local congregation can do to help cultivate this nature within itself.

Local congregations can attend to their corporate relationship with the Holy Spirit by using the congregational fruit of the Spirit from Newbigin as an evaluative matrix to determine the health of their relationship with the Spirit. This requires reflection, prayer, and discernment to evaluate these characteristics in the congregation, diagnose any deficiencies, and develop solutions to those deficiencies, all in the leading of the Holy Spirit. To attend to representing the kingdom of God, the local congregation must regularly ask whether what it does and says—both privately and publicly—represents or distorts the kingdom. If they find that they are distorting the kingdom, they must immediately stop this distortion and then prayerfully seek the guidance of the Spirit on how to correct this problem. To attend to living by the gospel, the local congregation must seek to cultivate a community foundation in the gospel that binds them together and defines them in society. This gospel foundation can be aided by biblical preaching, prayer, discipleship, care for one another, and regular study of scripture. It is up to the community to seek the guidance of the Holy Spirit for the best ways to cultivate this gospel life.

Another aspect of the elements of Newbigin's missionary ecclesiology within the congregation as hermeneutic of the gospel concept is their interconnectivity. It is not possible to have one of these elements in a local congregation without having the others. Being constituted by the Holy Spirit is the starting point because without the Holy Spirit forming and leading the followers of Jesus into the Body of Christ none of the others would be possible. But the active presence of the Holy Spirit continues to flow through the other two elements, binding them together. So, having one of these elements means having all of them. This could also be interpreted to mean that all three elements are similar, which they are not. Like the Trinity, they are relationally attached in the same nature (the missionary nature of the church), but they are distinct. One way of marking their distinction is to consider the relationship they focus upon. The constituting presence of the Holy Spirit focuses on the relationship of the congregation and God. Representing the kingdom focuses on the relationship of the congregation and the world. Living by the gospel focuses on the relationship of the congregation within itself. While all of these relationships can be found in each element, there is a primary relational focus for each.

Specifically for the twenty-first century North American Church, Newbigin's identifying of the local congregation as the hermeneutic of the gospel should be a hopeful challenge. Hopeful in its imagery of the missionary nature of the church. Challenging in that it should point out their need to recover this nature. In the fuller understanding of the congregation as hermeneutic of the gospel that I have shown here, the contemporary North American Church has detailed pieces that they can grasp and begin to prayerfully embrace as they seek to recover their missionary nature. And I pray that the church in North America, recovering its missionary nature, may experience revival not just in numbers (though certainly this), but in vitality as it seeks to live out its calling to "go and make disciples of all nations" (Matt 28:19).

FURTHER RESEARCH

Within this study, I have limited my conversation to the North American, English-speaking, Protestant Church (and a fairly Evangelical perspective of Protestantism at that), and one expression of Newbigin's missionary ecclesiology. This leaves open many more avenues of research on this topic, some of which would include:

(1) This interpretation of the congregation as hermeneutic of the gospel needs to be studied within individual congregations. Much like *Treasure in Clay Jars*, which found case studies of principles of missional churches within individual congregations, a study needs to be done of congregations to see how this interpretation of the hermeneutic of the gospel is practically lived. This study will not be easy and it will require developing a concise list of markers for each of these elements. Once identified, an in-depth investigation of individual congregations will be necessary to understand how these elements are expressed within those congregations.

So What?

(2) One of the other major expressions Newbigin uses for his missionary understanding of the nature of the church is the sign, instrument, and foretaste of the kingdom. Newbigin's use of the sign, instrument, and foretaste language includes the interconnectivity of the being of the community, doing the deeds of mission, and speaking the message of the gospel. This interconnectivity again speaks to the elements of Newbigin's missionary ecclesiology present within the sign, instrument, and foretaste imagery. While I have ventured to unpack this imagery in part in chapter 4, this expression needs further study. It would be a valuable research project, similar in scope to this one, to engage this expression of the missionary nature of the church, to coincide with this study, in order to give a more robust vision of Newbigin's missionary ecclesiology.

(3) One of the results of fulfilling its nature as the hermeneutic of the gospel is that local congregations will provide a new vision of society, one which is founded upon a plausibility structure that comes from the gospel. But this is not a return to Christendom, rather it is a society that seeks freedom, justice, and flourishing for all its members through Christian influence. In a forthcoming essay, George R. Hunsberger lays the groundwork for investigating what Newbigin means by a Christian vision for society,[27] but this needs further investigation. Newbigin's idea of a Christian vision for society may be an ill-formed vestige of modernist thinking, or it may be a further challenge to the twenty-first century Western Church to speak into a period of societal liminality with the truth of the gospel in order to shape society moving forward. It at least deserves a deep and thorough, book-length investigation.

(4) The concept of the biblically-based plausibility structure is one that Newbigin discusses several times throughout his writings. Thus, one area that needs further research is Newbigin's understanding of a biblical plausibility structure, particularly for Western society. Is this a plausibility structure with one interpretation of scripture, or does it allow for multiple interpretations in association with each other? And, how does this plausibility structure relate to Newbigin's call for the church to function as a tradition (in terms of what Polanyi describes a tradition to be) within plural societies?

(5) There needs to be a specific study regarding the corporate relationship between the congregation and the Holy Spirit. Too often the Western

---

27. Hunsberger, "Lesslie Newbigin and the Idea of a Christian Society"; Hunsberger, "Missional Voice and Posture of Public Theology."

Church has focused on the individual relationship with the Holy Spirit, but Newbigin is calling for an embrace of the reality of the corporate relationship. How a local congregation, as a whole, cultivates this relationship and the evidence of it within the life of the congregation—the congregational fruit of the Spirit—needs more investigation. There have been countless books and articles written about the Fruit of the Spirit, but viewing Newbigin's characteristics of the congregation as hermeneutic of the gospel as congregational fruit of the Spirit points to a need for further investigation that may provide invaluable wisdom for the life of local congregations. Understanding each of these characteristics more fully, unpacking the corporate relationship of the congregation and the Holy Spirit, and the meaning of this relationship for the life and ministry of the local congregation are all important ideas that need more study—both theologically and practically.

(6) Another key area of needed further study is the relevance and interpretation of the congregation as hermeneutic of the gospel within non-Western cultures and non-Protestant traditions. What has been unpacked here needs to be submitted to scholars and ministry leaders from churches in Africa, Asia, Latin America, and Oceania for them to analyze and dissect for their contexts. As well, Pentecostal, Orthodox, and Catholic brothers and sisters are invited to give feedback from within their tradition on this material. While I do believe that this concept has universal relevance, as a North American Protestant scholar it is not my place to say whether Newbigin's hermeneutic of the gospel concept is relevant and/or applicable within other regions of the world or Christian traditions. This research must be done by scholars and leaders who have intimate knowledge and a deeper understanding of their culture and context.

Bibliography

Behan, Shawn P. "Embracing Plurality: The Opportunity of Secularization." In *Against the Tide: Mission against Global Currents of Secularization*, edited by Craig Ott and W. Jay Moon, 15–35. Evangelical Missiological Society Series 27. Littleton, CO: Carey, 2019.

———. "A Hermeneutical Congregation: A New Reading of Lesslie Newbigin's Missional Ecclesiology through the 'Congregation as Hermeneutic of the Gospel' Principle." *Asbury Journal* 72 (2017) 110–26.

Blair, Fyfe. "Making Our Culture Attractive." *Candour* 4 (2006) 15–16.

Blauw, Johannes. *The Missionary Nature of the Church: A Survey of the Biblical Theology of Mission*. Cambridge: Lutterworth, 1962.

Bosch, David J. *Transforming Mission: Paradigm Shifts in Theology of Mission*. Maryknoll, NY: Orbis, 1991.

———. *Witness to the World: The Christian Mission in Theological Perspective*. Atlanta: John Knox, 1980.

Briscoe, Stuart. *The Fruit of the Spirit: Cultivating Christian Character*. Wheaton, IL: Shaw, 1993.

Cronshaw, Darren, and Steven Taylor. "The Congregation in a Pluralist Society: Rereading Newbigin for Missional Churches Today." *Pacifica* 27 (2014) 206–28.

Cruchley-Jones, Peter. "Entering Exile: Can There Be a Missiology for 'Not My People'?" In *A Scandalous Prophet: The Way of Mission after Newbigin*, edited by Thomas F. Foust et al., 23–36. Grand Rapids: Eerdmans, 2002.

Dietterich, Inagrace. "A Vision for the Sending of the Church in North America." *Missiology* 38 (2010) 29–36.

Dodds, Adam. "Newbigin's Trinitarian Missiology: The Doctrine of the Trinity as Good News for Western Culture." *International Review of Mission* 99 (2010) 69–85.

Fensham, Charles J. "The Methodology of Missiology in the Context of Turtle Island." *Missiology* 47 (2019) 300–314.

Flett, John G. "What Does It Mean for a Congregation to Be a Hermeneutic?" In *The Gospel and Pluralism Today: Reassessing Lesslie Newbigin in the 21st Century*, edited by Scott W. Sunquist and Amos Yong, 195–213. Downers Grove, IL: InterVarsity, 2015.

Forrester, Duncan B. "Lesslie Newbigin as Public Theologian." In *A Scandalous Prophet: The Way of Mission after Newbigin*, edited by Thomas F. Foust et al., 3–12. Grand Rapids: Eerdmans, 2002.

Bibliography

Foust, Thomas F. "Christology, Restoration, Unity: An Exploration of the Missiological Approach to Modern Western Culture according to Lesslie Newbigin and Dean E. Walker." PhD diss., University of Birmingham, 2002.

Foust, Thomas F., and George R. Hunsberger. "Bishop J. E. Lesslie Newbigin: A Comprehensive Bibliography." In *A Scandalous Prophet: The Way of Mission after Newbigin*, edited by Thomas F. Foust et al., 249–305. Grand Rapids: Eerdmans, 2002.

Foust, Thomas F., et al., eds. *A Scandalous Prophet: The Way of Mission after Newbigin*. Grand Rapids: Eerdmans, 2002.

Goheen, Michael W. *"As the Father Has Sent Me, I Am Sending You": J. E. Lesslie Newbigin's Missionary Ecclesiology*. Utrecht: Boekencentrum, 2000.

———. *The Church and Its Vocation: Lesslie Newbigin's Missionary Ecclesiology*. Grand Rapids: Baker Academic, 2018.

———. "The Missional Calling of Believers in the World: Lesslie Newbigin's Contribution." In *A Scandalous Prophet: The Way of Mission after Newbigin*, edited by Thomas F. Foust et al., 37–54. Grand Rapids: Eerdmans, 2002.

Gorman, Michael J. *Becoming the Gospel: Paul, Participation, and Mission*. Grand Rapids: Eerdmans, 2015.

———. *Cruciformity: Paul's Narrative Spirituality of the Cross*. Grand Rapids: Eerdmans, 2001.

———. *Inhabiting the Cruciform God: Kenosis, Justification, and Theosis in Paul's Narrative Soteriology*. Grand Rapids: Eerdmans, 2009.

Guder, Darrell L. *The Continuing Conversion of the Church*. Grand Rapids: Eerdmans, 2000.

———, ed. *Missional Church: A Vision for the Sending of the Church in North America*. Grand Rapids: Eerdmans, 1998.

Hughes, Robert S., III. "Lesslie Newbigin's Understanding of the Holy Spirit and the Church in Mission." PhD diss., Asbury Theological Seminary, 2013.

Hunsberger, George R. *Bearing the Witness of the Spirit: Lesslie Newbigin's Theology of Cultural Plurality*. Grand Rapids: Eerdmans, 1998.

———. "Biography as Missiology: The Case of Lesslie Newbigin." *Missiology* 27 (1999) 523–31.

———. "The Church in the Postmodern Transition." In *A Scandalous Prophet: The Way of Mission after Newbigin*, edited by Thomas F. Foust et al., 95–106. Grand Rapids: Eerdmans, 2002.

———. "Lesslie Newbigin's Idea of a Christian Society." In *Theology and Ethics for the Public Church: Mission in the 21st Century World*, edited by Samuel Yonas Deressa and Mary Sue Dehmlow Dreier, 123–40. Lanham, MD: Lexington/Fortress Academic, 2023.

———. "The Missional Voice and Posture of Public Theologizing." *Missiology* 34 (2006) 15–28.

———. "The Mission of Public Theology: An Exploration." *Swedish Missiological Themes* 93 (2005) 315–24.

———. "The Newbigin Gauntlet." In *The Church between Gospel and Culture: The Emerging Mission in North America*, edited by George R. Hunsberger and Craig Van Gelder, 3–25. Grand Rapids: Eerdmans, 1996.

———. "Renewing Faith during the Postmodern Transition." *TransMission Special Edition* (1998) 10–13.

Bibliography

———. *The Story That Chooses Us: A Tapestry of Missional Vision.* Grand Rapids: Eerdmans, 2015.

Hutton, Trevor. "Rooting the Practice of Evangelical Protestant Church Planting within a Trinitarian Theological Framework: With Particular Reference to Creation, Context, and Community." PhD diss., University of Manchester, 2018.

Kandiah, Krishna Rohan. "Towards a Theology of Evangelism for Late-Modern Cultures: A Critical Dialogue with Lesslie Newbigin's Doctrine of Revelation." PhD diss., King's College, 2005.

Kärkkäinen, Veli-Matti. "The Church in the Post-Christian Society between Modernity and Late Modernity: Lesslie Newbigin's Post-critical Missional Ecclesiology." In *Theology in Missionary Perspective: Lesslie Newbigin's Legacy,* edited by Mark T. B. Laing and Paul Weston, 125–54. Eugene, OR: Pickwick, 2012.

Kenneson, Philip D. *Life on the Vine: Cultivating the Fruit of the Spirit in Christian Community.* Downers Grove, IL: InterVarsity, 1999.

Kuyper, Abraham. "Sphere Sovereignty." Translated by George Kramps. Inauguration Address. Free University, Amsterdam, October 20, 1880.

Laing, Mark T. B. *From Crisis to Creation: Lesslie Newbigin and the Reinvention of Christian Mission.* Eugene, OR: Pickwick, 2012.

Laing, Mark T. B., and Paul Weston, eds. *Theology in Missionary Perspective: Lesslie Newbigin's Legacy.* Eugene, OR: Pickwick, 2012.

Leddy, Mary Jo. "The People of God as a Hermeneutic of the Gospel." In *Confident Witness—Changing World: Rediscovering the Gospel in North America,* edited by Craig Van Gelder, 303–13. Grand Rapids: Eerdmans, 1999.

LeMarquard, Grant. "Editorial: The Gospel in the Public Square." *Trinity Journal for Theology and Ministry* 4 (2010) 5–7.

Newbigin, Lesslie. "Authority: To Whom Shall We Go?" Sermon, St. Mary's, University Church at Cambridge, May 1979.

———. "The Basis and the Forms of Unity." *Mid-Stream* 23 (1984) 1–12.

———. *Behold, I Make All Things New.* Geneva: WCC, 1964.

———. "The Bible and Our Contemporary Mission." *Clergy Review* 69 (1984) 9–17.

———. "The Bible: Good News for Secularised People." Unpublished Keynote Address during the Europe/Middle East Regional Conference in Germany, April 1991.

———. "Bible Study on Romans 8." Unpublished Bible study given at the Conference on "Church in the Inner City." Birmingham, 1976.

———. "Can a Modern Society be Christian?" In *Christian Witness in Society: A Tribute to M. M. Thomas,* edited by K. C. Abraham, 95–108. Bangalore: Board of Theological Education, Senate of Serampore College, 1998.

———. "Can the West Be Converted?" *Princeton Seminary Bulletin* 6 (1985) 25–37.

———. "The Centrality of Jesus for History." In *Incarnation and Myth: The Debate Continued,* edited by Michael Goulder, 197–210. Grand Rapids: Eerdmans, 1979.

———. "Christ and the Cultures." *Scottish Journal of Theology* 31 (1978) 1–22.

———. "Christian Faith in a Secularized World." Unpublished manuscript.

———. "The Christian Layman in the World and in the Church." *National Christian Council Review* 72 (1952) 185–89.

———. *Christian Witness in a Plural Society.* London: British Council of Churches, 1977.

———. *Christ Our Eternal Contemporary.* Madras: CLS, 1968.

———. "The Church—'A Bunch of Escaped Convicts.'" *Reform* (1990) 6.

Bibliography

———. "The Church as a Servant Community." *National Christian Council Review* 91 (1971) 256–64.

———. "Church as Witness: A Meditation." *Reformed World* 35 (1978) 5–9.

———. "Church Union: Which Way Forward?" *National Christian Council Review* 89 (1969) 356–63.

———. "Co-operation and Unity." *International Review of Mission* 59 (1970) 67–74.

———. *Come Holy Spirit—Renew the Whole Creation.* Birmingham: Selly Oak Colleges, 1990.

———. *Context and Conversion.* London: Church Missionary Society, 1978.

———. "Conversion." *National Council Review* 86 (1966) 309–22.

———. "The Duty and Authority of the Church to Preach the Gospel." In *The Church's Witness to God's Design.* Vol. 2, *The Amsterdam Assembly Series,* 19–25. London: SCM, 1948.

———. "The Enduring Validity of Cross-Cultural Mission." *International Bulletin of Missionary Research* 12 (1988) 50–53.

———. "Evangelism and the Whole Mission of the Church." *Auburn Report* 10 (1998) 7–9.

———. "Faith and Faithfulness in the Ecumenical Movement." In *Faith and Faithfulness: Essays on Contemporary Ecumenical Themes,* edited by Pauline Webb, 1–7. Geneva: WCC, 1987.

———. "Faith and Order in India Now." *National Christian Council Review* 92 (1972) 433–36.

———. *Faith and Power: Christianity and Islam in "Secular" Britain.* With Lamin Sanneh and Jenny Taylor. Eugene, OR: Wipf & Stock, 2005.

———. *A Faith for This One World?* London: SCM, 1961.

———. *Faith in a Changing World.* Edited by Paul Weston. London: St. Paul's Theological Centre, 2012.

———. *The Finality of Christ.* London: SCM, 1969.

———. *Foolishness to the Greeks: The Gospel and Western Culture.* London: SPCK, 1986.

———. "From the Editor." *International Review of Missions* 54 (1965) 417–27.

———. "The Future of Mission and Missionaries." *Review and Expositor* 74 (1977) 209–18.

———. "The Gathering Up of History into Christ." In *The Missionary Church in East and West,* edited by Charles C. West and David M. Paton, 81–90. London: CSM, 1959.

———. *The Good Shepherd: Meditations on Christian Ministry in Today's World.* Rev. ed. Grand Rapids: Eerdmans, 1977.

———. "Gospel and Culture." Address given at the conference for the Danish Missions Council and the Danish Churches Ecumenical Council, Denmark, November 3, 1995.

———. "The Gospel and Modern Western Culture." Unpublished talk given to the Swedish Missions Council, 1993.

———. *The Gospel and Our Culture.* London: Catholic Missionary Education Center, 1990.

———. "The Gospel as Public Truth: Swanwick Opening Statement." In *The Gospel and Our Culture: The Gospel as Public Truth.* Documents from a National Consultation, Swanwick, July 1992.

———. "The Gospel as Public Truth." *Gospel and Our Culture* (1991) 1–2.

Bibliography

———. "The Gospel as Public Truth." *Gospel and Our Culture Movement Supplement* (1992) 1–2.

———. "The Gospel as True." *Trinity Journal for Theology and Ministry* 4 (2010) 22–34.

———. *The Gospel in a Pluralist Society.* Grand Rapids: Eerdmans, 1989.

———. "The Gospel in the Public Square." *Trinity Journal for Theology and Ministry* 4 (2010) 22–61.

———. "The Gospel in Today's Global City." *Selly Oak Occasional Paper* (1997) 1–9.

———. *The Holy Spirit and the Church.* Madras: CLS, 1972.

———. "Holy Spirit: The Believers Strike Oil." *Reform* (1990) 6.

———. *Honest Religion for Secular Man.* Eugene, OR: Wipf and Stock, 1966.

———. *The Household of God: Lectures on the Nature of the Church.* Eugene, OR: Wipf and Stock, 2008.

———. "Human Flourishing in Faith, Fact and Fantasy." *Religion and Medicine* 7 (1988) 400–412.

———. "Integration—Some Personal Reflections 1981." *International Review of Mission* 70 (1981) 247–55.

———. "Introduction" in *The Gospel as Public Truth: Applying the Gospel in the Modern World.* London: CEN, 1992.

———. *Is Christ Divided? A Plea for Christian Unity in a Revolutionary Age.* Grand Rapids: Eerdmans, 1961.

———. *Journey Into Joy.* Madras: CLS, 1972.

———. "Lay Presidency at the Eucharist." *Mid-Stream* 35 (1996) 177–82.

———. "Leading Off: A Christian Society?" *Leading Light* 2 (1995) 4, 18.

———. *Lesslie Newbigin, Missionary Theologian: A Reader.* Edited by Paul Weston. Grand Rapids: Eerdmans, 2006.

———. *The Light Has Come: An Exposition of the Fourth Gospel.* Grand Rapids: Eerdmans, 1982.

———. "Living Together." *Now* (1982) 18–19.

———. *Mission and the Crisis of Western Culture: Recent Studies.* Edited by Jock Stein. Edinburgh: Handsel, 1989.

———. "Ministry and Laity." *National Christian Council Review* 85 (1965) 479–83.

———. *The Mission and Unity of the Church.* Grahamstown: Rhodes University, 1960.

———. "A Missionary's Dream." *Ecumenical Review* 43 (1991) 4–10.

———. "Mission in an Ecumenical Perspective." Unpublished Manuscript. World Council of Churches Archives, 1962.

———. *Mission in Christ's Way: Bible Studies.* WCC Mission Series 8. Geneva: WCC, 1987.

———. "Mission in the 1980s." *International Review of Mission* 69 (1980) 575–76.

———. "Mission in the 1990s: Two Views." *International Bulletin of Missionary Research* 13 (1989) 98–102.

———. "The Mission of the Triune God." Unpublished manuscript, World Council of Churches Archives, 1962.

———. "Missions." Unpublished manuscript, 1991.

———. "The Nature of the Christian Hope." *Ecumenical Review* 4 (1952) 282–84.

———. "New Birth into a Living World." Unpublished Keynote Address, European Area Council of the World Alliance of Reformed Churches, September 1995.

BIBLIOGRAPHY

———. "Not Whole without the Handicapped." In *Partners in Life: The Handicapped and the Church*, edited by Geiko Müller-Fahrenholz, 17–25. Faith and Order Paper 89. Geneva: WCC, 1979.

———. "On Being the Church for the World." In *The Parish Church?*, edited by Giles S. Eccleston, 25–42. London: Mowbray, 1988.

———. "On the Gospel as Public Truth: Response to the Colloquium." Unpublished response to the neo-Calvinist colloquium at Leeds, August 1996.

———. *One Body, One Gospel, One World: The Christian Mission Today*. New York: IMC, 1958.

———. *The Open Secret: An Introduction to the Theology of Mission*. Rev. ed. Grand Rapids: Eerdmans, 1995.

———. *The Ordained Ministry and the Missionary Task*. Pamphlet. Geneva: WCC, 1962.

———. *The Other Side of 1984: Questions for the Churches*. Geneva: WCC, 1983.

———. "The Pastor's Opportunities: VI. Evangelism in the City." *Expository Times* 98 (1987) 355–58.

———. "Pastoral Ministry in a Pluralist Society." In *Witnessing Church*, 1–10 Madras: CLS, 1994.

———. "The Pattern of Ministry in a Missionary Church." Unpublished manuscript, October 1961.

———. "Politics and the Covenant." *Theology* 84 (1981) 356–63.

———. *Preaching Christ Today*. Birmingham: Overdale College, 1979.

———. "The Present Crisis and the Coming Christ." *Ecumenical Review* 6 (1954) 118–23.

———. *Proper Confidence: Faith, Doubt, and Certainty in Christian Discipleship*. Grand Rapids: Eerdmans, 1995.

———. "Recent Thinking on Christian Beliefs: VIII. Mission and Missions." *Expository Times* 88 (1977) 260–64.

———. "Reflections on an Indian Ministry." *Frontier* 18 (1975) 25–27.

———. *The Relevance of Trinitarian Doctrine for Today's Mission*. World Council of Church Commission on World Mission and Evangelism. London: Edinburgh House, 1963.

———. "Religion, Science, and Truth in the School Curriculum." *Theology* 91 (1988) 186–93.

———. "Religious Pluralism: A Missiological Approach." In *Theology of Religions: Christianity and Other Religions*, 227–44. Rome: Pontifical Gregorian University, 1993.

———. "Religious Pluralism and the Uniqueness of Jesus Christ." *International Bulletin of Missionary Research* 13 (1989) 50–52.

———. "Response to David M. Stone." *International Bulletin of Missionary Research* 12 (1988) 141–43.

———. "The Right to Fullness of Life." In *A Vision of Man: Essays on Faith, Theology, and Society*, edited by Samuel Amirtham, 339–47. Madras: CLS, 1978.

———. "Scripture as the Locus of Truth." *Trinity Journal for Theology and Ministry* 4 (2010) 35–48.

———. "A Sermon Preached at the Thanksgiving Service for the Fiftieth Anniversary of the Tambaram Conference of the International Missionary Council." *International Review of Mission* 77 (1988) 325–31.

———. *Set Free to Be a Servant: Studies in Paul's Letter to the Galatians*. Madras: CLS, 1969.

Bibliography

———. *Sign of the Kingdom*. Grand Rapids: Eerdmans, 1981.

———. *Signs amid the Rubble: The Purposes of God in Human History*. Compiled by Geoffrey Wainwright. Grand Rapids: Eerdmans, 2003.

———. *Sin and Salvation*. London: SCM, 1956.

———. "Some Thoughts on Britain from Abroad." *Christian News Letter* 12 (1947) 9–12.

———. *A South India Diary*. London: SCM, 1951.

———. *This Is Our Life*. Leeds: John Paul the Preacher's Press, 1978.

———. "The Trinity as Public Truth." In *The Trinity in a Pluralistic Age: Theological Essays on Culture and Religion*, edited by Kevin J. Vanhoozer, 1–8. Grand Rapids: Eerdmans, 1997.

———. *Truth and Authority in Modernity*. Valley Forge, PA: Trinity International, 1996.

———. *Truth to Tell: The Gospel as Public Truth*. Grand Rapids: Eerdmans, 1991.

———. *Unfinished Agenda: An Updated Autobiography*. London: SPCK, 1993.

———. *The Welfare State: A Christian Perspective*. Oxford: Oxford Institute for Church and Society, 1985.

———. "What Kind of Britain?" Unpublished London address, August 1994.

———. "What Kind of Society." *Trinity Journal for Theology and Ministry* 4 (2010) 49–61.

———. "Which Way for 'Faith and Order'?" In *What Unity Implies: Six Essays after Uppsala*, edited by Reinhard Groscurth, 115–32. World Council Studies 7. Geneva: WCC, 1969.

———. "Whose Justice?" *Ecumenical Review* 44 (1992) 308–11.

———. "Witness in a Biblical Perspective." *Mission Studies* 3 (1986) 80–84.

———. "Witness to Jesus Christ." In *Preaching Christ to Indian Today*, edited by P. D. Devanandan et al., 57–62. Madras: Diocesan, CLSI, 1956.

———. "Witness to the World." *Christian* (1987) 5–8.

———. *A Word in Season: Perspectives on Christian World Missions*. Grand Rapids: Eerdmans, 1994.

———. "The Work of the Holy Spirit in the Life of the Asian Church." In *A Decisive Hour for the Christian World Mission*, edited by Norman Goodall et al., 18–33. London: SCM, 1960.

———. "An X-Ray to Make God Visible in the World." *Reform* 7 (1990) 7.

Nikolajsen, Jeppe Bach. *The Distinctive Identity of the Church: A Constructive Study of the Post-Christendom Theologies of Lesslie Newbigin and John Howard Yoder*. Eugene, OR: Pickwick, 2015.

———. "Missional Church: A Historical and Theological Analysis of an Ecclesiological Tradition." *International Review of Mission* 102 (2013) 249–61.

Okesson, Gregg. "Christian Witness to Institutions: Public Missiology and Power." *Missiology* 44 (2015) 142–54.

———. *A Public Missiology: How Local Churches Witness to a Complex World*. Grand Rapids: Baker Academic, 2020.

Pieterse, Hendrick R. "A New Global Theology? Intercultural Theology and the Challenge of Public Discourse in a Global Church." *Missiology* 45 (2017) 138–55.

Porter, David Steven. "The Predicament of Place: Lesslie Newbigin and a Missionary Theology of Place." PhD diss., Duke Divinity School, 2017.

Prater, Arnold. *The Presence: The Ministry of the Holy Spirit*. Nashville: Thomas Nelson, 1993.

Bibliography

Rae, Murray. "The Congregation as Hermeneutic of the Gospel." In *Theology in Missionary Perspective: Lesslie Newbigin's Legacy*, edited by Mark T. B. Laing and Paul Weston, 189–202. Eugene, OR: Pickwick, 2012.

Robert, Dana. "Forty Years of the American Society of Missiology: Retrospect and Prospect." *Missiology* 42 (2014) 6–25.

Russell, A. Sue. "Mimesis, Alterity, and Liminality: Envisioning In-Christ Identity as the Social Dimension of Paul Eschatology." Presented at the Institute of Biblical Research annual meeting, Atlanta, November 20, 2015.

Sanderson, John W. *The Fruit of the Spirit*. Phillipsburg, NJ: P&R, 1985.

Schuster, Jürgen. "The Clue to History." In *Theology in Missionary Perspective: Lesslie Newbigin's Legacy*, edited by Mark T. B. Laing and Paul Weston, 33–48. Eugene, OR: Pickwick, 2012.

———. "The Significance of the Kingdom of God in Its Eschatological Tension for the Theology of Mission of Lesslie Newbigin." PhD diss., Trinity International University, 2006.

Shenk, Wilbert R. "Newbigin in His Time." In *The Gospel and Pluralism Today: Reassessing Lesslie Newbigin in the 21st Century*, edited by Scott W. Sunquist and Amos Yong, 29–47. Downers Grove, IL: InterVarsity Academic, 2015.

Smith, Stephen W. *Inside Job: Doing the Work within the Work*. Downers Grove, IL: InterVarsity, 2015.

Thorsen, Don. *The Wesleyan Quadrilateral: Scripture, Tradition, Reason, and Experience as a Model of Evangelical Theology*. Lexington, KY: Emeth, 2005.

Thurston, Bonnie. *Fruit of the Spirit: Growth of the Heart*. Collegeville, MN: Liturgical, 2000.

Van Engen, Charles. "Mission Theology in the Light of Postmodern Critique." *International Review of Mission* 86 (1997) 437–61.

Vandervelde, George. "The Church as Missionary Community: The Church as Central Disclosure Point of the Kingdom." *Trinity Journal for Theology and Ministry* 4 (2010) 112–29.

Vicedom, Georg F. *The Mission of God: An Introduction to a Theology of Mission*. Saint Louis: Concordia House, 1965.

Wainwright, Geoffrey. "Contemporary Ecumenical Challenges from the Legacy of Lesslie Newbigin." In *Theology in Missionary Perspective: Lesslie Newbigin's Legacy*, edited by Mark T. B. Laing and Paul Weston, 277–89. Eugene, OR: Pickwick, 2012.

———. *Lesslie Newbigin: A Theological Life*. Oxford: Oxford University Press, 2000.

Warner, Nigel Peter. "The Missionary Ecclesiology of Lesslie Newbigin and Its Implications for the Pastoral Care of the Church, with Particular Reference to His Work in the Period 1974–1998." MA diss., Anglia Polytechnic University, 2001.

Watson, David Lowes. "Christ All in All: The Recovery of the Gospel for Evangelism in the United States." In *The Church between Gospel and Culture: The Emerging Mission in North America*, edited by George R. Hunsberger and Craig Van Gelder, 177–97. Grand Rapids: Eerdmans, 1996.

Weng, Ng Kam. "Going Public with Lesslie Newbigin: Public Theology and Social Engagement in an Islamic Context." In *Theology in Missionary Perspective: Lesslie Newbigin's Legacy*, edited by Mark T. B. Laing and Paul Weston, 290–304. Eugene, OR: Pickwick, 2012.

Bibliography

West, Thomas Andrew. "'A Genuinely Missionary Encounter': The Proper Lens for Viewing Lesslie Newbigin's Theology." PhD diss., Southeastern Baptist Theological Seminary, 2017.

Weston, Paul. "Ecclesiology in Eschatological Perspective: Newbigin's Understanding of the Missionary Church." In *Theology in Missionary Perspective: Lesslie Newbigin's Legacy*, edited by Mark T. B. Laing and Paul Weston, 70–87. Eugene, OR: Pickwick, 2012.

———. "Lesslie Newbigin: Looking Forward in Retrospect." *Journal of Missional Practice* 5 (2015) 1–13.

———, ed. *Lesslie Newbigin, Missionary Theologian: A Reader*. Grand Rapids: Eerdmans, 2006.

———. "Mission and Culture Change: A Critical Engagement with the Writings of Lesslie Newbigin." PhD diss., London: King's College, 2001.

Wright, Christopher J. H. *Cultivating the Fruit of the Spirit: Growing in Christlikeness*. Downers Grove, IL: InterVarsity, 2017.

www.ingramcontent.com/pod-product-compliance
Lightning Source LLC
Chambersburg PA
CBHW071501150426
43191CB00009B/1395